Study and Revise
GCSE
English

Steve Eddy, Mary Hartley and Ruth Coleman

Acknowledgements

The Publishers would like to thank the following for permission to reproduce material in this book:

pp. 26–27 *Fair Do's* by David Nobbs © 1990, Jonathan Clowes Ltd, London, on behalf of David Nobbs Ltd; pp.28–29 *Of Mice and Men* by John Steinbeck © 2000, Penguin, Copyright John Steinbeck, 1937, 1965; pp. 31–32 *Cat's Eye* by Margaret Atwood © 1989, Bloomsbury Publishing Plc; pp. 34–35 *Lord of the Flies* by William Golding © 1954, Faber & Faber Ltd; pp. 37–38 'She Didn't Come Home' by Sue Grafton from *The Mammoth Book of Private Eye Stories* eds. Bill Pronzini and Martin H Greenberg © 1988, Robinson Publishing; p. 44 'Jane Austen's letter to James Stainer Clarke of 1 April 1816' *from Jane Austen's Letters*, edited by RW Chapman © vol 2, 1932, Oxford University press, Reprinted by permission of Oxford University Press; p. 45 Letter written by Mark Durk © Forest of Avon; pp. 47 and 51 *The Diary of a Young Girl: The Definitive Editions* by Anne Frank, edited by Otto H Frank and Mirjam Pressler, translated by Susan Massotty © 1997, Viking, The Anne Frank-Fonds, Basle, Switzerland, 1991. English translation Doubleday a division of Bantam Doubleday Dell Publishing Group Inc, 1995; p.48 *Fever Pitch* by Nick Hornby © 1992, Victor Gollancz, Nick Hornby, 1992; p.49 *So Late Into the Night: Byron's Letters and Journals* by G.G. Byron © 1976, John Murray (Publishers) Ltd.; p.52 *Long Walk to Freedom* by Nelson Mandela © 1995, Abacus; p.53 *Our Joyce* by Joyce Storey © 1992, Virago; p.54 *I Know Why the Caged Bird Sings* by Maya Angelou © 1984, Virago; p.55 *The Prince of Wales: A Biography* by Jonathan Dimbleby © 1994, Time Warner, Reprinted by permission of David Higham Associates Ltd.; p.56 *Charles – A Biography* by Anthony Holden © 1988, Weidenfield & Nicolson; p.58 *The Language of the Genes* by Steve Jones © 1993, HarperCollins; p.65 'Bay City Wonder' by Ruth Coleman © Spring/Summer 1991, Trailfinder magazine; p.66 *The Lost Continent: Travels in Small Town America* by Bill Bryson © 1994, Secker & Warburg; p.68 'Do You Have a Choice?' © Vegetarian Society; p.70 'The Cull of the Wild' © Vegetarian Society; p.72 'Drugs and Solvents: You and your child' © Department of Health; p.76 'Risk Grows as Swampy Digs Deeper' by Nick Shoon and Louise Jury in *The Independent* © 30 January 1997; p.77 Independent Television News: transcript of *News at Ten*, Thursday 30 January 1997 © ITV; p.78 'The nation digs you, Swampy', *The Independent* © 30 January 1997; p.79 'Right or wrong, the young at least show some guts' by Bel Mooney © 1 February 1997, *The Express*; p.80 'Against Nature' by Nick Trend © December 1996, *Candis Magazine*; p.81 'Drugs: The Other Road to Disaster' by Moyra Bremner © 4 December 1996, GUARDIAN; p.82 'Fury at Gallagher drug outburst' © *Daily Mail*, 30 January 1997; p.83 'Comment: Society must decide in the drugs debate', © *Daily Mail*, 1 February 1997; p.84 Front page of *The Guardian* © 4 December 1996, GUARDIAN; p.86 *Suicide Poster* © Crisis UK, by kind permission from Crisis UK (trading as Crisis). Charity no 1082947; p.86 *Appeal Advertisement* © International Fund for Animal Welfare; p.87 'A rapid reaction force for Bosnia' *Oxfam Appeal Advertisement* © Oxfam Publishing, reproduced with permission of Oxfam Publishing, 274 Banbury Road, Oxford, OX2 7DZ; pp. 89–92 'An Astrologer's Day' by R K Narayan from *Malgudi Days* © 1984, Penguin; pp. 93–94 'Dead Men's Path' by Chinua Achebe, from *Girls at War and Other Stories* © 1972, Heinemann Educational Books; p.96 'Poem at Thirty-Nine' by Alice Walker, from *Horses Make a Landscape More Beautiful* © 1985, The Women's Press; p.98 'Praise Song for My Mother' by Grace Nichols, from *The Fat Black Woman's Poems* © 1984, Virago; pp.100–101 *A View from the Bridge* by Arthur Miller © 1955, 1957 renewed 1983, 1985, published in volume form by Penguin Books; pp.112–113 'Romeo and Juliet, told by Juliet's Nurse' from *Shakespeare Without the Boring Bits* by Humphrey Carpenter © 1994, Viking, Humphrey Carpenter, 1994; p.128 'Not My Best Side' by U.A. Fanthorpe, from *Side Effects* © 1978, Peterloo Poets, U.A. Fanthorpe, "Side Effects" reproduced by permission of Peterloo Poets; p.130 'I Wouldn't Thank You for a Valentine' from *True Confessions and New Clichés* by Liz Lochhead © 1985, Polygon; p.131 'Valentine' from *Mean Time* by Carol Anne Duffy © 1993 Anvil Press Poetry, 'Valentine' is taken from *Mean Time* by Carol Anne Duffy published by Anvil Press Poetry in 1993; p.132 'Digging' from *Death of a Naturalist* by Seamus Heaney © 1966, Faber & Faber Ltd; p.132 'The Early Purges' from *Death of a Naturalist* by Seamus Heaney © 1966, Faber & Faber Ltd; p.134 'The Field-Mouse' from *Collected Poems* by Gillian Clarke © 1997, Carcanet Press Limited; p.134 'Night of the Scorpion' from *Collected Poems 1952–1988* by Nissim Ezekiel © 1992, OUP India, Reproduced by permission of Oxford University Press India, New Delhi.

Every effort has been made to trace copyright holders, but if any have been inadvertently overlooked the Publishers will be pleased to make the necessary arrangements at the first opportunity.

Although every effort has been made to ensure that website addresses are correct at time of going to press, Hodder & Stoughton Educational cannot be held responsible for the content of any website mentioned in this book. It is sometimes possible to find a relocated web page by typing the address of the home page for a website in the URL window of your browser.

Text © Steve Eddy, Mary Hartley and Ruth Coleman 2004

First published in this edition 2004
exclusively for WHSmith by
Hodder & Stoughton Educational
338 Euston Road
London NW1 3BH

All rights reserved. Apart from any use permitted under UK copyright law, no part of this publication may be reproduced or transmitted in any form or by any means, electronic or mechanical, including photocopying, recording or any information storage and retrieval system, without permission in writing from the Publisher.

Impression number   10 9 8 7 6 5 4 3 2
Year   2010 2009 2008 2007 2006 2005

Illustrations: Julian Mosedale, Andrea Norton

Prepared by *specialist* publishing services ltd, Milton Keynes

Printed and bound in the UK by Scotprint

A CIP record for this book is available from the British Library

ISBN 0 340 85858 3

Contents

Introduction		**iv**
1	**Launching into English Language**	**1**
	Ever-changing English	1
	Speaking and listening	2
	Reading	4
	Writing	7
2	**Literary prose published before 1914**	**10**
	Characterisation	10
	Context and tradition	14
	Setting	20
3	**Literary prose published after 1914**	**25**
	Openings	25
	Conflict	31
	Comparing texts from different periods	37
4	**Non-fiction**	**42**
	Letters	43
	Diaries	47
	Autobiography	53
	Biography	55
	Science writing	57
	Travel writing	60
	Information	68
5	**The media**	**74**
	What is meant by 'media'?	74
	Factual reporting and bias	76
	Opinion and argument	78
	Making an appeal	80
	From fact to comment	82
	Presentation	84
	Tugging at heartstrings	86

6	**Literature from other cultures**	**89**
	Short stories	89
	Poems	96
7	**Drama**	**100**
	The individual and society	100
	Macaroons and cucumber sandwiches	103
8	**Shakespeare**	**106**
	Background	107
	Style and language	108
	Antony and Cleopatra	110
	Character	112
	Comparisons	114
	Themes	116
	Performance	118
9	**Poetry**	**121**
	Before 1914	121
	Modern poetry	127
	Valentines	130
	Using your senses	132
	Encounters with animals	134
	Drafting	136
10	**Drafting and proofing**	**141**
	Proofreading	143
	Punctuation	144
	Spelling	146
	Confusions	148
Index		**151**

Introduction

Study and Revise GCSE English

Making the most of your memory

To do well in any subject, you have to make the most of your memory. Sadly, few people realise that they can help themselves remember to the key facts and techniques they need in an exam. So by starting to read this book, you've already given yourself a head-start over other students.

For effective learning and revision, you must understand how your memory works – and work with it. What happens after you've learned something? You might think that your recall steadily declines. But in fact your recall 10–20 minutes after a study session is better than it is immediately afterwards. This is because your brain has sorted out the information it's taken in. And if at this point you make yourself remember what you've learned, you'll reinforce your learning. That's why there are short tests in this book – to make you make yourself remember. For maximum benefit, take the test, then take a break. Better still, if you revise what you've learned a day later, then a week later, then a month later, it will stay with you for good.

Key skills

It's all the more important to train your memory now, because with new-style GCSE English exams you can't have helpful notes handwritten inside the text you take into the exam room. Even so, doing well in English is not just about memory. It's also about skills, especially speaking and listening, reading, and writing. Chapter 1 of this book introduces these skills. The rest of the book will help you to develop them.

Perhaps the biggest skill to develop in English is asking yourself questions. For example, a novelist might write: 'She fumbled with her papers.' Ask yourself why the author is telling us this. What does it reveal about the character. Is she nervous, bored, clumsy ...? If you're speaking, or writing, you need to ask a different kind of question: How can I have the desired effect on my audience?

Reading between the lines

One of the biggest failings that examiners report in students' work is a failure to 'read between the lines' – to see meanings that are hinted at. You need to look out for hidden meanings, but you also need to be able to make your own interpretations. Providing you base what you say on the evidence, you have a lot of room for personal interpretation. That's one reason why English can be so much fun. By helping you to develop your skills in understanding, interpreting and using language, this book will give you the confidence to enjoy it and to do your best in your English and English Literature exams.

Launching into English Language — Chapter 1

Overview

This chapter looks at what you need to know for GCSE English Language. By the end of the chapter you'll know about:

- What the National Curriculum says you should know.
- What your exam board requires.
- How to use this guide.
- How the English language has developed.
- Speaking and listening in different situations.
- Reading for different purposes and in different ways.
- What to look for in fiction and non-fiction.
- Writing – purpose, planning, structure, style.

The National Curriculum

The National Curriculum divides the study of English into three areas: Speaking and listening; Reading; and Writing. To do really well at GCSE you must show that you can:

- Speak clearly and purposefully in a variety of situations, using appropriate vocabulary and emphasis; contribute to discussion on the basis of listening and evaluation.
- Respond to a range of fiction and non-fiction texts, commenting on how authors achieve their effects through style, structure and presentation.
- Write in an interesting way, adapting your style to particular purposes, expressing opinions and arguments clearly (in non-fiction), and developing characters and settings (in fiction).

In addition, your punctuation and grammar should be good. Sentence structure is especially important. Good spelling is desirable, but it is better to take an occasional risk and gain marks for wide vocabulary than to avoid using words because you're not sure how to spell them.

Your exam board

All boards cover the National Curriculum, and all are covered by this guide. You'll find this guide helpful for Literature as well as Language, and your board may allow you to submit combined coursework.

Assessment will probably be 60 per cent exam-based, 40 per cent coursework (20 per cent Speaking and listening, 10 per cent Reading, and 10 per cent Writing).

This guide

To get the most from this guide:

- Be sure to read the 'Overview' and 'About this section' previews. They'll prepare you for what you're going to learn. The 'Section round-up' will reinforce what you've learnt in a section. At the end of a chapter the 'Checklist' will give more reinforcement and help you to identify the areas you still need to work on.
- Do as many of the tasks as you can manage. You'll find three types of task: Reading, Writing, and Speaking and listening (for which you will usually need a partner). Where extended writing is suggested, your teacher may let you use it as coursework.
- Let your teacher know that you're using this guide. If you need extra help with something covered in the guide, ask your teacher.
- Read selectively if you prefer. Use the Contents and Index. You can also flick through and read the clues and cures from 'Dr Wordsmith' scattered throughout this guide.

Ever-changing English
The melting-pot

About this section

This section looks at the origins and development of the English language.

English is an especially rich language because it springs from several sources (see map). It began with the Anglo-Saxons. Then came the Vikings, who spoke Old Norse, a language similar to Anglo-Saxon. Both languages were characterised by short, no-nonsense words: *earth*, *wood*,

Launching into English Language

blood and *guts* come from Anglo-Saxon; *get*, *hit*, *low* and *wrong* are from Old Norse, as are many *sk* words – such as *skin*, *sky* and *skein*.

After 1066 the Normans overran England. They spoke Norman French, which had been heavily influenced by Latin, the language of the Church, and a second language for educated people. Even now, most words for abstract ideas, such as *honour*, *education* and *civilisation*, come from Latin (usually via Norman French).

Chaucer to Shakespeare

The earliest English you are ever likely to read is that of Geoffrey Chaucer (born 1340), who wrote *The Canterbury Tales*. In Chaucer's day, Anglo-Saxon and French had largely merged, but the French influence was still strong:

> 'When that April with his showers sweete
> The drought of March hath pierced to the roote.'

This sounds clumsy unless we follow Chaucer's French-style pronunciation of *sweete* and *roote* like 'sweeter' and 'rooter', and *pierced* as two syllables. This had been lost by Shakespeare's time, and Samuel Johnson (1709–84) called Chaucer's verse 'rude', meaning awkward: he didn't know about the French pronunciation!

Shakespeare was a great populariser of words and coiner of phrases (see p. 108). Many of his phrases survive, but many of the words he used have changed their meaning.

Nice but sad

Much-used adjectives change meaning quickly. *Nice* comes from Latin *nescius* – 'ignorant'. In medieval English *nice* meant 'stupid'. Shakespeare used it meaning 'shy'. Gradually it came to mean 'fussy'. You know what it means now. *Sad* came from Old German *sadhaz* – 'full'. To Shakespeare it meant 'serious'. It gradually shifted to 'unhappy'. ✪ How do you use it now?

Borrowings and techno-speak

English has always 'borrowed' and absorbed words and phrases. Examples are *juggernaut* and *thug* (Hindi, India), *delicatessen* and *hoodlum* (German), and *aficionado* (Spanish). In addition, each technological development gives birth to new words and phrases, which are soon used in a more general sense. ✪ What technologies do the following come from? *Getting into gear*; *ticking over*; *lift-off*; *switch-off*; *interface*; *online*.

Your turn

Look up ten words in a good dictionary that gives derivations (look that up, too!). Write down where each comes from.

> ## Section round-up
>
> **This section has shown you that English is constantly gaining and losing words, changing meanings, and giving birth to new phrases.**

Speaking and listening

> ## About this section
>
> **This section looks at the different situations in which you speak and listen, and at appropriate styles of speech. It also gives hints on how to do well in oral coursework.**

You're the expert

Getting a good GCSE grade is easy compared to the incredible feat you've already achieved by learning to speak English as well as you have. (Even more so if it's your second language.)

However, you'll double your learning from everyday situations – from casual conversation to watching TV – if you become a more perceptive listener and understand the different communication styles required by different situations. Look at the situations pictured on the next page. Identify the **purpose** of communication in each (include the person not actually speaking), and how it will affect the **style** of speech used.

Purpose

The pictures on the next page identify the following purposes of communication:

- entertainment
- sharing experiences
- persuasion
- evaluation
- seeking and giving information
- expressing and sharing feelings
- complaining and justifying
- instruction and learning.

✪ What others can you think of?

Launching into English Language

Formal and informal

The BBC news is read in a relatively formal 'standard' English that will be widely understood. When people chat with friends, they're more likely to use 'non-standard' English, with differences in vocabulary and grammar from standard English. This will vary from one English-speaking culture to another – for example, the USA, the Caribbean, India and Pakistan – and from one part of Britain to another. A Bristolian might say 'Give it to I', instead of 'Give it to me'. A Liverpudlian might say 'I was made up', meaning 'I was really pleased.' Slang – including traditional Cockney rhyming slang – is non-standard. A regional accent is perfectly acceptable in standard English; local dialect words aren't.

Non-standard English is not wrong, but you have to be able to use standard English where the situation requires it. The high court judge in the picture below, left, needs your help. Translate what he says into standard English.

'Seems to me you're a right nasty piece of work. You go round nicking anything you can get your hands on, putting the frighteners on old dears so they cough up their dosh, and getting legless on the proceeds. Well, Sonny Jim, I'm going to bang you up for so long that by the time you get out you'll be ready to kick the bucket!'

Listening

Listening is a key skill. Some hints:

- **Just listening** (e.g. to a talk or debate). Make a mental note of the overall theme and anything you expect to find out. Jotting down keywords will help you to focus. Listen critically for facts and opinions (see p. 74). How is the argument/coverage developed? If questions are asked, are they really answered?

3

Launching into English Language

- **One to one.** Mentally note the ideas, facts and opinions the other person presents, and how the person seems to feel. **Paraphrasing** is a useful technique: it means summing up what the person has said, briefly: 'So you feel the job's too dangerous and you're not prepared to go on.'
- **In a group.** Follow the development of the discussion, including what individuals think and feel. Listen for misunderstandings. Don't let thinking what to say next stop you listening.

Asking questions

If interviewing or just getting to know someone new, it's usually better to ask 'open' questions, not 'closed' ones. The dialogue below gives examples. Kate's question is closed; Lucy's is open.

KATE: *Do you think road protesters do a useful job?*

JOHN: *Yes.*

LUCY: *What do you feel about the road protesters?*

JOHN: *I agree with what they're doing, but they need to improve their image.*

Now listen here!

With a partner, take it in turns to talk for a minute on a subject while the other person just listens. The listener then feeds back what the speaker has said as accurately as possible.

Section round-up

This section has taught you about the purposes of oral communication. It has also taught you about standard and non-standard English, and about communication skills, especially listening.

For your own notes

....

....

....

....

....

Reading

About this section

This section looks at the reading you already do, at how to read for different purposes and in different ways, and what to look for in fiction and non-fiction.

Your vast experience

You may not have been reading quite as long as you've been talking, but you've still read hundreds of thousands of words in your lifetime.

✪ See how many different types of reading you can identify on this page and the next. How would you adjust your reading style for each?

A43	
Brackley	10
Northampton	32
(Birmingham	60)

Dear Jo,
I don't think it's a good idea for us to see each other tonight. I need time to think.
Sorry, Ian

· THE ·
· JALAPENAS ·
Red Cross Hall
Saturday 4 August
8 till late – bar
£5.00
(£4.00 concessions)

Launching into English Language

Non-fiction

Non-fiction is any kind of writing intended to present facts, opinions or real-life experiences, as opposed to novels, poetry and drama. ✪ What different types of non-fiction can you identify below and over the page? What can you say about the writer's probable **intention** in each case?

In your exam you will be asked to read a piece of non-fiction. You may be asked to comment on its content, distinguish between fact and opinion, and analyse its style (or how it 'achieves its effects'). Bear in mind the author's intention. Remember, too, that non-fiction can use many of the techniques of fiction, such as **metaphor** (describing a thing as if it were something different but in some way similar; see p. 99) and **irony** (where the author says the opposite of what he or she really thinks, or pretends ignorance, for the sake of humour or ridicule). You could also be asked to compare it with another piece, perhaps from a 'pre-release' booklet. Ask your teacher what approach your exam board favours.

COGGINS A, 23 Niblet Terrace, 4	965 7723
A.J, 14 Lamyatt Rd, 3	961 4583
C.B, Stonecrop, Bingham	948 8932
D, 42 Sunset Boulevard, 8	965 3232
E.B, 8 Gardenia Place, 4	965 1854

Test yourself

Skimming is reading a piece of text quickly to get the general idea of what it's about. Try it with a news feature of about 200 words. Read it very quickly, aiming to answer the key questions: Who? What? When? Where?

Scanning is looking only for one thing, or for certain key features. When you cast your eyes over the contents of the fridge looking for a cherry yogurt, you're scanning. Try scanning a medium-length news piece looking for names of people and places.

Launching into English Language

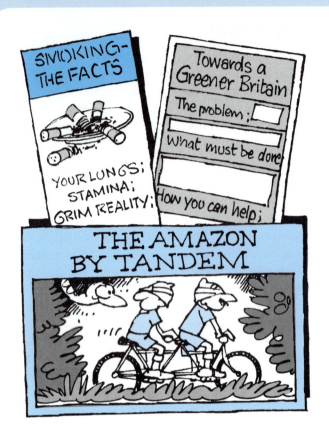

Dr Wordsmith's cure

Lost for words with which to refer to words? Here are some terms you should know:

- **noun** a 'thing' word: *dog, cat, love, tragedy*
- **adjective** a word you add to a noun to describe it: *fierce* dog; *fat* cat, *eternal* love
- **verb** a 'doing' word: *run, hate, do, terrify*
- **adverb** a word you **add** to a verb to say how something is done: *quickly, accurately*
- **prefix** a word, incomplete on its own, that goes before a word and adds a particular meaning to it; e.g. *pro* (for) in 'pro-reform', *anti* (against) in 'antisocial', and *pre* (before) in 'pre-1900'
- **suffix** a word, incomplete in itself, that goes at the end of a word and adds a particular meaning to it; e.g. *ation* in 'examination', and *fy* in 'terrify' and 'qualify'.

Fiction

Fiction means any writing that comes from the imagination rather than fact. In theory it includes poetry and drama, but it more often refers to novels and short stories.

Reading fiction is obviously important if you're studying Literature, but it's also important for English Language. You could well have to comment on a piece of fiction in your exam. If you find it hard to 'get into' novels, try this approach:

- Read the cover 'blurb' to get an idea of what to expect.
- Dip into the first chapter at random, reading a bit here, a bit there.
- Scan the first chapter for character names and write them down.
- Skim the first few paragraphs for their broad sense.
- Start to read more closely. Be prepared to re-read the opening if your mind wanders.
- Be an active reader. Ask yourself questions, such as, 'How will this character solve this problem? How would I solve it?'
- As you read on, make brief notes on the main characters. (This needn't take long.)

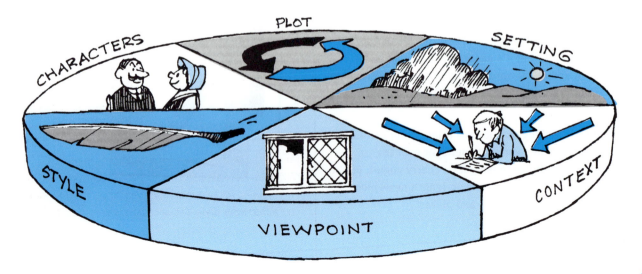

Launching into English Language

What to look for

There are several different things to consider in any novel, story or play.

- **Characterisation**. The characters and how we know about them (e.g. what they say and do, how the author describes them), their relationships, and how they develop. For example, do the characters learn anything?
- **Plot and structure**. What happens and how it is organised into parts or episodes. On a large scale, how does the story develop? Is there more than one story going on at once?
- **Setting and atmosphere**. The changing scene and how it reflects the story. In *Wuthering Heights* the rugged landscape and weather reflect the characters' emotional difficulties. In *Lord of the Flies* the jungle reflects human savagery.
- **Style and language**. The author's choice of words, and literary devices such as imagery (see p. 108), and how these reflect the mood.
- **Viewpoint**. How the story is told (e.g. through an imaginary narrator, or in the third person but through the eyes of one character – 'He was furious – how dare she!')
- **Social and historical context**. Influences on the author. Especially important for English Literature.

Section round-up

This section has encouraged you to consider what reading you already do, and suggested how you can read for different purposes and in different ways (remember skimming and scanning). It has told you what to look for in non-fiction (remember, especially, author's intention) and fiction (six points).

Writing

About this section

This section tells you how to tackle a piece of writing for English. It focuses on:

- **Purpose.**
- **Planning and structure.**
- **Beginnings and endings.**
- **Making your writing lively.**
- **Link words.**

Many of the points already made about oral work and reading apply to writing. In particular, if you read and note the techniques authors use, you'll become a better writer yourself.

What you'll have to do

Each of your exam papers will test you separately on reading and writing. You'll have to write your answer to the 'reading' question, but the focus will be on your reading of the text. The writing questions will test your ability to:

- argue, persuade or instruct
- inform, explain or describe.

You'll have a choice of questions, based on the reading part of the exam. In other words, you'll have something to start you off.

As to coursework, you'll have to do at least one piece of original writing. This could be, for example: a story, poetry, a play script, writing about your own experiences, or travel writing.

Purpose

In coursework, and almost certainly in the exam, you will have to bear in mind the exact purpose of the piece of writing, and who it is aimed at. Don't just think of yourself writing for the examiner or your teacher. In fact, it's a good idea to test out your coursework on other people and get feedback from them.

Some examples of purpose are given on pages 2–3. Remember, you may want to entertain, instruct, persuade or argue. You may be asked to 'Write an article for a teenage magazine' (or a children's magazine), to 'Write a letter to a newspaper', or 'Imagine you are an employee ... Write a memo to your boss.' ✪ How would you adapt your style and vocabulary in each case?

7

Launching into English Language

Planning and structure

Planning is the backbone of any piece of good writing. And if you plan properly, the structure will automatically follow on. The best way to plan is to use a visual approach, such as a spider diagram.

We'll take the example of Amir, faced with the exam question: '"The world would be a better place without cars." Write an essay arguing **either** for **or** against this statement.'

Amir could use a diagram to organise his arguments and number the order in which he wants to deal with each one.

Beginnings and endings

You'll find that the beginning comes more easily once you've planned properly, and once you know what your conclusion will be. Think of it like this: it's easier to begin a journey if you know your route and destination. It may help to draft the beginning and ending at the same time. Your ending could echo your beginning, giving the reader a sense of completion.

The beginning should capture the reader's attention, give an idea of what is to come, and arouse curiosity. Here are some possible beginnings for Amir's essay. ✪ What effects does each achieve? Which do you prefer?

> It's a grey Monday morning on the Walworth Road. Nazia pushes her toddler in the buggy. She's walking her 7-year-old son to a school half a mile from her home. At this hour of the day, her route is lined by a smoking, grumbling crocodile of cars, buses and lorries, all moving at slug pace, all pushing out a cocktail of chemical fumes into the air she and her children breathe.

> Isn't it wonderful to bowl along the open road, fresh air pouring in the window, serenaded by the sound system, while whitewashed cottages and rose gardens race past? But wait a minute …

> The last ten years have seen road traffic grow by 40 per cent, and thousands more miles of roadway built. Road transport produces 4.5 million tonnes of deadly carbon monoxide a year. Since 1979 diesel smoke has doubled. How does all this affect us?

How you end depends on your exact purpose. You might want to frighten people into action, or give them hope. By and large, you should aim to sum up your arguments and draw them to a short, punchy conclusion. You could echo the beginning, or leave the reader with something extra to think about. Here's a possible ending to match the third beginning above:

> Is the convenience of the car really worth the cost in human life and limb, stress, lung disease, and environmental destruction? Many people think not. But unless society as a whole decides this, by the year 2025 we will be faced with the nightmare of one and a half times as many cars on the road as we have now. How will we cope then?

Making your writing interesting

To write really interesting and persuasive non-fiction, you have to back your arguments with an appeal to the reader's imagination and emotions. Here's another version of the first beginning. ✪ Decide which you prefer, and why.

> It's Monday morning on the Walworth Road. Nazia pushes a buggy. She's walking her 7-year-old to a school half a mile from her home. At this hour of the day, there is a great deal of slow-moving traffic, all of it creating pollution.

Link words

Link words and phrases go between parts of a sentence, or at the beginning of a sentence, to smooth the flow of ideas and prepare the reader for what's coming next. They are particularly useful in writing argument. Here are the most important:

and	*whereas*	*nevertheless*
because	*which*	*despite*
or	*who*	*in addition*
but	*whom*	*what's more*
although	*however*	*moreover*

Try this

Write possible final paragraphs to match the first two beginnings above.

Make a plan for an essay arguing in favour of cars. You could start off by considering enjoyment, convenience and employment. Then write the opening.

Section round-up

Now you know about planning and structure, making your writing lively but smooth, and beginnings and endings.

Launching into English Language

Review

Checklist

Do you know:

		Yes	Not yet
1	What the National Curriculum covers – more or less (p. 1)?	☐	☐
2	What your specification covers (p. 1; ask your teacher for details)?	☐	☐
3	How to use this guide (p. 1)?	☐	☐
4	How the English language has developed (p. 2)?	☐	☐
5	About using formal and informal English (p. 3)?	☐	☐
6	About different styles of reading (pp. 4–5)?	☐	☐
7	What to look for in fiction and non-fiction (pp. 5–7)?	☐	☐
8	About purpose, planning, structure and style in writing (pp. 7–8)?	☐	☐

For your own notes

....

....

....

....

....

....

....

....

....

....

Chapter 2: Literary prose published before 1914

Overview

This chapter gives you examples of literary fiction published before the early twentieth century. It gives you an opportunity to read and respond to examples of work by major writers of previous eras. When you have worked through the chapter you will:

- Feel confident about reading literature from an earlier age.
- Be able to comment on character, plot and theme.
- Be able to comment on writers' use of language.
- Be able to make relevant comparisons.
- Be able to relate texts to their context.

Characterisation

About this section

This section introduces you to some fictional characters from novels written in the eighteenth and nineteenth centuries. When you have read the descriptions and worked through the suggestions you will be familiar with:

- Characterisation in novels from earlier centuries.
- Literary style before 1914.

Moll Flanders

The extract on page 11 is from *Moll Flanders*, a novel by Daniel Defoe published in 1722. We see Moll living in London. She has no money, and resorts to stealing.

Test your understanding

What is your first response to the passage? Look at the possible 'difficulties' listed in *Be prepared* in Medicine Box on this page.

Are there any unfamiliar words? You might have found: *whither*; *agoing*; *sally*; *jade*.

Hint: Even if you don't know what words like these mean, can you still understand the gist of what is being said? Apply some of the suggestions in *Ask yourself questions* in Medicine Box on this page. You will probably find that you can get the general meaning of a sentence even if it contains unfamiliar vocabulary.

Medicine Box

Ailment: It's too difficult. I can understand modern prose but my brain hurts as soon as I see a page of old-fashioned writing, and I can't make head or tail of it.

Dr Wordsmith's cure: The important thing is not to worry and to stay calm. What you are experiencing is quite common and understandable. As you know, language is constantly changing, and the language used in literary texts a century or more ago can seem very strange. The remedy for your condition is to **be prepared**, and to **ask yourself questions** to check your understanding.

Be prepared

Here are some of the differences you might find:

- unfamiliar words
- unfamiliar word order
- long sentences.

Ask yourself questions

Pause and ask yourself:

- What is being said?
- Who is doing, saying, thinking or feeling what?
- Can I put this in my own words?
- Can I explain to someone else what is being said?

Does the passage have words in an unfamiliar order?
You might have found: '… mixing with the crowd of people usually passing there, it was not possible to have been found out ….'

Hint: This part of the sentence describes how Moll mingles with the crowd to escape detection. Try to put it in your own words. Explain to a friend what is being said.

Are the sentences longer than you are used to?
Find some examples.

Your examples might include:

'However, I did the child no harm; I did not so much as fright it, for I had a great many tender thoughts about me yet, and did nothing but what, as I may say, mere necessity drove me to.'

Hint: If you find a long sentence difficult to grasp, try to break it up into its separate parts. Parts of a sentence separated by **semi-colons** (;) usually stand by themselves. Look for **conjunctions** (words like *and* and *for* that join parts of a sentence together). You should find each separate part of the sentence easier to follow.

Literary prose published before 1914

I went out now by daylight, and wandered about I knew not whither, and in search of I knew not what, when the devil put a snare in my way of a dreadful nature indeed, and such a one as I have never had before or since. Going through Aldersgate Street, there was a pretty little child had been at a dancing-school, and was agoing home all alone; and my prompter, like a true devil, set me upon this innocent creature. I talked to it, and it prattled to me again, and I took it by the hand and led it along till I came to a paved alley that goes into Bartholomew Close, and I led it in there. The child said, that was not its way home. I said, 'Yes, my dear, it is; I'll show you the way home.' The child had a little necklace on of gold beads, and I had my eye upon that, and in the dark of the alley I stooped, pretending to mend the child's clog that was loose, and took off her necklace, and the child never felt it, and so led the child on again. Here, I say, the devil put me upon killing the child in the dark alley, that it might not cry, but the very thought frightened me so that I was ready to drop down; but I turned the child about and bade it go back again, for that was not its way home; the child said, so she would; and I went through into Bartholomew Close, and then turned round to another passage that goes into Long Lane, so away into Charterhouse Yard and out into St John's Street; then crossing into Smithfield, went down Chick Lane, and into Field Lane, to Holborn Bridge, when, mixing with the crowd of people usually passing there, it was not possible to have been found out; and thus I made my second sally into the world.

The thoughts of this booty put out all the thoughts of the first, and the reflections I had made wore quickly off; poverty hardened my heart, and my own necessities made me regardless of anything. The last affair left no great concern upon me, for as I did the poor child no harm, I only thought I had given the parents a just reproof for their negligence, in leaving the poor lamb to come home by itself, and it would teach them to take more care another time.

This string of beads was worth about £12 or £14. I suppose it might have been formerly the mother's, for it was too big for the child's wear, but that, perhaps, the vanity of the mother to have her child look fine at the dancing-school, had made her let the child wear it; and no doubt the child had a maid sent to take care of it, but she, like a careless jade, was taken up perhaps with some fellow that had met her, and so the poor baby wandered till it fell into my hands.

However, I did the child no harm; I did not so much as fright it, for I had a great many tender thoughts about me yet, and did nothing but what, as I may say, mere necessity drove me to.

What impression of Moll's character do you gain from the extract ?

Hint: Look at what she does, and what she says about her actions.

Which of these statements do you agree with?

- Moll says she is tempted by the devil.
- Moll steals a little girl's clog.
- Moll kills the child to stop it crying.
- Moll's conscience is troubled by what she has done.
- Moll thinks the child's parents are to blame for allowing her to go home alone.
- Moll thinks the child shouldn't have been wearing the necklace anyway.
- Moll says she was driven to steal by necessity.

Draw a diagram or chart showing Moll's character. Start with 'actions' and 'thoughts'.

Literary prose published before 1914

Bleak House

You will meet a very different girl in this extract. It is taken from *Bleak House*, a novel by Charles Dickens, published in 1853.

In a poor room, with a sloping ceiling, and containing very little furniture, was a mite of a boy, some five or six years old, nursing and hushing a heavy child of eighteen months. There was no fire, though the weather was cold; both children were wrapped in some poor shawls and tippets, as a substitute. Their clothing was not so warm, however, but that their noses looked red and pinched, and their small figures shrunken, as the boy walked up and down, nursing and hushing the child with its head on its shoulder.

'Who has locked you up here alone?' we naturally asked.

'Charley,' said the boy, standing still to gaze at us.

'Is Charley your brother?'

'No. She's my sister, Charlotte. Father called her Charley.'

'Are there any more of you besides Charley?'

'Me,' said the boy, 'and Emma,' patting the limp bonnet of the child he was nursing. 'And Charley.'

'Where is Charley now?'

'Out a-washing,' said the boy, beginning to walk up and down again, and taking the nankeen bonnet much too near the bedstead, by trying to gaze at us at the same time.

We were looking at one another, and at these two children, when there came into the room a very little girl, childish in figure but shrewd and older-looking in the face – pretty-faced, too – wearing a womanly sort of bonnet much too large for her, and drying her bare arms on a womanly sort of apron. Her fingers were white and wrinkled with washing, and the soap-suds were yet smoking which she wiped off her arms. But for this, she might have been a child, playing at washing, and imitating a poor working-woman with a quick observation of the truth.

She had come running from some place in the neighbourhood, and had made all the haste she could. Consequently, though she was very light, she was out of breath, and could not speak at first, as she stood panting, and wiping her arms, and looking quietly at us.

'O, here's Charley!' said the boy.

The child he was nursing stretched forth its arms, and cried out to be taken by Charley. The little girl took it, in a womanly sort of manner belonging to the apron and bonnet, and stood looking at us over the burden that clung to her most affectionately.

'Is it possible,' whispered my guardian, as we put a chair for the little creature, and got her to sit down with her load: the little boy keeping close to her, holding to her apron, 'that this child works for the rest? Look at this! For God's sake look at this!'

It was a thing to look at. The three children close together, and two of them relying solely on the third, and the third so young and yet with an air of age and steadiness that sat so strangely on the childish figure.

'Charley, Charley!' said my guardian. 'How old are you?'

'Over thirteen, sir,' replied the child.

'O! What a great age!' said my guardian. 'What a great age, Charley!'

I cannot describe the tenderness with which he spoke to her; half playfully, yet all the more compassionately and mournfully.

'And do you live alone here with these babies, Charley?' said my guardian.

'Yes, sir,' returned the child, looking up into his face with perfect confidence, 'since father died.'

'And how do you live, Charley? O! Charley,' said my guardian, turning his face away for a moment, 'how do you live?'

'Since father died, sir, I've gone out to work. I'm out washing today.'

'God help you, Charley!' said my guardian. 'You're not tall enough to reach the tub!'

'In pattens I am, sir,' she said, quickly. 'I've got a high pair as belonged to mother.'

'And when did mother die? Poor mother!'

Literary prose published before 1914

'Mother died just after Emma was born,' said the child, glancing at the face upon her bosom. 'Then father said I was to be as good a mother to her as I could. And so I tried. And so I worked at home, and I did cleaning and nursing and washing for a long time before I began to go out. And that's how I know how; don't you see, sir?'

'And do you often go out?'

'As often as I can,' said Charley, opening her eyes and smiling, 'because of earning sixpences and shillings!'

'And do you always lock the babies up when you go out?'

'To keep 'em safe, sir, don't you see?' said Charley. 'Mrs Blinder comes up now and then, and Mr Gridley comes up sometimes, and perhaps I can run in sometimes, and they can play, you know, and Tom ain't afraid of being locked up, are you, Tom?'

'No-o!' said Tom, stoutly.

'When it comes on dark the lamps are lighted down in the court, and they show up here quite bright – almost quite bright. Don't they, Tom?'

'Yes, Charley,' said Tom, 'almost quite bright.'

'Then he's as good as gold,' said the little creature – O! in such a motherly, womanly way! 'And when Emma's tired he puts her to bed. And when he's tired he goes to bed himself. And when I come home and light the candle, and has a bit of supper, he sits up again and has it with me. Don't you, Tom?'

'O yes, Charley!' said Tom. 'That I do!' And either in this glimpse of the great pleasure of his life, or in gratitude and love for Charley, who was all in all to him, he laid his face among the scanty folds of her frock, and passed from laughing into crying.

It was the first time since our entry that a tear had been shed among these children. The little orphan girl had spoken of their father and their mother, as if all that sorrow were subdued by the necessity of taking courage, and by her childish importance in being able to work, and by her bustling, busy way. But now, when Tom cried; although she sat quite tranquil, looking quietly at us, and did not by any movement disturb a hair of the head of either of her little charges; I saw two silent tears fall down her face.

Try this

What do you gather from the passage about Charley and her way of life?

Hint: Look for descriptive details that help to create a full picture of the character and the circumstances of her life. You might include:

- details that show how cold the children are
- details that show how Charley is more like a woman than a young girl.

Show your ideas in a diagram. Include Charley's situation and her responsibilities.

Section round-up

You've survived the first close encounter with literary fiction written before 1914. You should now be familiar with:

- Some of the ways in which pre-1914 authors present characters.
- Literary style of earlier periods.

Literary prose published before 1914

Context and tradition

About this section

All novels reflect the conventions and cultural backgrounds of the world in which they are set. Because the world of a century or more ago was very different from today's world, you will come across ideas and attitudes that may seem strange. Remember that language isn't the only thing that changes. However, novels of all ages deal with common human experiences and emotions such as love, jealousy, hate. The following extracts all deal with love and marriage. When you have finished this section you will be able to:

- Discuss attitudes to love and marriage as shown in a variety of pre-1914 texts.
- Refer in detail to aspects of presentation and style.

Wuthering Heights

This extract is from *Wuthering Heights* by Emily Brontë, published in 1847. Catherine is telling Nelly, the housekeeper, that Edgar Linton has asked her to marry him. Cathy is torn between her feelings for Edgar and her love for Heathcliff, the orphan foundling she has grown up with.

I went into the kitchen and sat down. Heathcliff, as I thought, walked through to the barn. It turned out, afterwards, that he only got as far as the other side of the settle, when he flung himself on a bench by the wall, removed from the fire, and remained silent …

… Miss Cathy … put her head in, and whispered,

'Are you alone, Nelly?'

'Yes, Miss,' I replied.

She entered and approached the hearth. I, supposing she was going to say something, looked up. The expression of her face seemed disturbed and anxious. Her lips were half asunder, as if she meant to speak; and she drew a breath, but it escaped in a sigh, instead of a sentence.

I resumed my song, not having forgotten her recent behaviour.

'Where's Heathcliff?' she said, interrupting me.

'About his work in the stable,' was my answer.

He did not contradict me; perhaps he had fallen into a doze.

There followed another long pause, during which I perceived a drop or two trickle from Catherine's cheek to the flags.

'Is she sorry for her shameful conduct?' I asked myself. 'That will be a novelty, but she may come to the point as she will – I shan't help her!'

No, she felt small trouble regarding any subject, save her own concerns.

'Oh, dear!' she cried at last. 'I'm very unhappy!'

'A pity,' observed I, 'you're hard to please – so many friends and so few cares, and can't make yourself content!'

'Nelly, will you keep a secret for me?' she pursued, kneeling down by me, and lifting her winsome eyes to my face with that sort of look which turns off bad temper, even when one has all the right in the world to indulge it.

'Is it worth keeping?' I inquired, less sulkily.

'Yes, and it worries me, and I must let it out! I want to know what I should do – To-day, Edgar Linton has asked me to marry him, and I've given him an answer – Now, before I tell you whether it was a consent, or denial – you tell me which it ought to have been.'

'Really, Miss Catherine, how can I know?' I replied. 'To be sure, considering the exhibition you

14

Literary prose published before 1914

performed in his presence, this afternoon, I might say it would be wise to refuse him – since he asked you after that, he must either be hopelessly stupid, or a venturesome fool.'

'If you talk so, I won't tell you any more,' she returned, peevishly, rising to her feet. 'I accepted him, Nelly. Be quick, and say whether I was wrong!'

'You accepted him? Then, what good is it discussing the matter? You have pledged your word, and cannot retract.'

'But, say whether I should have done so – do!' she exclaimed in an irritated tone, chafing her hands together, and frowning.

'There are many things to be considered, before that question can be answered properly,' I said sententiously. 'First and foremost, do you love Mr Edgar?'

'Who can help it? Of course I do,' she answered.

Then I put her through the following catechism – for a girl of twenty-two, it was not injudicious.

'Why do you love him, Miss Cathy?'

'Nonsense, I do – that's sufficient.'

'By no means; you must say why.'

'Well, because he is handsome, and pleasant to be with.'

'Bad,' was my commentary.

'And because he is young and cheerful.'

'Bad, still.'

'And because he loves me.'

'Indifferent, coming there.'

'And he will be rich, and I shall like to be the greatest woman of the neighbourhood, and I shall be proud of having such a husband.'

'Worst of all! And, now, you say how you love him?'

'As everybody loves – You're silly, Nelly.'

'Not at all – Answer.'

'I love the ground under his feet, and the air over his head, and everything he touches, and every word he says – I love all his looks, and all his actions, and him entirely, and altogether. There now!'

'And why?'

'Nay – you are making a jest of it; it is exceedingly ill-natured! It's no jest to me!' said the young lady, scowling, and turning her face to the fire.

'I'm very far from jesting, Miss Catherine,' I replied. 'You love Mr Edgar because he is handsome, and young, and cheerful, and rich, and loves you. The last, however, goes for nothing – You would love him without that, probably, and with it, you wouldn't, unless he possessed the four former attractions.'

'No, to be sure not – I should only pity him – hate him, perhaps, if he were ugly, and a clown.'

'But there are several other handsome, rich young men in the world; handsomer, possibly, and richer than he is – What should hinder you from loving them?'

'If there be any, they are out of my way – I've seen none like Edgar.'

'You may see some; and he won't always be handsome, and young, and may not always be rich.'

'He is now; and I have only to do with the present – I wish you would speak rationally.'

'Well, that settles it – if you have only to do with the present, marry Mr Linton.'

'I don't want your permission for that – I shall marry him; and yet, you have not told me whether I'm right.'

'Perfectly right! if people be right to marry only for the present. And now, let us hear what you are unhappy about. Your brother will be pleased … the old lady and gentleman will not object, I think – you will escape from a disorderly, comfortless home into a wealthy, respectable one; and you love Edgar, and Edgar loves you. All seems smooth and easy – where is the obstacle?'

'Here! and here!' replied Catherine, striking one hand on her forehead, and the other on her breast. 'In whichever place the soul lives – in my soul, and in my heart, I'm convinced I'm wrong!'

Literary prose published before 1914

> 'That is very strange! I cannot make it out.'
>
> 'It's my secret; but if you will not mock at me, I'll explain it; I can't do it distinctly – but I'll give you a feeling of how I feel.'
>
> She seated herself by me again: her countenance grew sadder and graver, and her clasped hands trembled …
>
> … 'If I were in heaven, Nelly, I should be extremely miserable.'
>
> 'Because you are not fit to go there,' I answered. 'All sinners would be miserable in heaven.'
>
> 'But it is not for that. I dreamt, once, that I was there.'
>
> 'I tell you I won't harken to your dreams, Miss Catherine! I'll go to bed,' I interrupted again.
>
> She laughed, and held me down, for I made a motion to leave my chair.
>
> 'This is nothing,' cried she; 'I was only going to say that heaven did not seem to be my home; and I broke my heart with weeping to come back to earth; and the angels were so angry that they flung me out, into the middle of the heath on the top of Wuthering Heights, where I woke sobbing for joy. That will do to explain my secret, as well as the other. I've no more business to marry Edgar Linton than I have to be in heaven; and if the wicked man in there had not brought Heathcliff so low, I shouldn't have thought of it. It would degrade me to marry Heathcliff, now; so he shall never know how I love him; and that, not because he's handsome, Nelly, but because he's more myself than I am. Whatever our souls are made of, his and mine are the same, and Linton's is as different as a moonbeam from lightning, or frost from fire.'
>
> Ere this speech ended, I became sensible of Heathcliff's presence. Having noticed a slight movement, I turned my head, and saw him rise from the bench, and steal out noiselessly. He had listened till he heard Catherine say it would degrade her to marry him, and then he stayed to hear no farther.

Ask yourself some questions. ✪ What is Nelly like? What is Catherine like? What does Nelly think of Catherine? Why does Nelly question Cathy about her decision? What do you think of Cathy's answers?

✪ Which of these statements do you agree with? Find evidence to support your opinion.

- Catherine is always well-behaved.
- Catherine is usually sorry when she has done something wrong.
- Heathcliff is working in the stable while this conversation takes place.
- Nelly thinks Edgar is right to want to marry Cathy.
- Nelly thinks that all Cathy's reasons for marrying Edgar are poor ones.
- Catherine cares about Nelly's opinion.

Jot down your impressions as a diagram.

Ask yourself some questions. ✪ Do your impressions of Nelly and Cathy change? Do you think Cathy should marry Edgar? ✪ What do you think Heathcliff feels as he listens? What doesn't he hear Catherine say?

Hint: You get an insight into characters from the language they use. Look closely at the way Catherine describes her feeling that she belongs in Wuthering Heights, and the way she describes her feelings for Heathcliff.

A tip from Dr Wordsmith …

Many books present conflict or contrast between the characters. This often forms the basis for questions on a text. As you read, look for examples of ways in which characters are different from each other, and think about how this might affect what happens. Remember to notice what characters say and how they speak and behave.

Finish your diagram.

Your turn

What impression do you gain from the passage of Catherine and Nelly, and the relationship between them?

Hint: Use your diagram to draw your ideas together. Your answer should include some of the following points:

- Catherine is emotional and quick-tempered.
- Catherine wants to be reassured that she should marry Edgar.
- She wants to be taken seriously and dislikes being teased.

Literary prose published before 1914

- Catherine thinks social status is important.
- She would find it degrading to marry Heathcliff.
- Her feelings for Heathcliff are more passionate than her feelings for Edgar.
- Nelly is critical of Catherine and thinks she is spoilt.
- Nelly thinks that Catherine needs guidance.
- Nelly thinks that Catherine is marrying Edgar for the wrong reasons.

What do you find interesting about the language and style of the passage?

Hint: Use your diagram to gather some ideas. Look at how characters communicate, and at the use of images or powerful language. Your answer could include some of the following points:

- The first-person narrative
- The use of varied dialogue
- Catherine's images of heaven, angels, lightning and fire.

Write a description of Heathcliff's feelings as he listens, and leaves. Write in the first person, if you like.

Here are some different ways of beginning. Which one do you think is most effective? Why?

(a) 'During Cathy's conversation with Nelly I thought I ought to reveal that I was there on the other side of the settle, and could hear every word they said.'

(b) 'When Heathcliff hears Cathy say that she is going to marry Edgar Linton, he must feel really jealous.'

(c) 'She said it would degrade her to marry me. I can't explain the despair I feel every time I think of those words, and think of her marrying that weakling Linton.'

Discuss what might happen as the novel continues. Will Cathy marry Edgar? How do you think the marriage will turn out? What will Heathcliff do? Will he ever discover Cathy's true feelings for him? What might happen if he did?

Pride and Prejudice

On the next page is another passage about difficulties in love. This extract is from Jane Austen's novel *Pride and Prejudice*, published in 1813. Lady Catherine de Bourgh wants her nephew, Mr Darcy, to marry her daughter. She is alarmed because she has discovered that there may be a relationship between Mr Darcy and a young lady called Elizabeth Bennet. We see her here tackling Elizabeth on the subject.

Ask yourself some questions. ✪ Who wants Darcy and Miss de Bourgh to get married? What reasons does Lady Catherine give for objecting to Elizabeth as a possible wife for Darcy? What does she say will happen if Elizabeth were to marry Darcy? ✪ What impression have you gained of the characters of Lady Catherine and Elizabeth?

Record your responses and ideas.

Ask yourself some questions. ✪ Why does Lady Catherine think that a marriage between Darcy and her daughter would be so suitable? What further reasons does she give for objecting to Elizabeth? ✪ What reasons does Elizabeth give for refusing to do what she wants?

Practice time

Plan, write or discuss answers to these questions.

How does the writer direct our response to the characters?

Hint: Remember **WHE** – **W**hat is said, **H**ow it is said, and what the **E**ffect is. For each character, look at what she says and what it reveals of her ideas and beliefs. Think about the tone in which she speaks and the kind of language she uses. Decide what effect is intended and think about how you respond. Your answer could include some of these points:

Lady Catherine:

- values status, money and family connections
- snobbish
- pompous
- overbearing
- rude
- calls Elizabeth selfish and unfeeling, words that apply to herself
- seems ridiculous
- reader dislikes her and laughs at her.

Elizabeth:

- quick-witted
- argues soundly
- won't be bullied
- stands up for herself
- reader likes her and wants her to win the encounter.

17

Literary prose published before 1914

'Let me be rightly understood. This match, to which you have the presumption to aspire, can never take place. No, never. Mr Darcy is engaged to *my daughter*. Now what have you to say?'

'Only this; that if he is so, you can have no reason to suppose he will make an offer to me.'

Lady Catherine hesitated for a moment, and then replied, 'The engagement between them is of a peculiar kind. From their infancy, they have been intended for each other. It was the favourite wish of his mother, as well as of hers. While in their cradles, we planned the union; and now, at the moment when the wishes of both sisters would be accomplished, in their marriage, to be prevented by a young woman of inferior birth, of no importance in the world, and wholly unallied to the family! Do you pay no regard to the wishes of his friends? To his tacit engagement with Miss de Bourgh? Are you lost to every feeling of propriety and delicacy? Have you not heard me say, that from his earliest hours he was destined for his cousin?'

'Yes, and I had heard it before. But what is that to me? If there is no other objection to my marrying your nephew, I shall certainly not be kept from it, by knowing that his mother and aunt wished him to marry Miss de Bourgh. You both did as much as you could, in planning the marriage. Its completion depended on others. If Mr Darcy is neither by honour nor inclination confined to his cousin, why is not he to make another choice? And if I am that choice, why may not I accept him?'

'Because honour, decorum, prudence, nay, interest, forbid it. Yes, Miss Bennet, interest; for do not expect to be noticed by his family or friends, if you wilfully act against the inclinations of all. You will be censured, slighted, and despised, by every one connected with him. Your alliance will be a disgrace; your name will never even be mentioned by any of us.'

'These are heavy misfortunes,' replied Elizabeth. 'But the wife of Mr Darcy must have such extraordinary sources of happiness necessarily attached to her situation, that she could, upon the whole, have no cause to repine.'

'Obstinate, headstrong girl! I am ashamed of you! Is this your gratitude for my attentions to you last spring? Is nothing due to me on that score?

'Let us sit down. You are to understand, Miss Bennet, that I came here with the determined resolution of carrying my purpose; nor will I be dissuaded from it. I have not been used to submit to any person's whims. I have not been in the habit of brooking disappointment.'

'*That* will make your ladyship's situation at present more pitiable; but it will have no effect on *me*.'

'I will not be interrupted. Hear me in silence. My daughter and my nephew are formed for each other. They are descended on the maternal side, from the same noble line; and, on the father's, from respectable, honourable, and ancient, though untitled families. Their fortune on both sides is splendid. They are destined for each other by the voice of every member of their respective houses; and what is to divide them? The upstart pretensions of a young woman without family, connections, or fortune. Is this to be endured! But it must not, shall not be. If you were sensible of your own good, you would not wish to quit the sphere in which you have been brought up.'

'In marrying your nephew, I should not consider myself as quitting that sphere. He is a gentleman; I am a gentleman's daughter; so far we are equal.'

'True. You are a gentleman's daughter. But who was your mother? Who are your uncles and aunts? Do not imagine me ignorant of their condition.'

'Whatever my connections may be,' said Elizabeth, 'if your nephew does not object to them, they can be nothing to you.'

'Tell me once and for all, are you engaged to him?'

Though Elizabeth would not, for the mere purpose of obliging Lady Catherine, have answered this question, she could not but say, after a moment's deliberation,

'I am not.'

Lady Catherine seemed pleased.

'And will you promise me, never to enter into such an engagement?'

'I will make no promise of the kind.'

'Miss Bennet, I am shocked and astonished. I expected to find a more reasonable young woman. But do not deceive yourself into a belief that I will ever recede. I shall not go away, till you have given me the assurance I require.'

'And I certainly never shall give it. I am not to be intimidated into anything so wholly unreasonable. Your ladyship wants Mr Darcy to marry your daughter; but would my giving you the wished-for promise make their marriage at all more probable? Supposing him to be attached to me, would my refusing to accept his hand make him wish to bestow it on his cousin? Allow me to say, Lady Catherine, that the arguments with which you have supported this extraordinary application have been as frivolous as the application was ill-judged. You have widely mistaken my character, if you

Literary prose published before 1914

> think I can be worked on by such persuasions as these. How far your nephew might approve of your interference in his affairs, I cannot tell; but you have certainly no right to concern yourself in mine. I must beg, therefore, to be importuned no farther on the subject.'
>
> 'Not so hasty, if you please. I have by no means done. To all the objections I have already urged, I have still another to add. I am no stranger to the particulars of your youngest sister's infamous elopement. I know it all; that the young man's marrying her was a patched-up business, at the expense of your father and uncles. And is such a girl to be my nephew's sister? Is her husband, is the son of his late father's steward, to be his brother? Heaven and earth! – of what are you thinking? Are the shades of Pemberley to be thus polluted?'
>
> 'You can now have nothing farther to say,' she resentfully answered. 'You have insulted me, in every possible method. I must beg to return to the house.'
>
> And she rose as she spoke. Lady Catherine rose also, and they turned back. Her ladyship was highly incensed.
>
> 'You have no regard, then, for the honour and credit of my nephew! Unfeeling, selfish girl! Do you not consider that a connection with you must disgrace him in the eyes of everybody?'
>
> 'Lady Catherine, I have nothing farther to say. You know my sentiments.'

What does the passage tell you about society's attitude to love and marriage, and what the writer's view is?

Hint: Look at how the characters display certain attitudes and ideas. The reader rejects everything Lady Catherine says because she is such a ridiculous and unpleasant character. We cannot take her ideas seriously – we are supposed to mock them as the writer mocks her. It is likely, then, that the writer disagrees with the views expressed by this character. Your answer might include some of the following points.

Some people (like Lady Catherine) think that marriage:

- is an arrangement
- should be between people of similar backgrounds
- should be between people of equal wealth.

Other people (like Elizabeth) think that marriage should involve:

- feelings
- choice
- honour
- respect.

You could put on a dramatised reading of this scene. Work out what instructions you will give the readers about how they should speak and move.

A word from Dr Wordsmith ...

Be careful not to assume that the author's views are always the same as his or her characters'. Sometimes a writer gives a character attitudes and beliefs that the writer wishes to criticise. Often this is achieved through the technique known as **irony**, when there is a difference between what is said and what is meant.

Section round-up

Now that you have worked through this section you should be familiar with some of the ways in which writers pre-1914 deal with love and marriage:

- Aspects of characterisation.
- The idea that the writer and the characters are separate and can have different views.

Literary prose published before 1914

Setting

About this section

Descriptions of places or settings in stories are very important. Often they do more than just set the scene. Setting can help to create mood and atmosphere, and also tell you something about the characters. When you have finished this section you will be able to:

- Discuss the way some pre-1914 writers present places and settings.
- Comment on features of style.
- Offer personal response.

The Fall of the House of Usher

This extract is from the short story, 'The Fall of the House of Usher', by Edgar Allan Poe. The narrator of the story has received a letter from his childhood friend, Roderick Usher, asking him to visit. Here he sees his friend's house for the first time.

I scanned … the building. Its principal feature seemed to be that of an excessive antiquity. The discoloration of ages had been great. Minute fungi overspread the whole exterior, hanging in a fine tangled web-work from the eaves. Yet all this was apart from any extraordinary dilapidation. No portion of the masonry had fallen; and there appeared to be a wild inconsistency between its still perfect adaptation of parts and the crumbling condition of the individual stones. In this there was much that reminded me of the specious totality of old woodwork which has rotted for long years in some neglected vault, with no disturbance from the breath of the external air. Beyond this indication of extensive decay, however, the fabric gave little token of instability. Perhaps the eye of a scrutinizing observer might have discovered a barely perceptible fissure, which, extending from the roof of the building in front, made its way down the wall in a zigzag direction, until it became lost in the sullen waters of the tarn.

Noticing these things, I rode over a short causeway to the house. A servant in waiting took my horse, and I entered the Gothic archway of the hall. A valet, of stealthy step, thence conducted me, in silence, through many dark and intricate passages in my progress to the studio of his master. Much that I encountered on the way contributed, I know not how, to heighten the vague sentiments of which I have already spoken. While the objects around me – while the carvings of the ceilings, the sombre tapestries of the walls, the ebon blackness of the floors, and the phantasmagoric armorial trophies which rattled as I strode, were but matters to which, or to such as which, I had been accustomed from my infancy – while I hesitated not to acknowledge how familiar was all this – I still wondered to find how unfamiliar were the fancies which ordinary images were stirring up … The valet now threw open a door and ushered me into the presence of his master.

Literary prose published before 1914

The room in which I found myself was very large and lofty. The windows were long, narrow, and pointed, and at so vast a distance from the black oaken floor as to be altogether inaccessible from within. Feeble gleams of encrimsoned light made their way through the trellised panes, and served to render sufficiently distinct the more prominent objects around; the eye, however, struggled in vain to reach the remoter angles of the chamber, or the recesses of the vaulted and fretted ceiling. Dark draperies hung upon the walls. The general furniture was profuse, comfortless, antique, and tattered. Many books and musical instruments lay scattered about, but failed to give any vitality to the scene. I felt that I breathed an atmosphere of sorrow. An air of stern, deep, and irredeemable gloom hung over and pervaded all.

Over to you

What does the narrator find strange about the outside of the house?

Hint: Look at how he describes the way in which the building has aged.
You might notice:

- the building's extreme age and discoloration
- the fungi
- the crumbling stones
- no part of the building has fallen.

What impression is created by the description of the passages through which the narrator is taken?

Hint: Look for details of description.

Pick out adjectives. Think about the overall effect that is created. You might comment on:

- the sombre tapestries
- the ebon blackness of the floors
- the phantasmagoric armorial trophies
- the narrator's sense of his imagination being stirred up.

What words from this list might you use to describe the effect created?

*pleasant   attractive   gloomy   mysterious
foreboding   relaxed   tense   welcoming*

What effect is created by the description of the room itself?

Hint: Look at the description of the windows, the draperies and the furniture.

You might comment on:

- the high windows that give little light – 'feeble gleams'
- the light is 'encrimsoned'
- the trellised panes
- the high ceiling, 'vaulted and fretted'.

What words from this list could you use to describe the effect created?

*cosy   forbidding   shadowy   peaceful   troubled
easy   disturbed*

What kind of story does the description prepare us for?

Imagine that you are making a film of the story, and are looking for a house to represent the House of Usher.

(a) Give a full description of the kind of house you want.

(b) Give directions for shooting the scene you have just read. Think about what effect you want to create. Will you have camera close-ups? What about music? (If you are used to doing storyboards, you may like to try one.)

Literary prose published before 1914

Hard Times

This description is from *Hard Times* by Charles Dickens, published in 1854. The passage introduces the reader to Coketown, an industrial town in the north of England.

It was a town of red brick, or of brick that would have been red if the smoke and ashes had allowed it; but as matters stood it was a town of unnatural red and black like the painted face of a savage. It was a town of machinery and tall chimneys, out of which interminable serpents of smoke trailed themselves for ever and ever, and never got uncoiled. It had a black canal in it, and a river that ran purple with ill-smelling dye, and vast piles of building full of windows where there was a rattling and a trembling all day long, and where the pistons of the steam-engine worked monotonously up and down like the head of an elephant in a state of melancholy madness. It contained several large streets all very like one another, inhabited by people equally like one another, who all went in and out at the same hours, with the same sound upon the same pavements, to do the same work, and to whom every day was the same as yesterday and tomorrow, and every year the counterpart of the last and the next.

Practice time

What impression of Coketown is created here?

Hint: Look for details of description that can be linked together, such as sights and sounds. Notice the language and imagery that is used, and think about its effect. You could comment on:

- the effect of colour
- the effect of the similes 'like the painted face of a savage' and 'like the head of an elephant in a state of melancholy madness'
- the effect of the image 'interminable serpents of smoke'
- the effect of repetition of 'all', 'every', 'same'
- the length and rhythm of the last sentence.

Literary prose published before 1914

Far from the Madding Crowd

In this extract from *Far from the Madding Crowd*, published in 1874, the author Thomas Hardy describes Norcombe Hill on a windy night.

The hill was covered on its northern side by an ancient and decaying plantation of beeches, whose upper verge formed a line over the crest, fringing its arched curve against the sky, like a mane. Tonight these trees sheltered the southern slope from the keenest blasts, which smote the wood and floundered through it with a sound as of grumbling, or gushed over its crowning boughs in a weakened moan. The dry leaves in the ditch simmered and boiled in the same breezes, a tongue of air occasionally ferreting out a few, and sending them spinning across the grass.

The thin grasses, more or less coating the hill, were touched by the wind in breezes of differing powers and of almost differing natures – one rubbing the blades heavily, another raking them piercingly, another brushing them like a soft broom. The instinctive act of humankind was to stand and listen, and learn how the trees on the right and the trees on the left wailed or chanted to each other in the regular antiphonies of a cathedral choir; how hedges and other shapes then caught the note, lowering it to the tenderest sob; and how the hurrying gust then plunged into the south, to be heard no more.

Think about this

How does Thomas Hardy make the scene come alive?

Hint: Look for visual effects, and for words which express the sound and movement of the wind.

You could include:

- the 'arched curve' of the trees against the sky
- the simile 'like a mane'
- words such as 'grumbled', 'gushed', 'weakened moan'
- the way the trees 'wailed and chanted'.

How is Thomas Hardy's interest in time, change and the relationship between people and nature shown in the passage?

Hint: You could consider:

- the phrase 'ancient and decaying plantation of beeches'
- the way that the scene constantly changes (the movement of the leaves, the varying nature of the wind)
- the instinctive response of human beings to stand and listen
- the sense of awe conveyed through likening the sound of the wind to 'a cathedral choir'.

Literary prose published before 1914

Section round-up

Now you have worked through this section you should be familiar with:

- Ways of presenting places and settings.

- The use of language to create particular effects.

Review

This chapter has introduced you to writers and texts of earlier periods.

Checklist

Check that you now feel confident about:

		Yes	Not yet
1	Reading texts published before 1914.	❏	❏
2	Commenting on character.	❏	❏
3	Commenting on ideas presented in the text.	❏	❏
4	Discussing the use of language.	❏	❏

If you have answered 'Not yet' to any question, skim-read some of the hints and tips in the chapter. If you are still not sure, ask your teacher.

For your own notes

....

....

....

....

....

....

....

....

Literary prose published after 1914 — Chapter 3

Overview

This chapter gives you examples of novels and short stories published at any time from 1914 to the present day. As part of your exam work you will read, understand and appreciate high-quality fiction by major modern authors.

By the end of this chapter you will be able to:

- Read and understand a range of modern literary fiction.
- Comment on how authors achieve different effects in their writing.
- Show understanding of themes and characters.
- Give informed personal response to a variety of literary prose published after 1914.

Openings

About this section

This section gives you an opportunity to read the openings of two novels, and to think about how the authors create comic effects. When you have read the passages carefully and worked through some of the tasks, you should be able to show that you:

- Understand the openings of two modern novels.
- Can demonstrate understanding of the characters.
- Can show understanding of the writers' techniques and intentions.
- Can comment on the use of language.

Remind yourself of some of the aspects to think about when you read literary texts: character, setting, context, structure, plot and theme.

Fair Do's

This passage on the next page is the beginning of *Fair Do's*, a novel by David Nobbs, published in 1990.

Ask yourself some questions. ✪ What is happening? Who are the people? What are they like? ✪ How are they described? What kind of passage is it – funny, sad, exciting, mysterious? ✪ What is the Effect of the passage?

A tip from Dr Wordsmith …

Remember to use the technique introduced in Chapter 2, the WHE technique.
Ask yourself three questions as you read:

- **W**hat is the writer saying?
- **H**ow is it said?
- What **E**ffect is created?

Record your impressions: make notes or draw a diagram.

Literary prose published after 1914

The Church clock proclaimed the quarter. Several people on Gerry's side frowned. While a bride was expected to be late, a politician's wife was expected to be punctual enough to be only slightly late.

Leslie Horton, water-bailiff and organist, who hated to be called Les, thundered through his limited repertoire without subtlety.

Gerry smiled serenely at the new young vicar, who had not yet won the hearts of his congregation.

The long-haired Carol Fordinbridge was the first to mouth the possibility that had begun to form in a hundred barely credulous minds.

'Wouldn't it be awful if she didn't turn up?' she whispered.

The moment Leslie Horton had dreaded arrived. He had exhausted his programme of suitable pieces. The buzz of speculation in the congregation was growing steadily louder. Hats bobbled in horrified excitement. The new young vicar looked at Leslie Horton and shrugged with his eyes. Leslie Horton sighed with his shoulders and returned to the beginning of his repertoire.

The huge ribbed radiators had to fight valiantly against the stony chill of the abbey, even on this unseasonal day. With no joyous emotion to warm them, the ladies began to shiver. One of Rita's uncles had a sneezing fit.

The vicar advanced upon Gerry, who tried to smile confidently. His smile curled at the edges like a slice of tongue approaching its 'sell-by' date. The eyes of the congregation were upon them.

'If she isn't here soon,' whispered the vicar, 'I'll have to truncate the ceremony.'

'Truncate the ceremony?' hissed Gerry Lansdown. 'I don't want a truncated ceremony. I haven't paid a truncated licence fee.'

The vicar continued, 'I have another wedding later, the groom is a councillor, and I do not intend to have to delay an important wedding in my very first week here.'

Gerry Lansdown's hackles rose. His back arched. He was an insulted cat, ready for battle. But the vicar had gone.

The clock struck the half hour.

'Five more minutes,' whispered the vicar.

Gerry's lips twitched. 'Your precious councillor will have to wait, vicar,' he hissed. 'I think you should know that I just happen to be the prospective Social Liberal Democratic parliamentary candidate for Hindhead.'

The vicar smiled thinly. 'He's a serving councillor, not prospective. And he's chairman of the Tower Appeal Fund Committee. Five minutes.'

The hum of conversation grew louder still. Leslie Horton's playing grew slower. The sun lit up the garish battle scenes in the modern stained-glass window, dedicated to the King's Own Yorkshire Light Infantry.

The new young vicar made a signal to Gerry.

Gerry nodded resignedly. A crescent of blue, reflected from a stained-glass window, was falling across his face.

'Ladies and gentlemen,' said the vicar. 'It looks as if something has happened. I'm afraid we have no alternative, for the moment, as we have further nuptials pending on a tight schedule at this ever-popular venue, but to respectfully suspend the wedding for the moment. Mr Horton, would you please play us out?'

Leslie Horton, water-bailiff and organist, who hated to be called Les, would wonder to the end of his days why he played 'The Wedding March' at that moment.

The wedding guests stood uneasily in the tactless sunshine. The women had to hold onto their hats as another gust announced the fragility of the fine weather. The men found no opportunity to wear their top hats and wondered why they had hired them. The funny little man with big ears who turned up unbidden at all the weddings walked slowly away, shaking his head.

Literary prose published after 1914

All those who were saddened by the turn of events wore long faces, to prove that they were saddened. All those who weren't saddened wore even longer faces, to hide the fact that they weren't saddened. The photographer, from Marwoods of Moor Street, cast a last baleful glance at Gerry, before shuffling off with his unused tripod.

Out of the inhospitable gravel on the south side of the church there grew a lone tree, a sickly, unshapely ash. Around this tree a munificent council had placed a round slatted seat. Onto this seat jumped Gerry Lansdown. His face was pale. His eyes were hot. His complacency was a distant memory.

'Ladies and gentlemen,' he cried, and silence fell instantly. Everyone wanted to hear what he would say. What could he say? 'Ladies and gentlemen. It seems that something has delayed Rita ... or something. Until we find out what ... and bearing in mind that many of you have travelled a long way, many from Hindhead and some from even further afield ... and as the reception ... er ... and it seems criminal to waste all that lovely food.' Gerry's voice gained assurance as he touched on political matters. 'We in the Social Liberal Democratic party believe that all waste of food is totally unjustified in a world where so many haven't enough to eat ... so, whatever has happened, if indeed it has, I think the best course will be to proceed with the reception as if nothing had happened ... I mean, as if nothing hadn't happened. Thank you.'

Task time

Here are some examples of the kind of question you may get in your exam. If you have time you could practise writing complete answers to the questions, or if you prefer you could make a spider diagram to help you plan full answers.

What impression does the passage give you of the vicar's character?

You could include these points:

- He thinks Gerry is less important than the next wedding's groom.
- The next groom is financially important to the abbey.
- The vicar sees the abbey as an attractive venue rather than a religious centre.

What impression does the passage give you of Gerry Lansdown's character?

You could include these points:

- Gerry is confident at first – he smiles 'serenely'.
- He is angry – he 'hissed' – and wants what he has paid for.
- Gerry is self-important and tries to use his position as prospective candidate.

- His speech turns into a political speech.
- The pauses and breaks as he speaks suggest his nervousness.

How does the writer use language to make the passage funny?

You could include these points:

- the descriptions of people's typical 'wedding' behaviour
- the way Leslie Horton's playing is described
- the inappropriateness of the Wedding March
- the inappropriateness of the vicar's and Gerry's language
- expressions such as the simile 'curled at the edges like a slice of tongue approaching its "sell-by" date'.

Think of a ceremony you have attended, such as a wedding or a christening, or a celebration like a birthday party. Prepare a short talk about it to give to your group or class. Try to include details of people's behaviour. You could write it up as a piece of personal writing.

Literary prose published after 1914

Of Mice and Men

This passage is from the opening of *Of Mice and Men*, a novel by John Steinbeck published in 1937. The story is set in California during the American Depression, a period during which millions of people experienced unemployment, poverty and near starvation. George and Lennie are itinerant workers on their way to new jobs.

… two men emerged from the path and came into the opening by the green pool. They had walked in single file down the path, and even in the open one stayed behind the other. Both were dressed in denim trousers and in denim coats with brass buttons. Both wore black, shapeless hats and both carried tight blanket rolls slung over their shoulders. The first man was small and quick, dark of face, with restless eyes and sharp, strong features. Every part of him was defined: small, strong hands, slender arms, a thin and bony nose. Behind him walked his opposite, a huge man, shapeless of face, with large, pale eyes, with wide, sloping shoulders; and he walked heavily, dragging his feet a little, the way a bear drags his paws. His arms did not swing at his sides, but hung loosely.

The first man stopped short in the clearing, and the follower nearly ran over him. He took off his hat and wiped the sweatband with his forefinger and snapped the moisture off. His huge companion dropped his blankets and flung himself down and drank from the surface of the green pool; drank with long gulps, snorting into the water like a horse. The small man stepped nervously beside him.

'Lennie!' he said sharply. 'Lennie, for God's sakes don't drink so much.' Lennie continued to snort into the pool. The small man leaned over and shook him by the shoulder. 'Lennie. You gonna be sick like you was last night.'

Lennie dipped his whole head under, hat and all, and then he sat up on the bank and his hat dripped down on his blue coat and ran down his back. 'Tha's good,' he said. 'You drink some, George. You take a good big drink.' He smiled happily.

George unslung his bundle and dropped it gently on the bank. 'I ain't sure it's good water,' he said. 'Looks kinda scummy.'

Lennie dabbled his big paw in the water and wiggled his fingers so the water arose in little splashes; rings widened across the pool to the other side and came back again. Lennie watched them go. 'Look, George. Look what I done.'

George knelt beside the pool and drank from his hand with quick scoops. 'Tastes all right,' he admitted. 'Don't really seem to be running, though. You never oughta drink water when it ain't running, Lennie,' he said hopelessly. 'You'd drink out of a gutter if you was thirsty.' He threw a scoop of water into his face and rubbed it about with his hand, under his chin and around the back of his neck. Then he replaced his hat, pushed himself back from the river, drew up his knees, embraced them, looked over to George to see whether he had it just right. He pulled his hat down a little more over his eyes, the way George's hat was.

George stared morosely at the water. The rims of his eyes were red with sun glare. He said angrily: 'We could just as well of rode clear to the ranch if that bastard bus driver knew what he was talkin' about. "Jes' a little stretch down the highway," he says. "Jes' a little stretch." God damn near four miles, that's what it was! Didn't wanta stop at the ranch gate, that's what. Too God damn lazy to pull up. Wonder he isn't too damn good to stop in Soledad at all. Kicks us out and says: "Jes' a little stretch down the road." I bet it was *more* than four miles. Damn hot day.'

Lennie looked timidly over to him. 'George?'

'Yeah, what ya want?'

'Where we goin', George?'

The little man jerked down the brim of his hat and scowled over at Lennie. 'So you forgot that awready, did you? I gotta tell you again, do I? Jesus Christ, you're a crazy bastard!'

'I forgot,' Lennie said softly. 'I tried not to forget. Honest to God I did, George.'

28

Literary prose published after 1914

'OK – OK. I'll tell ya again. I ain't got nothing to do. Might jus' as well spen' all my time tellin' you things and then you forget 'em, and I tell you again.'

'Tried and tried,' said Lennie, 'but it didn't do no good. I remember about the rabbits, George.'

'The hell with the rabbits. That's all you ever can remember is them rabbits. OK! Now you listen and this time you got to remember so we don't get in no trouble. You remember settin' in that gutter on Howard Street and watchin' that blackboard?'

Lennie's face broke into a delighted smile. 'Why sure, George. I remember that … but … what'd we do then? I remember some girls come by and you says … you says … '

'The hell with what I says. You remember about us goin' into Murray and Ready's, and they give us work cards and bus tickets?'

'Oh, sure, George, I remember that now.' His hands went quickly into his side pockets. He said gently: 'George … I ain't got mine. I musta lost it.' He looked down at the ground in despair.

'You never had none, you crazy bastard. I got both of 'em here. Think I'd let you carry your own work card?'

Lennie grinned with relief. 'I … I thought I put it in my side pocket.' His hand went into the pocket again.

George looked sharply at him. 'What'd you take outa that pocket?'

'Ain't a thing in my pocket,' said Lennie cleverly.

'I know there ain't. You got it in your hand. What you got in your hand – hidin' it?'

'I ain't got nothin', George. Honest.'

'Come on, give it here.'

Lennie held his closed hand away from George's direction. 'It's on'y a mouse, George.'

'A mouse? A live mouse?'

'Uh-uh. Jus' a dead mouse, George. I didn't kill it. Honest! I found it. I found it dead.'

'*Give it here*,' said George.

'Aw, leave me have it, George.'

'Give it here!'

Lennie's closed hand slowly obeyed. George took the mouse and threw it across the pool to the other side, among the brush. 'What you want of a dead mouse, anyways?'

'I could pet it with my thumb while we walked along,' said Lennie.

'Well, you ain't petting no mice while you walk with me. You remember where we're goin' now?'

Lennie looked startled and then in embarrassment hid his face against his knees. 'I forgot again.'

'Jesus Christ,' George said resignedly. 'Well – look, we're gonna work on a ranch like the one we come from up north.'

'Up north?'

'In Weed.'

'Oh, sure. I remember. In Weed.'

'That ranch we're goin' to is right down there about a quarter-mile. We're gonna go in an' see the boss. Now, look – I'll give him the work tickets, but you ain't gonna say a word. You jus' stand there and don't say nothing. If he finds out what a crazy bastard you are, we won't get no job, but if he sees ya work before he hears ya talk, we're set. Ya got that?'

'Sure, George. Sure I got it.'

'OK. Now when we go in to see the boss, what you gonna do?'

'I … I,' Lennie thought. His face grew tight with thought. 'I … ain't gonna say nothin'. Jus' gonna stan' there.'

'Good boy. That's swell. You say that over two, three times so you won't forget it.'

Lennie droned to himself softly: 'I ain't gonna say nothin' … I ain't gonna say nothin' … I ain't gonna say nothin'.'

'OK,' said George. 'An' you ain't gonna do no bad things like you done in Weed, neither.'

Literary prose published after 1914

Over to you

Practise writing or planning answers to the following questions.

What do you learn from the passage about George and Lennie, and the relationship between them?

Hint: Use a coloured pencil to highlight references to George and a different colour to highlight references to Lennie. You could make your points under headings:

Physical attributes

George: small, quick, restless

Lennie: huge, slow, heavy

Find examples of animal imagery used to describe Lennie.

Personalities and relationship

George:
- irritable
- kind
- feels responsible for Lennie
- can think ahead

Lennie:
- gentle
- relies on George
- forgetful
- childlike
- trusts and admires George

Find words and lines from the passage to illustrate the above points.

Previous events

You could include references to events that happened before we meet George and Lennie:
- It is likely that Lennie accidentally killed the pet mouse he carried in his pocket.
- Lennie did something bad when they were working on the ranch in Weed.

Dr Wordsmith says ...

If you select and analyse appropriate details from the text and show how the writer uses language to gain particular effects, you are more likely to get a high grade. You might find these phrases helpful:

- 'An amusing effect is created by the writer's use of ...'
- 'The writer makes effective use of contrast in the description of ...'

What particular effects does the writer's use of language create?

You could consider these aspects:

The dialogue between the characters

- colloquial expressions
- George's forceful language
- Lenny's simple sentences

Descriptive details

- clothes and equipment
- sense of physical discomfort and hardship.

You may be asked to compare different texts. In what ways are the two passages in this section similar, and in what ways are they different?

Hint: Think about how you would describe the overall tone or feeling of each passage. Are the characters presented in the same way? How do you respond to each extract as the beginning of a novel? Do you think they are likely to be the same kind of novel? Remember that your own response is what matters – but you must support it with reference to the text.

Make a chart comparing the two passages.

Section round-up

Well done! You have shown that you can:
- **Read with understanding.**
- **Select and comment on appropriate details.**
- **Appreciate writers' use of language.**

Literary prose published after 1914

Conflict

About this section

This section gives you two passages which describe incidents from childhood. They both deal with conflict between friends.

By the end of this section you will be able to:

- Discuss different ways of presenting characters in texts.
- Comment on linguistic features of texts.
- Compare writers' concerns and their effect on the reader.

Medicine Box

Ailment: I feel panicky because I don't know what to look for in the passage.

Dr Wordsmith's cure: No need to panic. Here's something that will help: read the passage quickly once, then look at the questions you will have to answer. Then read the passage more slowly and carefully, making notes which will help you write your answer. The notes could be in the form of spider diagrams.

Cat's Eye

The following passages are taken from *Cat's Eye*, a novel by Margaret Atwood published in 1989. Part of the novel deals with the narrator's childhood, and in particular her relationship with one of her friends.

Grace is waiting there and Carol, and especially Cordelia. Once I'm outside the house there is no getting away from them. They are on the school bus, where Cordelia stands close beside me and whispers into my ear: 'Stand up straight! People are looking!' Carol is in my classroom, and it's her job to report to Cordelia what I do and say all day. They're there at recess, and in the cellar at lunchtime. They comment on the kind of lunch I have, how I hold my sandwich, how I chew. On the way home from school I have to walk in front of them, or behind. In front is worse because they talk about how I'm walking, how I look from behind. 'Don't hunch over,' says Cordelia. 'Don't move your arms like that.'

They don't say any of the things they say to me in front of others, even other children: whatever is going on is going on in secret, among the four of us only. Secrecy is important, I know that: to violate it would be the greatest, the irreparable sin. If I tell I will be cast out forever.

But Cordelia doesn't do these things or have this power over me because she's my enemy. Far from it. I know about enemies. There are enemies in the schoolyard, they yell things at one another and if they're boys they fight. In the war there were enemies … You throw snowballs at enemies and rejoice if they get hit. With enemies you can feel hatred, and anger. But Cordelia is my friend. She likes me, she wants to help me, they all do. They are my friends, my girlfriends, my best friends. I have never had any before and I'm terrified of losing them. I want to please.

Hatred would have been easier. With hatred, I would have known what to do. Hatred is clear, metallic, one-handed, unwavering; unlike love.

The telephone rings. It's Grace. 'You want to come out and play?' she says, in her neutral voice that is at the same time blank and unsoft, like glazed paper. I know Cordelia is standing beside her. If I say no, I will be accused of something. If I say yes, I will have to do it. I say yes.

'We'll come and get you,' Grace says.

My stomach feels dull and heavy, as if it's full of earth. I put on my snowsuit and boots, my knitted hat and mittens. I tell my mother I'm going out to play. 'Don't get chilled,' she says.

31

Literary prose published after 1914

The sun on the snow is blinding. There's a crust of ice over the drifts, where the top layer of snow has melted and then refrozen. My boots make clean-edged footprints through the crust. There's no one around. I walk through the white glare, towards Grace's house. The air is wavery, filled with light, overfilled; I can hear the pressure of it against my eyes. I feel translucent, like a hand held over a flashlight or the pictures of jellyfish I've seen in magazines, floating in the sea like watery flesh balloons.

At the end of the street I can see the three of them, very dark, walking towards me. Their coats look almost black. Even their faces when they come closer look too dark, as if they're in shadow.

Cordelia says, 'We said we would come and get you. We didn't say you could come here.'

I say nothing.

Grace says, 'She should answer when we talk to her.'

Cordelia says, 'What's the matter, are you deaf?'

Their voices sound far away. I turn aside and throw up onto a snowbank. I didn't mean to do it and didn't know I was going to. I feel sick to my stomach every morning, I'm used to that, but this is the real thing, alphabet soup mixed with shards of chewed-up cheese, amazingly red and orange against the white of the snow, with here and there a ruined letter.

Cordelia doesn't say anything. Grace says, 'You better go home.' Carol, behind them, sounds as if she's going to cry. She says, 'It's on her face.' I walk back towards my house, smelling the vomit on the front of my snowsuit, tasting it in my nose and throat. It feels like bits of carrot.

I lie in bed with the scrub-pail beside me, floating lightly on waves of fever. I throw up several times, until nothing but a little green juice comes out. My mother says, 'I suppose we'll all get it,' and she's right. During the night I can hear hurrying footsteps and retching and the toilet flushing. I feel safe, small, wrapped in my illness as if in cotton wool.

I begin to be sick more often. Sometimes my mother looks into my mouth with a flashlight and feels my forehead and takes my temperature and sends me to school, but sometimes I'm allowed to stay home. On these days I feel relief, as if I've been running for a long time and have reached a place where I can rest, not forever but for a while. Having a fever is pleasant, vacant. I enjoy the coolness of things, the flat gingerale I'm given to drink, the delicacy of taste, afterwards.

I'm in the kitchen, greasing muffin-tins for my mother. I see the patterns the grease leaves on the metal, I see the moons of my nails, the raggedy flesh. My fingers go around and around.

My mother makes the batter for the muffins, measuring the salt, sifting the flour. The sifter sounds dry, like sandpaper. 'You don't have to play with them,' my mother says. 'There must be other little girls you can play with instead.'

I look at her. Misery washes over me like a slow wind. What has she noticed, what has she guessed, what is she about to do? She might tell their mothers. This would be the worst thing she could do.

'When I was little and the kids called names, we used to say, "Sticks and stones will break my bones but names will never hurt me," ' she says. Her arm goes vigorously around, mixing, efficient and strong.

'They don't call me names,' I say. 'They're my friends.' I believe this.

'You have to learn to stand up for yourself,' says my mother. 'Don't let them push you around. Don't be spineless. You have to have more backbone.' She dollops the batter into the tins.

I think of sardines and their backbones. You can eat their backbones. The bones crumble between your teeth; one touch and they fall apart. This must be what my own backbone is like: hardly there at all. What is happening to me is my own fault, for not having more backbone.

My mother sets down the bowl and puts her arms around me. 'I wish I knew what to do,' she says. This is a confession. Now I know what I've been suspecting: as far as this thing is concerned, she is powerless.

I know that muffins have to be baked right away, right after they've been ladled out, or they'll be flat and ruined. I can't afford the distraction of comfort. If I give in to it, what little backbone I have left will crumble away to nothing.

I pull away from her. 'They need to go into the oven,' I say.

Literary prose published after 1914

Your turn

If you have worked through the previous section, you may have noticed that quite often the first questions on a passage are to do with the content of the passage and the characters, and the last questions are to do with language and the effects created. Plan or write responses to these questions.

What do you learn from the passage about the narrator and her feelings about Cordelia?

Hint: Use a diagram or chart to gather your ideas. Find the key words in the question and underline or circle them with a coloured pencil to remind you to keep to the point.

You could include some of these points:

- The narrator feels like a victim.
- She can't escape from the girls.
- She has to endure their comments and criticisms.
- She accepts that this way of behaving is their secret.
- She accepts that the bullying is for her own good.
- She thinks Cordelia is her friend.
- She wants to please.
- She is physically tense and sick.
- She is relieved when she is allowed to stay home.
- She blames herself.
- She realises that her mother can't help her.

What do you learn from the passage about Cordelia, Carol and Grace?

Hint: Remember you must comment on **all three** characters named in the question, even if there is not the same amount to say about each of them. Your answer could include some of the following points:

- Cordelia enjoys power.
- She gives out the tasks.
- Cordelia uses a range of bullying tactics.
- Grace adds her own contribution to the verbal bullying.
- Grace speaks only after Cordelia has started the attack.
- Grace and Carol might be shaken when the narrator is sick.

Comment on the writer's use of language to convey feelings and atmosphere.

Hint: Look for examples of descriptive words and phrases. You might find some effective **similes** or **images**. Think about what effect they have, what feelings the words are creating. You could comment on the following:

- the description of hatred as 'clear, metallic' – **what** do the words make you see?
- the description of the narrator's feelings as she approaches Grace's house – what is the **effect** of words like 'light', 'translucent', 'floating'? Why is the 'darkness' of the three other girls emphasised?
- the image of the frail, brittle sardine bones and **how** it relates to the narrator.

Write a story or a description which involves some characters bullying another. You could write a play script if you prefer.

A word from Dr Wordsmith ...

There are different ways of using quotations in your answers.

(a) You can put long quotations in a separate paragraph. This works best if you want to give a close analysis of the language. Be careful, though – you mustn't copy out chunks of text just to fill up space. The depth and quality of your comment is essential.

(b) You can insert quotations in your sentences. This technique helps you to highlight the key words you need, and it keeps the flow of your answer going. Watch out – if you use too many inserted quotations it can be very distracting for the reader, and can actually make your meaning less clear.

Literary prose published after 1914

Lord of the Flies

This extract is taken from the novel *Lord of the Flies* by William Golding, published in 1954. A group of schoolboys is stranded on a desert island. Some of them, led by Jack, have the job of hunting pigs for food. This group is also responsible for keeping a fire going to provide a smoke signal for any passing ships. Here, Jack's group has let the fire go out and has hunted and killed a pig. In the meantime, a ship has passed by, and there was no signal for it to see.

Ralph flung back his hair. One arm pointed at the empty horizon. His voice was loud and savage, and struck them into silence.

'There was a ship.'

Jack, faced at once with too many awful implications, ducked away from them. He laid a hand on the pig and drew his knife. Ralph brought his arm down, fist clenched, and his voice shook.

'There was a ship. Out there. You said you'd keep the fire going and you let it out!' He took a step towards Jack who turned and faced him.

'They might have seen us. We might have gone home –'

This was too bitter for Piggy, who forgot his timidity in the agony of his loss. He began to cry out, shrilly:

'You and your blood, Jack Merridew! You and your hunting! We might have gone home –'

Ralph pushed Piggy on one side.

'I was chief; and you were going to do what I said. You talk. But you can't even build huts – then you go off hunting and let out the fire –'

He turned away, silent for a moment. Then his voice came again on a peak of feeling.

'There was a ship –'

One of the smaller hunters began to wail. The dismal truth was filtering through to everybody. Jack went very red as he hacked and pulled at the pig.

'The job was too much. We needed everyone.'

Ralph turned.

'You could have had everyone when the shelters were finished. But you had to hunt –'

'We needed meat.'

Jack stood up as he said this, the bloodied knife in his hand. The two boys faced each other. There was the brilliant world of hunting, tactics, fierce exhilaration, skill; and there was the world of longing and baffled common-sense. Jack transferred the knife to his left hand and smudged blood over his forehead as he pushed down the plastered hair.

Ask yourself some questions. ✪ Who are the main characters? Who is the leader? ✪ How are Ralph and Jack different from each other? ✪ What does each feel at this moment?

Hint: You could highlight the important ideas about the characters with a different coloured pen for each.

Show your ideas about the characters in a diagram.

Piggy began again.

'You didn't ought to have let that fire out. You said you'd keep the smoke going – '

This from Piggy, and the wails of agreement from some of the hunters, drove Jack to violence. The bolting look came into his blue eyes. He took a step, and able at last to hit someone, stuck his fist into Piggy's stomach. Piggy sat down with a grunt. Jack stood over him. His voice was vicious with humiliation.

'You would, would you? Fatty!'

Ralph made a step forward and Jack smacked Piggy's head. Piggy's glasses flew off and tinkled on the rocks. Piggy cried out in terror:

'My specs!'

He went crouching and feeling over the rocks but Simon, who got there first, found them for him. Passions beat about Simon on the mountain-top with awful wings.

Literary prose published after 1914

'One side's broken.'

Piggy grabbed and put on the glasses. He looked malevolently at Jack.

'I got to have them specs. Now I only got one eye. Jus' you wait – '

Jack made a move towards Piggy who scrambled away till a great rock lay between them. He thrust his head over the top and glared at Jack through his one flashing glass.

'Now I only got one eye. Just you wait – '

Jack mimicked the whine and scramble.

'Jus' you wait – yah!'

Piggy and the parody were so funny that the hunters began to laugh. Jack felt encouraged. He went on scrambling and the laughter rose to a gale of hysteria. Unwillingly Ralph felt his lips twitch; he was angry with himself for giving way.

He muttered.

'That was a dirty trick.'

Jack broke out of his gyration and stood facing Ralph. His words came in a shout.

'All right, all right!'

He looked at Piggy, at the hunters, at Ralph.

'I'm sorry. About the fire, I mean. There. I – '

He drew himself up.

'I – apologize.'

The buzz from the hunters was one of admiration at this handsome behaviour. Clearly they were of the opinion that Jack had done the decent thing, had put himself in the right by his generous apology and Ralph, obscurely, in the wrong. They waited for an appropriately decent answer.

Ask yourself some questions. ✪ Why does Jack hit Piggy? Why is his behaviour here accepted by most of the boys?

✪ What do you think about his apology? ✪ What is Ralph feeling?
Keep adding to your diagram.

Yet Ralph's throat refused to pass one. He resented, as an addition to Jack's misbehaviour, this verbal trick. The fire was dead, the ship was gone. Could they not see? Anger instead of decency passed his throat.

'That was a dirty trick.'

They were silent on the mountain-top while the opaque look appeared in Jack's eyes and passed away.

Ralph's final word was an ungracious mutter.

'All right. Light the fire.'

With some positive action before them, a little of the tension died. Ralph said no more, did nothing, stood looking down at the ashes round his feet. Jack was loud and active. He gave orders, sang, whistled, threw remarks at the silent Ralph – remarks that did not need an answer, and therefore could not invite a snub; and still Ralph was silent. No one, not even Jack, would ask him to move and in the end they had to build the fire three yards away and in a place not really as convenient. So Ralph asserted his chieftainship and could not have chosen a better way if he had thought for days. Against this weapon, so indefinable and so effective, Jack was powerless and raged without knowing why. By the time the pile was built, they were on different sides of a high barrier.

When they had dealt with the fire another crisis arose. Jack had no means of lighting it. Then to his surprise, Ralph went to Piggy and took the glasses from him. Not even Ralph knew how a link between him and Jack had been snapped and fastened elsewhere.

Ask yourself some questions. ✪ Why doesn't Ralph accept Jack's apology? ✪ How does Ralph make it clear that he is chief? What about the 'barrier'? Does it refer to more than the pile of wood? ✪ What is the importance of Ralph taking Piggy's glasses from him?

Finish your diagram. You might like to show how the relationships between the boys change during the course of the passage as a flow chart.

35

Literary prose published after 1914

Time to practise

Think about how you would answer the following questions. You could write full answers if you have time, or write plans.

What do you learn from the passage about (a) Ralph (b) Jack (c) Piggy?

Hint: Use your diagram to gather your ideas. You could include some of the following points:

- Ralph is angry and emotional.
- He sees the fire and rescue as a priority.
- Ralph values common sense.
- Ralph won't be distracted from what he is saying.
- Ralph turns away from Jack and forms an alliance with Piggy.
- Jack knows he is in the wrong and is embarrassed.
- Jack sees hunting as a priority.
- Jack values excitement and the challenge of the chase.
- Jack is violent, and takes his anger out on Piggy.
- Jack knows how to get the others on his side.
- Piggy is weaker than the other two.
- Piggy supports Ralph and dislikes Jack.
- Piggy is the object of jokes and ridicule.
- Ralph acknowledges Piggy.

Imagine that you are one of the boys who went hunting with Jack. Write your diary account of the day's events. Remember to include details from the passage.

What do you think about the ways in which the writers present conflict in the passages from *Cat's Eye* and *Lord of the Flies*? You could consider:

- **the subject matter**
- **how sympathetic you are to the characters**
- **the way the story is told.**

Hint: This kind of question gives you a lot of scope for showing your understanding of writers' techniques. Ask yourself some questions. ✪ **W**hat is the conflict about? ✪ **H**ow do I know what the characters are like? ✪ **E**ffect: Does the writer want me to sympathise with any particular character? Your answer might include some of the following points:

Cat's Eye
- ongoing situation – not a particular incident
- first-person narration
- sympathy with narrator – see events from her point of view

Lord of the Flies
- passage focuses on particular incident – more dramatic?
- third-person narrative
- insight into all characters' feelings

Dr Wordsmith says …

You will get high marks if you can show how texts are structured. Comments on the different effects of first-person narration and third-person narration, as you have practised in the last question, will gain you credit.

Section round-up

In this section you have shown that you can:

- **Analyse character.**
- **Discuss features of presentation.**
- **Use quotations effectively.**
- **Understand the structure of texts.**

Literary prose published after 1914

Comparing texts from different periods

About this section

The last part of this chapter gives you an opportunity to compare a literary text from the twentieth century with one written at the end of the nineteenth century.

By the end of this section you will be able to:

- Discuss texts written in different periods.
- Appreciate distinctive qualities of style and language.
- Select appropriate details to support points.

How many detective series can you think of, either in books, on television or in films? You may be surprised to hear that crime stories featuring private detectives and police detectives have been popular for a couple of centuries. This section gives you a chance to meet two fictional detectives, one from the nineteenth century and one who is probably starting a new case at this very moment!

She Didn't Come Home

This passage is adapted from 'She Didn't Come Home', a short story by the American writer Sue Grafton, published in 1986.

My name is Kinsey Milhone. I'm female, thirty-two, twice divorced, 'doing business' as Kinsey Milhone Investigations in a little town ninety-five miles north of Los Angeles. Mine isn't a walk-in trade like a beauty salon. Most of my clients find themselves in a fix and then seek my services, hoping I can offer a solution for a mere thirty bucks an hour, plus expenses. Robert Ackerman's message was waiting on my answering machine that Monday morning at nine when I got in.

'Hello. My name is Robert Ackerman and I wonder if you could give me a call. My wife is missing and I'm worried sick. I was hoping you could help me out.' In the background, I could hear whiney children, my favourite kind. I made a pot of coffee before I called him back.

A little person answered the phone. There was a murmured child-size hello.

'Hi,' I said. 'Can I speak to your daddy?'

'Yes.' Long silence.

'Today?' I asked.

The receiver was clunked down on a tabletop and in due course Robert Ackerman picked up the phone.

'It's Kinsey Milhone, Mr Ackerman. I just got your message. Can you tell me what's going on?'

'Oh yeah ...' He was interrupted by a piercing shriek that sounded like one of those policemen's whistles you use to discourage obscene phone callers. I listened patiently while he dealt with the errant child.

'Sorry,' he said when he came back on the line. 'Look, is there any way you could come out to the house? I've got my hands full and I just can't get away.'

I took his address and brief directions, then headed out to my car.

Robert and the missing Mrs Ackerman lived in a housing tract that looked like it was built in the forties before anyone ever dreamed up the notion of family rooms, country kitchens, his'n'hers solar spas. What we had here was a basic box. When Robert answered the door I could just about see the whole place at a glance. He had a baby propped on his hip like a grocery bag. Another child clung to his right leg, while a third rode his tricycle at various walls and doorways, making loud sounds with his mouth.

Robert ran a distracted hand across his head. 'I'm sorry everything is such a mess, but my wife hasn't been here for two days. I've called the police and checked the hospitals. I'm scared something's happened to her. I'm going crazy with anxiety. Someone has to find out where she is.'

'Mr Ackerman ...'

'You can call me Rob.'

Clients always say that. I mean, unless their names are something else.

'Rob,' I said, 'the police are your best bet. They've got a vast machinery they can put to work and it won't cost you a cent.'

Literary prose published after 1914

> 'You charge a lot, huh?'
>
> 'Thirty bucks an hour plus expenses.'
>
> He thought about that for a moment. 'Could you maybe put in ten hours? I got three hundred bucks we were saving for a trip to the San Diego Zoo.'
>
> I pretended to think about it, but the truth was, I couldn't say no. Anyway, the kids were starting to whine and I wanted to get out of there. I waived the retainer and said I'd send him an itemized bill when the ten hours were up. I wanted to reduce my contact with the short persons who were crowding round him now, begging for sweets. I thought about Lucy Ackerman whose three strapping sons had legs the size of my arms. If I were she, I knew where I'd be. Long gone.

Your turn

Write or plan answers to the following questions.

What impression do you get from the passage about the character of Kinsey Milhone?

Hint: Read the passage again. Underline or make notes on the important things you learn. You could think about:

- money
- children
- way of working.

Comment on the way the writer uses language.

Hint: Try to describe the effect or tone of the passage in one or two words or phrases. Your comments might include:

- the colloquial style
- the use of dialogue
- the sarcastic or sardonic tone.

The Adventure of the Speckled Band

Now you are about to meet another private detective – but a very different character. In this extract from *The Adventure of the Speckled Band* by Sir Arthur Conan Doyle, published in 1892, Sherlock Holmes meets a client for the first time. The story is narrated by Dr Watson, Holmes's friend.

As you read, jot down notes to record your impressions of character and style.

> It was early in April in the year '83 that I woke one morning to find Sherlock Holmes standing, fully dressed, by the side of the bed. He was a late riser, as a rule, and as the clock on the mantelpiece showed me that it was only a quarter-past seven, I blinked up at him in some surprise, and perhaps just a little resentment, for I was myself regular in my habits.
>
> 'Very sorry to knock you up, Watson,' said he, 'but it's the common lot this morning. Mrs Hudson has been knocked up, she retorted upon me, and I on you.'
>
> 'What is it, then – a fire?'
>
> 'No; a client. It seems that a young lady has arrived in a considerable state of excitement, who insists upon seeing me. She is waiting now in the sitting-room. Now, when young ladies wander about the metropolis at this hour of the morning, and knock sleepy people up out of their beds, I presume that it is something very pressing which they have to communicate. Should it prove to be an interesting case, you would, I am sure, wish to follow it from the outset. I thought, at any rate, that I should call you and give you the chance.'
>
> 'My dear fellow, I would not miss it for anything.'
>
> I had no keener pleasure than in following Holmes in his professional investigations, and in admiring the rapid deductions, as swift as intuitions, and yet always founded on a logical basis, with which he unravelled the problems which were submitted to him. I rapidly threw on my clothes and was ready in a few minutes to accompany my friend down to the sitting-room. A lady dressed in black and heavily veiled, who had been sitting in the window, rose as we entered.
>
> 'Good-morning, madam,' said Holmes cheerily. 'My name is Sherlock Holmes. This is my intimate friend and associate, Dr Watson, before whom you can speak as freely as before myself.

Literary prose published after 1914

'Ha! I am glad to see that Mrs Hudson has had the good sense to light the fire. Pray draw up to it, and I shall order you a cup of hot coffee, for I observe that you are shivering.'

'It is not cold which makes me shiver,' said the woman in a low voice, changing her seat as requested.

'What, then?'

'It is fear, Mr Holmes. It is terror.' She raised her veil as she spoke, and we could see that she was indeed in a pitiable state of agitation, her face all drawn and gray, with restless, frightened eyes, like those of some hunted animal. Her features and figure were those of a woman of thirty, but her hair was short with premature gray, and her expression was weary and haggard. Sherlock Holmes ran her over with one of his quick, all-comprehensive glances.

'You must not fear,' said he soothingly, bending forward and patting her forearm. 'We shall soon set matters right, I have no doubt. You have come in by train this morning, I see.'

'You know me, then?'

'No, but I observe the second half of a return ticket in the palm of your left glove. You must have started early, and yet you had a good drive in a dog-cart, along heavy roads, before you reached the station.'

The lady gave a violent start and stared in bewilderment at my companion.

'There is no mystery, my dear madam,' said he, smiling. 'The left arm of your jacket is spattered with mud in no less than seven places. The marks are perfectly fresh. There is no vehicle save a dog-cart which throws up mud in that way, and then only when you sit on the left-hand side of the driver.'

More for you

The following questions will help you to check your understanding. If you like, you could record the information as a diagram.

What methods of detection does Sherlock Holmes apply?

Hint: Look at the way Holmes works out how and when the lady travelled. Does he work through intuition? Guesswork? Logic? Deduction?

What do you gather from the passage about Sherlock Holmes's way of life?

Hint: Pick out details that tell you where and how he lives. You might look at these points:

- shares accommodation with Dr Watson
- late riser
- housekeeper Mrs Hudson – duties include lighting fire, making coffee
- lives in London.

'Whatever your reasons may be, you are perfectly correct,' said she. 'I started from home before six, reached Leatherhead at twenty past, and came in by the first train to Waterloo. Sir, I can stand this strain no longer; I shall go mad if it continues. I have no one to turn to – none, save only one, who cares for me, and he, poor fellow, can be of little aid. I have heard of you, Mr Holmes; I have heard of you from Mrs Farintosh, whom you helped in the hour of her sore need. It was from her that I had your address. Oh, sir, do you not think that you could help me, too, and at least throw a little light through the dense darkness which surrounds me? At present it is out of my power to reward you for your services, but in a month or six weeks I shall be married, with the control of my own income, and then at least you shall not find me ungrateful.'

Holmes turned to his desk and, unlocking it, drew out a small casebook, which he consulted.

'Farintosh,' said he. 'Ah yes, I recall the case; it was concerned with an opal tiara. I think it was before your time, Watson. I can only say, madam, that I shall be happy to devote the same care to your case as I did to that of your friend. As to reward, my profession is its own reward; but you are at liberty to defray whatever expenses I may be put to, at the time which suits you best. And now I beg that you will lay before us everything that may help us in forming an opinion upon the matter.'

Literary prose published after 1914

> 'Alas!' replied our visitor, 'the very horror of my situation lies in the fact that my fears are so vague, and my suspicions depend so entirely upon small points, which might seem trivial to another, that even he to whom of all others I have right to look for help and advice looks upon all that I tell him about as the fancies of a nervous woman. He does not say so, but I can read it from his soothing answers and averted eyes. But I have heard, Mr Holmes, that you can see deeply into the manifold wickedness of the human heart. You may advise me how to walk amid the dangers which encompass me.'
>
> 'I am all attention, madam.'

Now try this

Why does the lady choose Sherlock Holmes to help her?

Hint: Look at what she says about Mrs Farintosh.

Does Sherlock Holmes need to earn a living through detection?

Think about the two passages you have just read in this section and the similarities and differences between them. Make a chart to show the differences in:

(a) the characters of Kinsey Milhone and Sherlock Holmes

(b) the style and language of the passages.

Hint: Use all the information you have recorded so far. You could include some of the following points:

- the character and background of each detective
- their different ways of speaking
- the different length of sentences in each passage
- the different types of crime they deal with
- the different positions and roles of women
- their different attitudes to their clients
- the use of formal/informal language.

Give a short talk outlining the differences and similarities between the beginnings of these stories. Say which one you would choose to continue reading. Remember to give your reasons.

What about creating your own detective? Make notes for a description of him or her, and come up with a few lines of dialogue or descriptions of typical cases.

A word from Dr Wordsmith ...

Some of the differences between these texts are explained by the social and historical contexts in which they were written. The style and content of the Sue Grafton extract reflect the social background of contemporary America, and the extract is an example of the popularity of toughness and realism in detective fiction. The Conan Doyle extract reflects the social conventions of England in an earlier period. The longer sentences and formal dialogue are typical of late Victorian style.

Section round-up

In this section you have shown that you can:

- Compare texts from different periods.
- Appreciate style and characterisation.
- Understand the social and historical context of texts.
- Select relevant details.

Literary prose published after 1914

Review

This chapter has introduced you to writers and texts of later periods.

Now that you've finished the chapter, use this checklist to measure your confidence rating.

Checklist

Do you feel confident about:

		Yes	Not yet
1	Reading a range of literature published since 1914?	❑	❑
2	Commenting on the different effects of language?	❑	❑
3	Appreciating style and characterisation?	❑	❑
4	Giving a personal response based on the text?	❑	❑

If your answer to any of these questions is 'Not yet', look back at the chapter. If you are still unsure, ask your teacher for help.

For your own notes

....

....

....

....

....

....

....

41

Chapter 4: Non-fiction

Overview

When you have worked your way through this chapter you should be well on the way to being able to:

- Read, understand and enjoy a variety of non-fiction.
- Tell the difference between fact and opinion.
- See similarities and differences in the way information is presented and write about it.
- Follow an argument and say how effective it is.
- Make your own arguments convincing.
- Spot similarities and differences in various material.
- Pick out relevant details from different material and compare them.
- Analyse the way writers use language and structure for different effects.
- See how language varies and changes over time and between writers.
- Write your own non-fiction for a wide variety of purposes and audiences.

About non-fiction

Have you ever felt strongly about something and then felt angry when you have seen some **printed information** that presents an opposite, or in your opinion, an unjust or incorrect point of view?

Have you ever misunderstood an **instruction** in an exam when you were asked to do a particular thing but it turned out you should have done something else?

Dr Wordsmith says ...

- Remember that quality is always more important than quantity.
- Write legibly and always check your work for correct spelling, punctuation and grammar.
- Make sure you organise your ideas into well-constructed sentences and paragraphs.

Check anything you are not sure about with your teacher.

Have you ever been unable to understand **directions** because they were not written or spoken clearly?

If you answered 'yes' to any of these questions, take heart – you are not alone. Most of us make such mistakes, or are on the receiving end of such mistakes, much of the time. Like the examiner of your GCSE English exam paper, if these things have happened to you, you will appreciate the importance of clear, accurate instructions.

Non-fiction is around us all a great deal of the time. It greets you in the morning **newspaper**, on the **cereal packet** as you eat your breakfast, on **advertising hoardings**, **bus timetables** and in a host of other places. We also come into everyday contact with **statistics**, **leaflets**, **listings**, **fliers**, **spreadsheets**, **textbooks**, **notices**, **rulebooks** – and that's before we think about other media such as **radio**, **television** and the **Internet**.

Non-fiction in everyday life serves a variety of purposes. Newspapers, magazines, leaflets, radio, television and the Internet keep us informed with **reports** and **descriptions** of places or events. Leaflets or adverts persuade us to buy or do certain things. We rely on **reviews** of films and books to help us decide if we want to see or buy them, and we might consult an encyclopaedia for information. We learn to distinguish between what is invented and what is non-fiction, and what is fact and what is opinion.

Non-fiction

When we hear of a person's exceptional achievements, expertise in a field that interests us, or remarkable courage in adverse circumstances, we read their **diaries**, **letters** or accounts of their lives or special abilities which we find in the **biography** and **autobiography** sections of libraries and bookshops. If we want to explore a new interest we might look for a **manual** to tell us about it.

A need for a holiday might inspire us to read **travel books** and **brochures** or **guide books**. Our ability to understand and produce non-fiction is an essential life skill and an important tool to enable us to function effectively in everyday life. This chapter focuses on a wide variety of non-fiction and the many forms it takes, and will help you to understand and produce your own effective non-fiction.

You could make a chart of examples of types of non-fiction as you work your way through the chapter.

Letters

About this section

You will take a detailed look at letters and letter writing to:

- **Clarify the conventions of letter writing.**
- **See how writers use language and structure for their effects.**
- **Try out some different styles yourself.**

Millions of letters are sent and received in all parts of the world every day. They are written by businesses, public authorities and private individuals for all sorts of reasons. Some people's letters are so convincing, interesting, revealing or just plain enjoyable that they have volumes of their letters published.

Make a list of as many reasons as you can think of for writing letters.

Just to remind you ...

It goes without saying that you should use your best handwriting and fresh stationery for writing letters, particularly formal ones. Ripped-out pages of school exercise books or scrap paper with stains from the bottom of a coffee cup might do for a friend, but certainly not for anyone else!

Good letters will always contain appropriate details laid out in a generally accepted manner. For example, unless you are writing to a friend or close relative, you should probably make sure your letter looks something like this.

> Your address
> Postcode
> Date
>
> Their address
> Postcode
>
> Dear (title of addressee)
>
> Re: if any
>
> This is the 'contact' part of the letter. It could be a request, a complaint, an application, an invitation, an enquiry, a confirmation, a brief note, etc ...
>
> Yours sincerely
>
> Signature (if used)
> Your name, printed if signature used

Remember to include a stamped, self-addressed envelope (SAE) if requested or if you are writing to a charity. Always be polite, clear and concise – even if you're complaining about something – and sign off with a term corresponding to the title of the addressee (e.g. 'Yours faithfully' if you are writing to 'Dear Sir/Madam' and 'Yours sincerely' if you are writing to the addressee by name). Make sure your name is legible. This is particularly important if you use a signature which resembles a spider in motion – print your name beneath it.

Non-fiction

Writing for a range of purposes

The most difficult part of writing a letter is making sure that you use language which fits the purpose, and creates the right overall tone. This letter is such an example. It is from the writer Jane Austen (1775–1817) to James Stainer Clarke (c.1765–1834), Chaplain, Librarian and Historiographer to the Prince Regent who became King George IV. James Clarke grovelled to the extravagant prince, whom Jane disliked. Look at how she makes a **polite but assertive refusal** to take up a suggestion she has received from Clarke to write 'an historical romance illustrative of the history of the august House of Coburg' – the name given to the prince's family.

Thanks, but ... no thanks

Pick out or underline with a coloured pen, the polite, respectful words and phrases Jane Austen uses in the first paragraph of this letter.

Pick out or underline with a different coloured pen, the language in the second paragraph which indicates that Jane Austen was modest.

Rewrite the second paragraph of Jane Austen's letter in contemporary language. Take care to be as polite as she is but remain firm.

Write a brief letter which politely, but assertively, refuses an offer. This could be a lecture on the most boring topic you can think of, or use your imagination to think of any other offer that you could most definitely refuse!

My dear Sir,

I am honoured by the Prince's thanks and very much obliged to yourself for the kind manner in which you mention the work. I have also to acknowledge a former letter forwarded to me from Hans Place. I assure you I felt very grateful for the friendly tenor of it, and hope my silence will have been considered, as it was truly meant, to proceed only from an unwillingness to tax your time with idle thanks. Under every interesting circumstance which your own talents and literary labours have placed you in, or the favour of the Regent bestowed, you have my best wishes. Your recent appointments I hope are a step to something still better. In my opinion, the service of a court can hardly be too well paid, for immense must be the sacrifice of time and feeling required by it.

You are very very kind in your hints as to the sort of composition which might recommend me at present, and I am fully sensible that an historical romance, founded on the House of Saxe Coburg, might be much more to the purpose of profit or popularity than such pictures of domestic life in country villages as I deal in. But I could no more write a romance than an epic poem. I could not sit seriously down to write a serious romance under any other motive than to save my life; and if it were indispensable for me to keep it up and never relax into laughing at myself or other people, I am sure I should be hung before I had finished the first chapter. No, I must keep to my own style and go on in my own way; and though I may never succeed again in that, I am convinced that I should totally fail in any other.

I remain, my dear Sir,

Your very much obliged, and very sincere friend,

J. Austen

Chawton, near Alton, April 1, 1816.

Non-fiction

Writing to persuade, argue and advise

This letter is written to **persuade** people to do something.

Look at how it achieves its effect. In the first paragraph this is explained for you. See if you can explain the effect of the persuasive language and techniques highlighted in the rest of the letter. Comment on each example in the circle provided.

Write a letter to householders to *advise* them that their electricity/water supply will be turned off for two hours next week. Be sure to anticipate the reader's reaction to help you find the right tone.

Write a letter of complaint to the manufacturer of a faulty item you bought. Remember to develop your *argument* logically and to give evidence to back up your claim.

Makes it clear what the subject of the letter is

Polite way to say 'persuade'

A free day out – quite an incentive

You don't have to do anything to be entitled to a prize – wow!

30 September 2002

FORESTS FOR THE COMMUNITY
FOREST OF AVON

Dear Headteacher

Christmas Card Recycling 2002/03 for Tree Planting

It may seem rather early to be receiving your first Christmas greeting! However, I would like to invite you to help us to raise money for tree planting in the Forest of Avon as you may have done in other recent years. As before, participating schools will be automatically entered into a draw for which the award will be a free Nature Study Day for 60 children at the Wildlife Trust's Willsbridge Mill.

Arrangements will be very easy this year. Quite simply, your staff and pupils save the cards and later in January we will arrange for them to be collected. Your involvement will cost you nothing, and it could be made into a curriculum opportunity for environmental education. The Forest will benefit by receiving £1000 or more from the volume of card taken out of the waste stream by Avon children.

We hope to involve more than half of the 475 schools in the area this year, so if you have not joined in before, please do this time. I would also be very glad to know if any classes within your school are studying recycling, woodlands, or related topics this term or early next, in order to discuss publicity opportunities for both your school and the Forest of Avon. All you have to do to participate in the project and be entered for the draw is to return the tear-off strip below by return of post, and not later than 22 November. Further details will follow ...

Thank you in anticipation of your involvement.

Yours sincerely,

Mark Durk
Director

....

We would like to recycle our Christmas cards to raise money for tree planting in the Forest of Avon. Please enter our school into the draw to win a free Nature Study Day with the Wildlife Trust at Willsbridge Mill.

Headteacher:...

School:...

Address:..

....

Tel:..

Non-fiction

Keeping it brief ...

Now look at this letter written by Charles Dickens, or Boz as he nicknamed himself. He was writing to an admirer who offered him suggestions for his work and had perhaps sent a sculpture of a head and shoulders. The letter was written in 1841 in the style of a character from one of his novels – Alfred Jingle from *The Pickwick Papers*.

> My Dear Hall.
>
> Post just going – compression of sentiments required – Bust received – likeness <u>amazing</u> – recognisable instantly if encountered on the summit of the Great Pyramid – Scotch anecdote most striking and most distressing – dreamed of it – babies well – wife ditto – yours the same, I hope? Seaport sketches, one of those ideas that improves in promise as they are pondered on – <u>Good</u>, I am certain – Ever faithfully, and at present hastily –
>
> Boz.

Using email

You've probably heard the idea that you can be more informal in emails than you would be on paper. Obviously, email, rather than paper, is a form of communication that you may use with friends and so you may not worry about spelling errors. In any other context, however, you should apply the same amount of care. The important differences are:

- Be brief – think of your communication as a message or short note rather than a letter.

- Email communications can enable instant exchange. Such swiftness can be useful when organising something at short notice, for example.

- It is polite to make an entry in the subject field – the equivalent of the reference information that you give under the name of the person addressed in a formal letter. The subject should be a clear summary of the content of the message.

- Remember that it is easier to trace the sender of a rude email than the sender of a letter. It is also easy to send an email in haste. If in doubt save it in drafts until later.

- Be careful what you say in an email. The person you are sending it to may not be the person who downloads it at the other end.

Finding the right tone

When being brief, as in emails, it is easy to give the wrong impression. A joke could be taken the wrong way or you may not make yourself clear and cause offence. You could use emoticons such as smilies 😊 to reinforce your point but this is best reserved for friends. It is better to try to express yourself in words that give the right impression.

Your turn

Write a letter in which 'compression of sentiments is required' using prose instead of hyphenated point form. Try thanking someone who sent you this book to help you with your GCSEs.

Rewrite one paragraph of the letter on page 45 in the style of Alfred Jingle.

Working with others

You and a friend have decided to organise a charity sports match. The headteacher has given you permission to use a school computer to email invitations to everyone in the school and to ask for sponsorship. A relative and a neighbour have said they will circulate your email where they work, too. Your task is to write one email that will be suitable for all audiences and get you the right response. Think carefully about how you will use text and background colour, fonts, sizes, etc. to present your request.

Try using ICT-based research techniques to find out about forms of communication that came before paper-based correspondence and email. Write a paragraph on each form and put them in chronological order. Try looking up smoke signals, pigeon post, the fax, telegraph, the postal service, marathon runners.

Section round-up

After reading this section, you should be able to show how you can comment on and achieve certain effects in letter writing.

Non-fiction

Diaries

About this section

You will find out about some famous diarists, and:
- See how language changes over time.
- Make comparisons between styles of diary.
- Write some 'uplifting' diary entries of your own.

Do you keep a diary? Many people do, sometimes just for parts of their lives such as when they travel or live abroad for a time. Other people just seem to be compelled to keep a daily or frequent record of what happens in their lives. A diary can help you to organise your thoughts, allow you to reflect on something that has happened during the day, provide you with a measure to see how much you change over time, or simply be a more reliable record than your memory.

Diary as friend

A famous diarist was Anne Frank, the Jewish girl whose family spent two years hiding from the Nazis in secret rooms within her father's factory in occupied Amsterdam. In 1944 they were discovered and Anne and her sister were sent to a concentration camp where they both died. Her diary was a thirteenth birthday present, and her gift for writing soon becomes apparent. In this extract, Anne talks about the nature of keeping a diary and explains how she regards it as a friend.

Over to you

Writing a diary proved to be one of the devices Anne used to keep her spirits up while she was in captivity. What three reasons does she give for keeping a diary?

Many of the entries in Anne's diary are intensely personal. Although she says in this extract 'since I'm not planning to let anyone else read this stiff-backed notebook grandly referred to as a "diary", unless I should ever find a real friend', millions of copies have been published all over the world. In your opinion, does the fact that her diary became an important and moving account of a life touched by war justify the intrusion, or should her personal thoughts and feelings have been respected and the diary allowed to die with her?

Write an answer to this question bearing in mind how you would feel about your diary being published after your death.

Saturday, 20 June 1942

Writing in a diary is a really strange experience for someone like me. Not only because I've never written anything before, but also because it seems to me that later on neither I nor anyone else will be interested in the musings of a thirteen-year-old schoolgirl. Oh well, it doesn't matter. I feel like writing, and I have an even greater need to get all kinds of things off my chest.

'Paper has more patience than people.' I thought of this saying on one of those days when I was feeling a little depressed and was sitting at home with my chin in my hands, bored and listless, wondering whether to stay in or go out. I finally stayed where I was, brooding. Yes, paper <u>does</u> have more patience, and since I'm not planning to let anyone else read this stiff-backed notebook grandly referred to as a 'diary', unless I should ever find a real friend, it probably won't make a bit of difference.

Now I'm back to the point that prompted me to keep a diary in the first place: I don't have a friend.

Non-fiction

A Fan's Life

Writer Nick Hornby adapts the diary format in an ingenious way in his book *Fever Pitch*, published in 1992. A devoted football fan, he tells the story of his obsession in match reports beginning when he witnessed his first match at age 11. The result is a very successful example of writing to entertain:

Just Like a Woman

Cambridge United v Exeter City 29/4/78

With twenty minutes to go, Exeter went into the lead, and my girlfriend (who together with her girlfriend and her girlfriend's boyfriend had wanted to experience at first hand the dizzy glory of promotion) promptly did what I had always presumed women were apt to do at moments of crisis: she fainted. Her girlfriend took her off to see the St John's Ambulancemen; I meanwhile, did nothing, apart from pray for an equaliser, which came, followed minutes later by a winner. It was only after the players had popped the last champagne cork at the jubilant crowd that I started to feel bad about my earlier indifference.

I had recently read *The Female Eunuch*, a book which made a deep and lasting impression on me. And yet how was I supposed to get excited about the oppression of females if they couldn't be trusted to stay upright during the final minutes of a desperately close promotion campaign? And what was to be done about a male who was more concerned about being a goal down to Exeter City of the Third Division than he was about somebody he loved very much? It all looked hopeless.

Thirteen years later I am still ashamed of my unwillingness, my *inability*, to help, and the reason I feel ashamed is partly to do with the awareness that I haven't changed a bit. I don't want to look after anybody when I'm at a match; I am not *capable* of looking after anybody at a match. I am writing some nine hours before Arsenal play Benfica in the European Cup, the most important match at Highbury for years, and my partner will be with me: what happens if *she* keels over? Would I have the decency, the maturity, the common sense, to make sure that she was properly looked after? Or would I shove her limp body to one side, carry on screaming at the linesman, and hope that she is still breathing at the end of ninety minutes, always presuming, of course, that extra time and penalties are not required?

Analyse the extract

To see how Nick Hornby achieves an entertaining piece of writing you could consider this extract in chunks.

Paragraph 1: Deals with what happened.

How does the writer give a sense of the immediate? Is there anything in the text to suggest that he might have acted differently if the fainting had occurred at the start of the match? (Think about time, the nature of football matches in their closing stages and what he says in the third paragraph.)

How does the writer show his preconceived ideas about the way women behave?

What does this say about how he views the difference between men and women?

Identify the techniques and phrases that show the match was more important than his girlfriend's health.

Paragraph 2: Deals with his dilemma.

Nick Hornby mentions *The Female Eunuch*, a book by Germaine Greer that did much to draw attention to the argument that men had dominated women throughout history. Identify two phrases which reveal that he is both in sympathy with this argument and that he finds it difficult to accept.

Paragraph 3: Deals with what might happen in the future.

Why are some words in italics?

List the three qualities that Nick Hornby gives to show that he knows how he should behave if his partner faints.

The final sentence could easily have ended after the words '... ninety minutes'. What is the effect of adding 'always presuming, of course, that extra time and penalties are not required?'

Non-fiction

Before you move on ...
Pause to reflect on:
- how a writer's inner conflict can be used to literary effect
- how humour can arise from serious issues.

More about diaries

Some writers use a diary as a refreshing break from writing in a more literary style. Virginia Woolf wrote hers at teatime while the evening was still ahead of her, and she found that using a diary helped to solve problems which arose in her work.

A diary is also a place where you can write what you like, ignoring all the rules of writing for a reader, because it is usually meant to be private. Look at the extract on the right from the diary of the poet Lord Byron – it betrays his great love of women, that he did most things in a hurry and most hearteningly, that he had terrible problems with punctuation!

An historical record

Samuel Pepys was a young man about London in the mid-seventeenth century. He kept what has become a famous diary for about ten years, during which time he worked for the Admiralty. The main reason for his diary's fame is that it is a rare surviving account of everyday life in the England of those times. Several key events in England's history took place during the time of Pepys. He witnessed the epidemic of bubonic plague known as the Black Death in 1665, and several pages of his diary are devoted to a fascinating record of the Great Fire of London in 1666. On the next page is part of the entry in his diary for 2 September, the day the fire started.

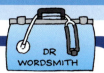

Dr Wordsmith says ...

Don't over-use the hyphen or dash – it can look lazy. The main use of a hyphen is to link words which belong together such as up-to-date, or on-screen. The hyphen is also used to show a break in a word which comes at the end of a line. When you wish to mark a pause or a break you will normally use a comma, but the occasional use of what is more commonly called the dash (–) can be effective. A dash is also – sometimes – used instead of brackets.

Extract from diary of Lord Byron

23 September [1816]. The whole town of Brientz were apparently gathered together in the rooms below – pretty music – & excellent Waltzing – none but peasants – the dancing much better than in England – the English can't Waltz – never could – nor ever will. – One man with his pipe in his mouth – but danced as well as the others – some other dances in pairs – and in fours – and very good. – I went to bed but the revelry continued below late & early. – Brientz but a village. – Rose early. – Embarked on the Lake of Brientz. – Rowed by women in a long boat – one very young & very pretty – seated myself by her – & began to row also – presently we put to shore & another woman jumped in – it seems it is the custom here for the boats to be manned by women – for of five men & three women in our bark – all the women took an oar – and but one man.

Non-fiction

> *2 September. Lord's Day. Some of our maids sitting up late last night to get things ready against our feast today, Jane called us up, about 3 in the morning, to tell us of a great fire they saw in the City. So I rose, and slipped on my nightgown and went to her window, and thought it to be on the back side of Markelane at the furthest; but being unused to such fires as fallowed, I thought it far enough off, and so went to bed again and to sleep. About 7 rose again to dress myself, and there looked out at the window and saw the fire not so much as it was, and further off. So to my closet to set things to rights after yesterday's cleaning. By and by Jane comes and tells me that she hears that above 300 houses have been burned down tonight by the fire we saw, and that it was now burning down all Fishstreet by London Bridge. So I made myself ready presently, and walked to the Tower and there got up upon one of the high places. Sir J. Robinson's little son going up with me; and there I did see the houses at that end of the bridge all on fire, and an infinite great fire on this and the other side the end of the bridge – which, among other people, did trouble me for poor little Michell and our Sarah on the Bridge. So down, with my heart full of trouble, to the Lieutenant of the Tower, who tells me that it begun this morning in the King's bakers house in Pudding Lane, and that it hath burned down St Magnes Church and most part of Fishstreete already. So I down to the waterside and there got a boat and through bridge, and there saw a lamentable fire. Poor Michell's house, as far as the Old Swan, already burned that way and the fire running further, that in a very little time it got as far as the Stillyard while I was there. Everybody endeavouring to remove their goods, and flinging into the river or bringing them into lighters that lay off. Poor people staying in their houses as long as till the very fire touched them, and then running into boats or clambering from one pair of stair by the waterside to another. And among other things, the poor pigeons I perceive were loath to leave their houses, but hovered about the windows and balconies till they were some of them burned their wings, and fell down.*

Your turn

The account begins with the information that maids in the Pepys household are preparing for a feast when one of them, called Jane, delivers the news about the fire. This makes the account unmistakably personal rather than public. Pick out or underline some other details that demonstrate this.

Pepys visits the Lieutenant of the Tower to find out what's going on. With a partner, role-play the conversation that might have taken place. Make a list of points first and refer to them if you need prompting.

The language we use today is considerably different from the language Pepys uses. For example, he says 'So I made myself ready presently', when we would probably say 'So I got ready'. Pepys says 'there I did see', where we might say 'there I saw'. Look at these examples from the same extract and then write out a more modern way of saying them. Look back at the extract if you need to remind yourself of the context in which the phrases appear.

(a) 'So to my closet to set things to rights'

(b) 'with my heart full of trouble'

(c) 'So I down to the waterside'

(d) 'the poor pigeons I perceive were loath to leave their houses'

Now rewrite the first three sentences of the account in your own modern English. What does this exercise tell you about the way language changes?

Hint: Look at tense, order of subject, nouns and verbs in sentence and punctuation.

Very little equipment or advice about fire fighting was available in seventeenth-century London. If you had the unenviable task of sending out town criers or making up a simple poster, what advice would you give?

Non-fiction

In adversity ...

Now look at this extract from Anne Frank's diary, written three days after her fifteenth birthday.

Friday, 26 May 1944

My dearest Kitty,

At long, long last, I can sit quietly at my table before the crack in the window frame and write you everything, everything I want to say.

I feel more miserable than I have in months. Even after the break-in I didn't feel so utterly broken, inside and out. On the one hand, there's the news about Mr van Hoeven, the Jewish question (which is discussed in detail by everyone in the house), the invasion (which is so long in coming), the awful food, the tension, the miserable atmosphere, my disappointment in Peter. On the other hand, there's Bep's engagement, the Whitsun reception, the flowers, Mr Kugler's birthday, cakes and stories about cabarets, films and concerts. That gap, that enormous gap, is always there. One day we're laughing at the comical side of life in hiding, and the next day (and there are many such days), we're frightened, and the fear, tension and despair can be read on our faces.

Miep and Mr Kugler bear the greatest burden for us, and for all those in hiding – Miep in everything she does and Mr Kugler through his enormous responsibility for the eight of us, which is sometimes so overwhelming that he can hardly speak from the pent-up tension and strain. Mr Kleiman and Bep also take very good care of us, but they're able to put the Annexe out of their minds, even if it's only for a few hours or a few days. They have their own worries, Mr Kleiman with his health and Bep with her engagement, which isn't looking very promising at the moment. But they also have their outings, their visits to friends, their everyday lives as ordinary people, so that the tension is sometimes relieved, if only for a short while, while ours never is, never has been, not once in the two years we've been here. How much longer will this increasingly oppressive, unbearable weight press down on us?

... Miep sent us a currant loaf with 'Happy Whitsun' written on top. It's almost as if she were mocking us, since our moods and cares are far from 'happy'.

We've all become more frightened since the van Hoeven business. Once again you hear 'shh' from all sides, and we're doing everything more quietly. The police forced the door there; they could just as easily do that here too! What will we do if we're ever ... no, I mustn't write that down. But the question won't let itself be pushed to the back of my mind today; on the contrary, all the fear I've ever felt is looming before me in all its horror.

... I've asked myself again and again whether it wouldn't have been better if we hadn't gone into hiding, if we were dead now and didn't have to go through this misery, especially so that the others could be spared the burden. But we all shrink from this thought. We still love life, we haven't yet forgotten the voice of nature, and we keep hoping, hoping for ... everything.

Let something happen soon, even an air raid. Nothing can be more crushing than this anxiety. Let the end come, however cruel; at least then we'll know whether we are to be the victors or the vanquished.

Yours, Anne M. Frank

Now try this

Pick out or underline five words or phrases that show how bad things have become, for example, 'more miserable', 'utterly broken'.

How far does Anne consider other people? How mature would you say her attitude is?

What effect has two years in hiding had on Anne, her family and her protectors?

How does this extract make you feel?

It has been said that a good piece of writing should 'flow like honey'. How far do you think this applies to Anne's style of writing?

Hint: Think about how easy the passage was to read. Did you stumble over any words? Is the tone prose-like or conversational? Does the style invite you to comment or to reply somehow? Does her style engage your attention?

Non-fiction

An account

Now look at this extract from *Long Walk to Freedom*, Nelson Mandela's autobiography, based on his prison diary. (For notes on autobiography see pp. 53–54.)

Prison not only robs you of your freedom, it attempts to take away your identity. Everyone wears a uniform, eats the same food, follows the same schedule. It is by definition a purely authoritarian state that tolerates no independence or individuality. As a freedom fighter and as a man, one must fight against the prison's attempt to rob one of these qualities.

From the courthouse, I was taken directly to Pretoria Local, the gloomy red-brick monstrosity that I knew so well. But I was now a convicted prisoner, not an awaiting-trial prisoner, and was treated without even the little deference that is afforded to the latter. I was stripped of my clothes and Colonel Jacobs was finally able to confiscate my kaross. I was issued the standard prison uniform for Africans: a pair of short trousers, a rough khaki shirt, a canvas jacket, socks, sandals and a cloth cap. Only Africans are given short trousers, for only African men were deemed 'boys' by the authorities.

I informed the authorities that I would under no circumstances wear shorts and told them I was prepared to go to court to protest. Later, when I was brought dinner, stiff cold porridge with half a teaspoonful of sugar, I refused to eat it. Colonel Jacobs pondered this and came up with a solution: I could wear long trousers and have my own food, if I agreed to be put in isolation. 'We were going to put you with the other politicals,' he said, 'but now you will be alone, man. I hope you enjoy it.' I assured him that solitary confinement would be fine as long as I could wear and eat what I chose.

For the next few weeks, I was completely and utterly isolated. I did not see the face or hear the voice of another prisoner. I was locked up for twenty-three hours a day, with thirty minutes of exercise in the morning and again in the afternoon. I had never been in isolation before, and every hour seemed like a year. There was no natural light in my cell; a single bulb burned overhead twenty-four hours a day. I did not have a wristwatch and I often thought it was the middle of the night when it was only late afternoon. I had nothing to read, nothing to write on or with, no one to talk to. The mind begins to turn in on itself, and one desperately wants something outside oneself on which to fix one's attention. I have known men who took half-a-dozen lashes in preference to being locked up alone. After a time in solitary, I relished the company even of the insects in my cell, and found myself on the verge of initiating conversations with a cockroach.

Over to you

What are the stated and unstated (explicit and implicit) reasons why Mandela refuses to wear the standard prison uniform for Africans?

What effect does the incident with the cockroach have on the passage?

What period of time elapses during this extract? How might the account have differed if it had been written as a diary?

Now compare this extract with the previous one, by Anne Frank. What circumstances do the two have in common?

From these extracts, what do you learn about the personalities of these two people and how they coped with adversity?

Imagine that you have managed to get stuck in a lift on a Friday afternoon. No one will rescue you until Monday morning. All you have with you is some water to drink, a pen and some paper. Make notes of your diary entries for Friday, Saturday and Sunday and then write a paragraph for one of the days.

Section round-up

If you've survived the hardships you've read about in this section you're well on the way to understanding how language changes over time, how to work with different texts, and how to appreciate other people's experiences.

Non-fiction

Autobiography

About this section

You will look at how writers present their lives, in particular:

- **How they look back on incidents that occurred.**

- **How they analyse the attitudes that surrounded them.**

Autobiographies are accounts of people's lives which are written by the subjects themselves, not by other writers. Autobiographies are often written by quite ordinary people, not just the famous. Such works may somehow typify an era, or be written with such an engaging style that the simplest of details contains much to interest the reader. Some celebrities may simply feel they do not have the skills to write their own story so they become the **biographer's** subject or employ a 'ghost writer' whose name does not appear on the published **autobiographical** work.

Two women

Look at these extracts from the autobiographies of two women growing up in the 1930s and 1940s. Joyce Storey (1) is white and grew up in Bristol. Maya Angelou (2) is black and grew up in the United States of America.

1 Looking back, it seems amazing to me how ignorant we were. It's so difficult to describe in today's climate of freedom. But we were, for example, woefully ignorant of sexual matters. Nobody told us anything. Grown-ups suffered from crippling shyness in discussing anything 'in front of the children'. There were half-embarrassed, half-giggling references to the Stork or being found under a gooseberry bush. But people were not only very Victorian in their attitudes, but as I realise now, incredibly ignorant about the workings of their own bodies. Small wonder then, that in answer to my anxious question, my Mother would often shake her head and sniff,

'You'll find out soon enough, my girl.'

So, I knew nothing of the great secret of how babies happened. We girls whispered together in that flat, sharing grossly inaccurate information, and nothing that I heard persuaded me in favour of marriage or being a wife and mother. Rather the reverse. And what I did know, what I had already found out, appalled me. All my uncles were often the worse for drink and sexually and physically abused their wives. The women in our family often wore the cowed and care-worn look of the constantly afraid – except that is, for my own Mother. My Dad never hit any of us, but then he was seen as being 'weak'!

If it got to the point where a woman couldn't stand it any more, there was nowhere for her to go. The woman who left her husband and went back to her Mother was sharply told,

'You made your bed, now you must lie on it.'

And Father would say,

'No man must interfere between man and wife,' and pack his errant daughter off home again.

And if an unmarried girl got into trouble, she was a bad girl. She got a thrashing from her father and if the man would not marry her, she was often sent away to a Home. Most women would feel a kind of sympathy for her and you would often hear the comment,

'Poor little bitch.'

But they could do nothing constructive, and she would be pointed out in the street as a kind of horrible example and her shame perpetuated.

So I think it was a kind of act of rebellion that we put the doll's head in the pee-pot. We all knew that there was some sort of inevitability about our lives that we couldn't avoid, so that hanging on to this innocence was a memory we would cherish forever. The days when we giggled over silly things and life held no responsibility, no drudgery, when the days were long and the sun shone were to be spun out as long as possible.

We were aware of our parent's struggle, but we hoped with youthful optimism that their lot would not be ours; by this simple act of defiance we were saying that we would not tolerate what they accepted without question. Reading trashy stories about girls who married rich men was an escape from harsh reality. Even the films transported us into a realm of fantasy and held us spellbound with stories of the poor girl who married the millionaire. When I dreamed and sighed and told my mother I would only marry a rich man so that I could have my wall-to-wall carpets and my red velvet curtains, she would reply, with a curl of her lips and almost with contempt,

'Don't get ideas above your station, my girl. Just remember you are nothing and what you read in books or see in films never happens in real life.'

Non-fiction

2 Two days after V-Day, I stood with the San Francisco Summer School class at Mission High School and received my diploma. That evening, in the bosom of the now-dear family home, I uncoiled my fearful secret and in a brave gesture left a note on Daddy Clidell's bed. It read: *Dear Parents, I am sorry to bring this disgrace on the family, but I am pregnant. Marguerite.*

The confusion that ensued when I explained to my stepfather that I expected to deliver the baby in three weeks, more or less, was reminiscent of a Molière comedy. Except that it was funny only years later. Daddy Clidell told Mother that I was 'three weeks gone'. Mother, regarding me as a woman for the first time, said indignantly, 'She's more than any three weeks.' They both accepted the fact that I was further along than they had first been told but found it nearly impossible to believe that I had carried a baby, eight months and one week, without their being any the wiser.

Mother asked, 'Who is the boy?' I told her. She recalled him, faintly.

'Do you want to marry him?'

'No.'

'Does he want to marry you?' The father had stopped speaking to me during my fourth month.

'No.'

'Well, that's that. No use ruining three lives.' There was no overt or subtle condemnation. She was Vivian Baxter Jackson. Hoping for the best, prepared for the worst, and unsurprised by anything in between.

Daddy Clidell assured me that I had nothing to worry about. That 'women been gittin' pregnant ever since Eve ate that apple.' He sent one of his waitresses to I. Magnin's to buy maternity dresses for me. For the next two weeks I whirled around the city going to doctors, taking vitamin shots and pills, buying clothes for the baby, and except for the rare moments alone, enjoying the imminent blessed event.

With attitude

Comparing these extracts, pick out examples of the difference in attitude between British and American fathers towards their daughters' unwanted pregnancies.

From these extracts, what differences can you find in the way that unmarried pregnant girls were treated in the two countries?

Make a list of points which demonstrate how far and in what way you think attitudes have changed in Britain since the war. You could make two columns headed 'Then' and 'Now'.

How do you think social, historical and cultural factors affect a writer's work?

Hint: Think about how free a person is or could be to think for themselves, the attitudes of publishers, their own families, neighbours ...

Think of an incident or event in your life which sticks out in your mind. It may be prominent because you fell flat on your face, caught the wrong train, scored a home goal, or did something you were particularly proud of. Write a page of your autobiography recording this incident or event in a way which will amuse, entertain or engage a reader. Drawing a spider diagram of the factors involved and how they relate to one another may help you to get started. Ask your teacher if you can include this task in your coursework.

Section round-up

Now you should be able to look at some of the factors which affect writers' lives, analyse the attitudes that surrounded them and write about your own life.

Non-fiction

Biography

About this section

You will look at two separate biographies of the same person to compare detail and style, and try some biographical writing of your own.

Biographies are accounts of people's lives which they did not write themselves. Biographies tend to be written about famous people. Few members of the Royal Family will escape a biographer's attention, for example.

Similarly, many people are interested in reading about the lives of writers, artists and politicians, and those who have led particularly difficult lives, are gifted in some way, or have overcome great hardship or oppression with unusual courage.

Compare these extracts from two different biographies of Prince Charles, which feature the same event (the first by Jonathan Dimbleby, *The Prince of Wales, a Biography*, the second by Anthony Holden, *Charles – a Biography*). The occasion is the 150th anniversary of the Royal Institute of British Architects (RIBA) in May 1984. Instead of praising British architecture as everyone expected, the Prince caused a stir by making a speech which criticised architects and town planners, and referred to one proposed development as 'a giant glass stump', and another as 'a monstrous carbuncle on the face of a much-loved and elegant friend'.

1

At Hampton Court Palace, that most splendid of all the royal residences, there was a heady, celebratory atmosphere that May evening among all but a select few of the RIBA leadership, who had discovered – by accident, only that afternoon – what the Prince intended to say. Sensing the scale of the controversy he was about to cause, Charles had 'leaked' an advance copy of his speech to his friend Charles Douglas-Home, editor of *The Times* – and also, to avoid accusations of favouritism, to Peter Preston, editor of the *Guardian*. Douglas-Home, as requested, had kept it to himself, sharing its contents with his own architecture correspondent only when *en route* to Hampton Court. Preston, as is the way of more conventional editors, had passed it on to his staff. When a *Guardian* reporter sought the response of the RIBA president, Michael Manser, only a few hours before the speech was due to be delivered, he was so thunderstruck that he considered boycotting the evening. Manser's inquiries to Buckingham Palace revealed total confusion: the press office had never heard of the RIBA gold medal and Edward Adeane had to confess that his boss had not shown him the final version of his speech.

For days the Prince's own staff, especially Edward Adeane, had been trying to talk him out of the assault he proposed to make, as had others of his advisers and friends. Its strength and passion, apart from appearing an unseemly abuse of hospitality, would incur the enmity of a British professional institute under royal patronage; it would involve him in an already heated public debate, in an area which was wholly new ground to him. To Adeane, the speech had become a resignation issue.

The night before, Charles himself had become sufficiently concerned about his speech to lose sleep over it. As he tossed and turned, a particular phrase occurred to him which inspired renewed confidence. While drafting the most striking phrase in the entire tirade, he had been thinking in terms of 'warts' or 'pimples'. Now the word 'carbuncle' – used by his step-mother-in-law, Raine Spencer, in a recent book on British spas – swam into the royal psyche and helped it at last find rest. Next morning, as Adeane still urged caution, the Prince of Wales was adamant. He had found a cause about which he cared; he was convinced he was in the right and he was determined to speak his mind.

Non-fiction

2 He did not complete his final draft until the early hours of the day itself, after which he instructed his staff to dispatch it to the editors of *The Times*, the *Guardian* and the *Observer*.

On the afternoon of 30 May, officials at RIBA were jolted out of their complacence about the royal contribution to their celebration by a telephone call from the *Guardian* to Patrick Harrison, the secretary of RIBA, warning him that the speech was to be 'difficult'. Harrison asked the *Guardian* to send round a copy. When he saw it, Manser was horrified: it was not so much difficult as a 'secret bombshell', as he would later describe it. Harrison was deputed to ring the Palace, where a junior press officer disclaimed any knowledge of what the Prince was to say. Harrison protested that, 'It was the wrong speech at the wrong time.' And he demanded, 'Who leaked it to the *Guardian*?' According to RIBA, the Prince's office was conciliatory, and his private secretary promised to try to dissuade the Prince from his course. Later, Edward Adeane even rang Manser and apparently pledged to do what he could on the journey between Buckingham Palace and Hampton Court. Not for the first time, Adeane failed to measure his man; not for the first time, they had a fierce argument in which Adeane (according to the memory of his colleagues) sought to impress on the Prince that he was overstepping the mark; and not for the first time, was overruled.

Manser and his colleagues waited queasily for their guest of honour to arrive. As he got out of the car, the Prince observed with apparent innocence, 'You've got a good turn-out of press here.' Manser led him to the platform and welcomed him to the celebration, still hoping that Adeane had prevailed upon the Prince at least to tone the speech down. His hopes were soon dashed. After congratulating Correa on 'his supreme skill' as an architect and his 'imaginative concern' for the poor of the Third World, the Prince moved swiftly to deliver his broadside.

Now test your recall

From the two extracts, what can you deduce about Edward Adeane and his relationship with the Prince?

Why do you think the Prince leaked the speech to the press?

'From these extracts, the first biographer seems to have been allowed closer access to the Prince's private thoughts than the second.' What evidence can you find to support or refute this statement?

Do you find one extract more readable than the other? If so, why?

Hint: How often did you get stuck? How many words did you come across which you didn't understand? How long were the sentences? Was any of the writing unnecessarily complicated?

In a group of three, take it in turns for each person to be interviewed by the other two, each taking notes of what the subject says. Write up a short biographical piece on the two you interview. Compare the two accounts that have been written about the same person. How do they differ? Is one more accurate than the other? What differences are there in style?

Hint: Is one more critical than the other? Do they use neutral or 'gushing' language, present tense or past tense?

Think of someone you know who interests you. Interview them and make brief notes which you could use if you were to become their official biographer. You could extend this task by writing a paragraph which conveys something about the subject's personality, manner and general uniqueness in a way that you think would engage the interest of a reader.

Section round-up

Now you should understand some of the factors at work in biographical writing.

Non-fiction

Science writing

Nobody goes through life without wondering what might be found in Space, or how life began. Our knowledge and understanding of the world comes through science – a branch of knowledge based on observable fact. Yet science can be difficult to the untrained mind. Our medium for sharing this and all other knowledge is, of course, language. Good science writing must therefore simplify ideas that are sometimes complicated but often captivating.

The extracts below are from the writings of three scientists who have all tried to make science understandable and enjoyable to non-scientists. You will also notice another feature of science writing for a wide audience – the absence of technical scientific terms and, for example, Latin names for genera and species of plants and animals.

Each extract is concerned with the evolution of species by the action of natural selection – the theory observed and tested by nineteenth-century naturalist Charles Darwin. The extracts also have in common the development of a case either by argument or by chronology. See if you can see this development as you read them.

First read the extracts, marking any words or phrases that you find difficult to understand. Look these up until you are satisfied that you understand each extract and the very simple idea that species develop or die out according to how well they adapt to their changing environment.

Tree of Life

The affinities of all the beings of the same class have sometimes been represented by a great tree. I believe this simile largely speaks the truth. The green and budding twigs may represent existing species; and those produced during former years may represent the long succession of extinct species. At each period of growth all the growing twigs have tried to branch out on all sides and to overtop and kill the surrounding twigs and branches, in the same manner as species and groups of species have at all times overmastered other species in the great battle for life. Of the many twigs which flourished when the tree was a mere bush, only two or three, now grown into great branches, yet survive and bear the other branches; so with the species which lived during long-past geological periods, very few have left living and modified descendants. From the first growth of the tree, many a limb and branch has decayed and dropped off; and these fallen branches of various sizes may represent those whole orders, families, and genera which have now no living representatives, and which are known to us only in a fossil state… So it is that the great Tree of Life fills with its dead and broken branches the crust of the earth, and covers the surface with its ever-branching and beautiful ramifications.

Charles Darwin

The Origin of Species, the book from which this extract was taken, was first published in 1859. It was considered by many to contain outrageous, blasphemous theories that challenged the existence of God. Many copies were burned. The book proved to be one of the most significant ever written, however, and most of its findings have since been accepted as an accurate account of how life develops.

Now try this

What literary device does Darwin use in this extract?

In your opinion, how successful is this device given that it is used in such an extended form?

Find the evidence to suggest that the author is expressing an opinion rather than fact.

What word does Darwin use to give the idea of fierce competition?

Non-fiction

The Language of the Genes

The engine – if not the engineer – of evolutionary change is natural selection, the preservation of favoured types in the struggle for life. Change is inevitable in any system, be it genes or language, in which there are errors of transmission from one generation to the next. Although change of this kind is certainly evolution, it is evolution at random. It cannot lead to progress from simple to complicated of the kind which Darwin was interested in and which gave rise to humans from their modest predecessors. Natural selection takes advantage of the fact that, each generation, inheritance makes mistakes. Because some are better at coping with what life throws at them, they copy themselves more successfully. Darwin's mechanism sorts out the best from what mutation supplies. It gives a direction to evolution and allows a living system to escape from the inevitability of extinction. This is as true for humans as for any other creature.

Steve Jones

Now try this

What mechanical image does the writer, Steve Jones, use?

Why does the writer mention language as well as genes?

Choose two other words that the writer could have used instead of 'modest'.

The Living Planet

It was, after all, some 600 million years ago that simple animals began to swim in the ancient seas; and over 200 million years since amphibians and reptiles invaded the land. Birds developed feathers and wings and took to the air a few million years afterwards and mammals evolved fur and warm blood around the same time. Sixty-five million years ago, the reptiles fell into their still-mysterious decline and mammals assumed the dominance of the land which they still hold today. So 50 million years ago, as the island continent of India approached Asia, all the major groups of animals and plants that we know today, and indeed almost all the large families within those groups, were already in existence. Each of the continents had its own multitudinous complement of inhabitants, though India, having been isolated as an immense island since just after the decline of the reptiles, was undoubtedly much poorer in advanced groups of animals than Asia. When the two eventually met and the new mountains began to rise some 40 million years ago, the animals and plants from the two old continents began to spread into the new uncolonised extension to their territory.

David Attenborough

Now try this

Would you say this passage is more descriptive or explanatory?

Is this passage more concerned with what happened or why it happened?

From what you have read in this passage, is there any aspect of evolution that is still not understood?

Non-fiction

Compare the texts

Which extract is the easiest to understand? Give reasons for your answer.

Which extract is the hardest to understand? Remember to give your reasons.

What differences in language do you notice between the two passages that are recently written and the one that is over a century old?

In which extract is the idea that humans are no different from other species most clearly expressed?

From the list below, choose the words that most fit each author's style. (You may also want to use their opposites or choose your own.) Then write three sentences to sum up each style:

informative	*descriptive*	*economical*
lyrical	*succinct*	*journalistic*
straightforward	*conversational*	*authoritative*
reverential	*repetitive*	*listing*
inspiring	*clear*	*precise*
instructive	*captivating*	*smooth*
absorbing	*fascinating*	*persuasive*
easy		

In your view, which of the three extracts is the most literary?

Which extract, do you think, is the most concerned with science?

In which extract is concern with history most apparent?

Each of the words below are about change but have different meanings. Research and write one sentence to define each one: *evolution*, *revolution* and *devolution*.

Section round-up

Now you should have a good idea of some of the factors to be considered when reading and writing about factual matters.

For your own notes

59

Non-fiction

Travel writing

> **About this section**
>
> You'll be going places to think about the language and effect of travel writing for particular purposes and different audiences.

Travel writing is a popular type of non-fiction. What better than to sit back on a rainy evening and follow an intrepid explorer through a jungle or up a snowy mountain? Travel writers do not have to be adventurous, however – there are probably as many ways to entertain and engage a reader with travel writing as there are travel books. As a major world industry, the travel and tourism agencies also generate a great deal of literature promoting their destinations. Develop a diagram as you work your way through this section. You could start with: home, abroad, methods of transport, adventures and holidays.

Currying flavour

Compare these two brief descriptions of Delhi, the capital of India, where there is an old part of the city and a more modern part.

 A 'Delhi. Capital of kingdoms and empires. Now, a sprawling metropolis with a fascinating blend of the past and the present. A perfect introduction to the composite culture of an ancient land. A window to the kaleidoscope that is India.'

 B 'Delhi is a fantastic place, fascinating and filthy in the extreme. Old Delhi is full of snake charmers, bear wrestlers, opium dens and dead bodies lying in the gutter. But New Delhi is beautiful, modern, airy, green and lush. Amazing.'

One of these descriptions comes from the Government of India's Department of Tourism, and the other from an airmail letter written by a 16-year-old schoolboy to his parents (he had told them he was going to pick grapes in France, and returned from India four years later!)
 Which do you think is which?

Under the microscope

The contrast between these pieces clearly demonstrates that we write for different purposes and different audiences. Let's look at them individually and then compare them.

A

Content

- Summarises Delhi's importance – 'Capital', and historical past – 'kingdoms and empires', 'blend of past and present', without lots of dull detail.
- Uses persuasive words to praise it – 'fascinating', 'perfect'.
- Describes Delhi in romantic terms which give an impression rather than solid information – 'composite culture of an ancient land', 'kaleidoscope that is India'.
- Is also trying to be truthful. The only words that seem to detract from the glossy image of Delhi that is being presented seem to be 'sprawling metropolis'.
  ✪ Would 'radiating' or 'expanding' be a more flattering adjective? Can you think of any others that could be used to qualify the word 'metropolis'?

Purpose
The idea of this description, which appears as a caption to a colourful picture of dancers, is to entice the reader to visit India.

Audience
Any adult who is faintly interested in visiting India and who will lose interest if they have to wade through acres of small print to find out about it.

Language
The five collections of words in this description are statements not sentences. They are short and simple and are meant to have impact, in much the same way as newspaper headlines may be arresting without being correct grammatical units.

Non-fiction

Content

- Uses few words to convey a fairly full first impression.
- Concentrates on the feel of the place, with actual details of who and what can be found there, rather than dealing with its historical context or relative importance as a city.
- Contains contrasts – 'fascinating and filthy'.
  ✪ Can you spot any other?

Hint: There are two towns.

Purpose
The description is part of a letter to convey an impression. No one's job depends on what is said, and India's economy will not suffer from the reference to the dead bodies!

Audience
It is a private matter. ✪ Do you think the description would have shocked the writer's parents?

Language
The present tense and the list of things to be found there make the description come alive. The alliteration of the letter 'f', at the beginning of three out of eight words, adds structure and rhythm. It is interesting that the description of Old Delhi lists four paired words, and the description of New Delhi, five single ones which give the impression of clean straightforwardness. The sentence structure in this description is more conventional, although the writer starts a sentence with 'But'. Ending the description with 'Amazing' as a sentence on its own emphasises the quality of awesome surprise.

You would not be expected to examine such short extracts in as much detail as this so don't worry when you try this for yourself in the next task. Before you move on, pick out one fact and one opinion from each description of Delhi.

For your own notes

Non-fiction

It's a mystery

An unsolved mystery as famous as the Loch Ness Monster is that of the legendary Yeti or Abominable Snowman. Compare content and style in these accounts by two explorers, Eric Shipton (1) and Don Whillans (2), on two different Himalayan mountains, 20 years apart.

1 During the course of a dozen expeditions in the Himalayas I have come across several sets of those mysterious footprints which the Sherpas have said were made by the Yeti or 'Abominable Snowman'. Before 1951 I had not taken more than a mild interest in the phenomena; for although the Sherpas had always displayed deep concern at the appearance of the tracks and I myself could offer no rational explanation, the footprints themselves were so indistinct, so distorted by melting, that it was impossible even to gauge the size of the feet that had made them.

In 1951 Michael Ward, Sonam Tensing and I crossed a 20,000-foot pass into a piece of unexplored country which we discovered later to be the upper basin of a river called the Menlung. At about four o'clock in the afternoon we were making our way down a long glacier below the pass when we came across footprints in the snow. Sonam Tensing, a quiet, sober man approaching middle age, whom I had known for many years, became very excited and immediately identified them as those of a Yeti. Unlike other Yeti footprints I had seen, these were fresh.

We followed the tracks for about two miles. Over most of that distance the snow overlying the glacier ice was soft and deep, and thus the tracks appeared as elongated holes often partly filled with loose snow. But in many places, particularly near the edges of crevasses, the snow was barely an inch deep, and here the tracks showed perfect imprints of the feet, the toes, the heels, and the contours of the soles revealed in sharp relief, quite unspoiled by melting. Moreover we found several places where the creature, whatever it was, had jumped across a narrow crevasse, and we could see clearly that on landing on the other side it had dug its toes in to prevent itself from slipping back. Each footprint was about a foot long. It was November and the nights were very cold, and early that morning the snow would have been very hard; since then there had been a great deal of melting. From this and the appearance of the tracks it was obvious that the creature had passed that way very recently, certainly not more than a few hours before.

Since seeing those tracks I cannot dismiss the yeti as a legend. Whatever made them, it was not a bear. But I have no constructive theory to offer.

Non-fiction

2 It was just as we put down our loads that I heard a noise on the ridge behind me. Pemba Tharkay looked up and simply said, 'Yeti coming.'

I whipped round just in time to see a dark object dropping behind a ridge, and as it vanished two lines of black crows flew up – these are very common in the Himalayas, and the noise we had heard must have been their squawking. But the object was something else; definitely bigger than a bird, though I couldn't be sure what it was since it was now getting dark. I was quite disturbed by the way Pemba mentioned the Yeti. He just made a flat statement, and I felt that if this Yeti did exist this was just the kind of place it would appear. But I didn't continue looking – which was a mistake – because we needed to pitch the tents before dark. I just mentioned to Pemba that I thought that what I had seen was more than a couple of crows and then completely forgot about the incident.

The following day Mike and I went off to make a reconnaissance for a permanent Base Camp and left the two Sherpas at the Machapuchare site. At first we climbed up onto the moraine bank intending to traverse the top of it, but there were too many ups and downs – so I dropped back into the valley between the moraine bank and the mountain where there was a smooth, easy slope.

There had been an avalanche down it several weeks earlier, but it didn't look as if there was going to be any further danger. I had been walking for a few minutes when I was stopped dead by the appearance of a set of deep tracks coming down the mountainside on the left of the valley. I realized immediately that this was the exact point where this whatever-it-was had dropped down behind the ridge the previous evening. The snow had been very soft and whatever it was had made deep tracks in a similar manner to ourselves. Anyhow, I took a picture of the tracks going up the mountainside and called Mike over. There were one or two scratch-marks like claw-marks on the snow, and Mike said, 'Oh, it's a bear.'

But there were one or two things that didn't look like a bear to me. I didn't form any opinions at that stage but just looked at all the tracks and the features. It wasn't possible to get a picture of one clear footprint because the snow had tumbled into each hole, which was at least a foot deep. I thought they were about the size of a small man, about my own size foot, which is size 6. We then carried on a little farther up the valley but by this time the cloud had come down and we couldn't really see the South Face of Annapurna, so Mike and I went back to the camp and rejoined the Sherpas. I examined the tracks through the binoculars and estimated that they came down to an altitude of around 13,000 feet, and vanished over the crest of the ridge at 15,000 feet. Mike was going back to join the main party at Pokhara and he left me that evening to get back to the Hinko Cave to rejoin the two coolies we had left there. He planned to take them back to the nearest village, load them up with food and send them back up to the Hinko Cave, since by this time I hoped to complete my little reconnaissance and planned to return to the Cave to await the main party.

That night, after Mike had departed, I began to ponder about the tracks. It did occur to me that it was possible that this creature, whatever it was, might still be around, so I stuck my head outside the tent. It was bright moonlight and the moon was shining straight onto the hillside where the tracks were. It was even possible to read small print, it was so bright. The hillside had gentle undulations, rather like an easy ski slope, and I made a mental note of where I could see dark spots which were possibly rocks or trees. If any of these moved they could only be some kind of living creature. It was a fantastically cold night – I was in two sleeping-bags but was still cold. Even so I kept my head sticking outside the tent, and after a time noticed that one of these dark spots appeared to have moved. I couldn't be sure, but I continued watching and then, without a doubt, it started to move quite quickly. There was a monocular in the tent which I focused on the dark, moving shape. It was then that I could definitely distinguish limbs and a kind of bounding movement. It was going directly uphill towards another clump of

63

Non-fiction

trees and it was obvious, just by the movements, that it was a reasonably powerful animal and that it was bounding along on all fours. It disappeared into the shadow of a tree, which was leafless, it being winter, and then reappeared wandering from one clump of trees to the next, but it was in a slightly shadowy portion of the hillside at the base of a kind of dune and I couldn't see it clearly. However, when it reached the topmost tree it came into the moonlight. It gave me the impression that it was hunting for food, and then, as if it had decided to abandon its search, it started diagonally downwards across the hillside heading for some cliffs.

Once it started to move out in the moonlight I could get a better idea of what it was. It was on all fours and it was bounding along very quickly across the snow, heading for the shelter of the cliffs. That was the point at which I thought, that thing is an ape or ape-like creature. Then it just disappeared into the shadow of the rocks and I felt then that that was the last I was ever going to see of this creature, whatever it was. There had been a peculiar atmosphere about the place ever since we had arrived at the Machapuchare Base Camp – and now this seemed to have gone.

The following morning I went up to make a full reconnaissance to the permanent Base Camp site and I took the two Sherpas along. I thought I'd see their reaction at the point where I'd photographed the tracks the day before. The tracks were so obvious that it was impossible not to make any comment, but they walked straight past and didn't indicate that they had seen them. I had already mentioned that I had seen the Yeti, not knowing exactly what it was, but they pretended they didn't understand and ignored what I said.

I am convinced that they believe the Yeti does exist, that it is some kind of sacred animal which is best left alone; that if you don't bother it, it won't bother you. I feel very much the same way myself. If it's not a bear and is one of these legendary creatures, and if it's managed to survive so long and under such bitterly cold conditions, it deserves to be left alone.

When I got back from looking at the Face, I had another indication of the Sherpas' attitude to the Yeti. They had come back in front of me and were playing around, sliding down the snow hummocks on plastic bags; this is a favourite game of theirs.

I suggested, 'Why don't you go over to the other side of the valley, the slope's a lot better there.' But before the words were out of my mouth, Kancha chipped in, 'It's no good over there, Sahib; been over there, no good.'

But it was obvious they hadn't been anywhere near there, for there were no tracks. I suddenly realized that this was the hillside where we had seen the Yeti, and that the two Sherpas would not go there for this reason.

Are you ready?

Comparing both accounts, describe the reaction of the Sherpas to the presence of the Yeti.

Why is it difficult to authenticate either the sightings or tracks of the Yeti?

At what time of day and altitude does it seem possible to locate the Yeti?

Who do you think each author is addressing? How do their styles differ?

Hint: Do they invite you to become involved or just tell a story? Is either expecting an answer?

Write a short entry on the Yeti for a non-fiction book to be titled *Unsolved Mysteries of the 20th Century*. Think about who you are writing it for. Should it be informative, exciting, arouse the curiosity of the reader? How much of what you write can be fact and how much opinion? Think about how it would differ from an account for a scientific journal.

Imagine you are the Yeti that Shipton mentions and that Whillans saw. Describe your lifestyle, food and habitat, and what you think of these invaders within your territory. Decide who you are writing the account for – you should try to make your account entertaining, engaging and original.

Eric Shipton says that he has 'no constructive theory to offer' about the tracks he sees. You are a zoologist convinced you have solved the mystery. Present your well-argued theory in an article for a respected broadsheet newspaper. If your teacher approves, some of this material could be included in your coursework.

Non-fiction

Exploring America

Compare the style and content of these two pieces of travel writing about different parts of the United States of America.

Bay City Wonder

Whoever said 'See Rome and die' had obviously not been to San Francisco. Poised on a promontory at the edge of a bay in Northern California, this must be one of the world's most beautiful cities. Mists and fogs roll in from the ocean and hug the tops of downtown highrises. Perhaps you have landed in the middle of a modern-day fairytale.

There is a boldness about any city which continues to grow despite being located on one of the world's most active fault-lines. The city's second major earthquake this century was in October 1989. There is a feeling that San Francisco is on borrowed time. Fitted with special shock absorbers which will apparently accommodate the movement likely to be caused during a tremor, many of the buildings claim to be quake-proof. Shockwave damage from the last quake was restricted to the very north-eastern edge of the city and part of the arterial Bay Bridge collapsed.

Several bridges span sections of the San Francisco Bay area, and afford spectacular views of the mountains to the north and to the east. The bridges are impressive feats of engineering. The most famous is the Golden Gate, actually more rusty red in colour than its grand title suggests. This was, however, the gateway to treasures further inland where many a miner hoped to find his fortune in the goldrush of the mid-nineteenth century. The highly successful football team is even called the San Francisco Forty-Niners after these founding fathers of the modern city.

This spirit of confidence and defiance is reflected in the city's willingness to erect controversial buildings. The Transamerica Pyramid is a distinctive landmark. It towers high on the skyline like a great tapering white rocket. The new Marriott building uses sweeping curves of blue glass which change colour with the weather. I thought it looked like a Wurlitzer jukebox. Wherever I looked, this building would persistently force itself into my view.

The island of Alcatraz, site of the infamous penitentiary, sticks up in the Bay a little way in from the Golden Gate. The icy waters may have deterred inmates from taking the plunge, but it doesn't stop bobbing seals from swimming in to size up the tourists and scavenge discarded morsels at Fisherman's Wharf. Even the occasional whale has been lured into the Bay area. On its journey south from Canadian seas in search of the warmer waters of Baja California, one lost whale has twice become stuck at the mouth of the Sacramento River which flows into the Bay. Tapes of whale songs were successful in helping this disorientated creature back on to its original route!

San Francisco is an easy city to get around. Being small, much of it can be seen on foot. The transportation network allows for transfers between bus, tram, light rail and cable cars. A trip from Market Street to Fisherman's Wharf by one of the original cable cars is fun.

From a cable car, you can jump down in Chinatown. The largest Chinese community in the west is located here, a wonderful place to pick up some bargains. Seek out a dim sum breakfast and taste a multitude of small and varied dishes.

For nightlife the Italian area, Northpoint, is the place to go. Amid a clutch of good bookshops, live jazz beckons you into small bars to while away some time. After a few evening hours you will understand why America's artists and writers have often 'hung out' here.

From San Francisco many other of the west coast's attractions are open to you. Nearby is Big Sur and the haunts frequented by beatnik writer Jack Kerouac. Or make a trip to Cannery Row, immortalised in the novel of the same name by John Steinbeck. You might meet Clint Eastwood at Carmel or take in some Bach at the festival in July. There is a Jazz Festival in September at Monterey. Across the Bay in Berkeley, students at the University of California set trends before your eyes. Be tempted to a drink at the pier there as the sun goes down.

Further inland Yosemite National Park offers stunning views. The giant sequoias there will make you feel a mere inch or two tall. Log cabins are available for climbers, wildlife enthusiasts and ramblers wishing to explore the vast mountains.

All this from just one destination must be a bargain so see Rome by all means, but make sure you visit San Francisco first. After all, it may not be there for much longer …

65

Non-fiction

The Lost Continent

At the town of Holly Springs stood a sign for Senatobia, and I got briefly excited. Senatobia! What a great name for a Mississippi town! All the stupidity and pomposity of the Old South seemed to be encapsulated in those five golden syllables. Maybe things were picking up. Maybe now I would see chain-gangs toiling in the sun and a prisoner in heavy irons legging it across fields and sloshing through creeks while pursued by bloodhounds, and lynch mobs roaming the streets and crosses burning on lawns. The prospect enlivened me, but I had to calm down because a state trooper pulled up alongside me at a traffic light and began looking me over with that sort of casual disdain you often get when you give a dangerously stupid person a gun and a squad car. He was sweaty and overweight and sat low in his seat. I assume he was descended from the apes like all the rest of us, but clearly in his case it had been a fairly gentle slope. I stared straight ahead with a look that I hoped conveyed seriousness of purpose mingled with a warm heart and innocent demeanour. I could feel him looking at me. At the very least I expected him to gob a wad of tobacco juice down the side of my head. Instead, he said, 'How yew doin'?'

This so surprised me that I answered, in a cracking voice, 'Pardon?'

'I said, how yew doin'?'

'I'm fine,' I said. And then added, having lived some years in Britain, 'Thank you.'

'Y'on vacation?'

'Yup.'

'Hah doo lack Miss Hippy?'

'Pardon?'

'I say, hah doo lack Miss Hippy?'

I was quietly distressed. The man was armed and Southern and I couldn't understand a word he was saying to me.

'I'm sorry,' I said. 'I'm kind of slow, and I don't understand what you're saying.'

'I say' – and he repeated it more carefully – 'How doo yew lack Mississippi?'

It dawned on me. 'Oh! I like it fine! I like it heaps! I think it's wonderful. The people are so friendly and helpful.' I wanted to add that I had been there for an hour and hadn't been shot at once, but the light changed and he was gone, and I sighed and thought, 'Thank you, Jesus.'

I drove on to Oxford, home of the University of Mississippi, or 'Ole Miss', as it's known. The people named the town after Oxford in England in the hope that this would persuade the state to build the university there, and the state did. This tells you most of what you need to know about the workings of the Southern mind. Oxford appeared to be an agreeable town. It was built around a square, in the middle of which stood the Lafayette County Courthouse, with a tall clock-tower and Doric columns, basking grandly in the Indian summer sunshine. Around the perimeter of the square were attractive stores and a tourist information office. I went into the tourist information office to get directions to Rowan Oak, William Faulkner's home. Faulkner lived in Oxford for the whole of his life, and his home is now a museum, preserved as it was on the day he died in 1962. It must be unnerving to be so famous that you know they are going to come in the moment you croak and hang velvet cords across all the doorways and treat everything with reverence. Think of the embarrassment if you left a copy of *Reader's Digest Condensed Books* on the bedside table.

Behind the desk sat a large, exceptionally well-dressed black woman. This surprised me a little, this being Mississippi. She wore a dark two-piece suit, which must have been awfully warm in the Mississippi heat. I asked her the way to Rowan Oak.

'You parked on the square?' she said. Actually she said, 'You pocked on the skwaya?'

'Yes.'

'Okay, honey you git in yo' car and you makes the skwaya. You goes out the other end, twoads the university, goes three blocks, turns rat the traffic lats, goes down the hill and you there, un'stan?'

'No.'

She sighed and started again. 'You git in yo' car and you makes the skwaya —'

'What, I drive around the square?'

'That's rat, honey. You makes the skwaya.' She was talking to me the way I would talk to a French person. She gave me the rest of the instructions and I pretended to understand, though they meant almost nothing to me. All I kept thinking was what funny sounds they were to be emerging from such an elegant-looking woman. As I went out the door she called out, 'Hit doan really matter anyhow cuz hit be's closed now.' She really said hit; she really said be's.

I said, 'Pardon?'

'Hit be's closed now. You kin look arond the grounz if you woan, but you caint go insod.'

I wint outsod thinking that Miss Hippy was goan be hard work.

Non-fiction

Now try this

Bay City Wonder

What device does the writer use to introduce and conclude the piece. Do you think it is effective?

Pick out six features of interest in San Francisco, and six words which describe the city.

What kind of atmosphere is created in this piece?

Hint: Think about threats, spirit and fun.

Would it make you want to go there? Give reasons for your answer.

The Lost Continent

Did this extract make you laugh? If so, why?

How does the author, Bill Bryson, exploit language to create effect?

Would this account tempt you to go to Mississippi? Give reasons for your answer.

Did you need to read what the policeman or the smart woman said more than once to understand the accent? Imagine the piece without the use of the southern drawl. What effect would it have on the passage?

From what he shares with the reader about the policeman, what does Bill Bryson imply about Mississippi and the people who live there? What does it tell you about him?

Could this piece have been written for *The Senatobia Times*? How do you think residents of Senatobia would feel about this account of their town?

With a partner, try reading aloud the conversation between Bill Bryson and the woman in the tourist office. Then swap over, substituting a different accent for her southern drawl. How does this alter the effect of the passage?

Now compare the two pieces

One piece is written for a travel magazine produced by a travel agent. It is a short overview of a place, spoken of in very favourable terms.

In contrast, the other piece does not particularly flatter the place, in fact you could say it is quite disparaging towards it. In which piece are you most aware of the writer? Why?

Imagine you are a travel writer and have been asked to write a short travel article on Oxford, Mississippi, for the same magazine that published *Bay City Wonder*, even though you have probably never been there. How will you sell the place for the tourism market? For example, will you mention:

- the link with Oxford, England?
- that it is a university town?
- that it is 'agreeable'?
- the smart woman in the tourist office?
- the kind of attitude Bill Bryson expected to encounter in Mississippi?
- the difficulty a non-American might have with understanding the accent?
- that William Faulkner lived there?
- that the town has some fine buildings and a formal town plan?

Make a list of any further points that you would (or wouldn't!) mention. How important is accuracy of information in writing of this kind? Why?

Section round-up

Now you should have a good idea of how to suit travel writing to its audience and purpose. You should also be able to write short travel pieces of your own for different purposes.

For your own notes

Non-fiction

Information

About this section

You will look at a variety of leaflets and compare them. This will help you to:

- Distinguish between fact and opinion (see also p. 74).
- Comment on impact, content and presentation.
- Devise material to persuade, argue, advise.
- Write to inform, explain, describe.

Look at this flier (small poster) from the Vegetarian Society. It is part of their campaign for students to have the right to a vegetarian meal at school if they wish.

Now try this

Give three reasons why the Vegetarian Society thinks you should be able to have a vegetarian meal at school if you wish.

Make a list of actions you could take to make sure such choice is possible.

List two facts and two opinions given in this leaflet.

Comment on the content, language and layout of the leaflet.

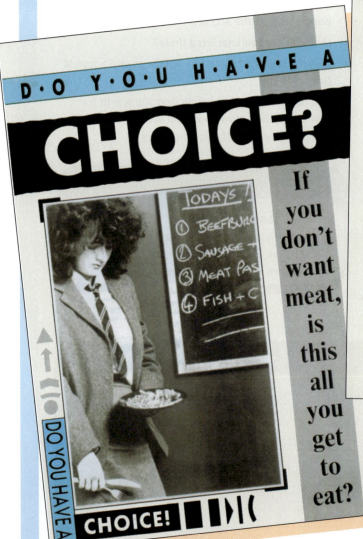

Non-fiction

Medicine Box

Ailment: I don't know how to comment on leaflets.

Dr Wordsmith's cure: No problem. Just sip this medicine slowly.

Impact: Is it 'pick-uppable' or so dull that just looking at it makes you yawn?

Title/headings: Are these catchy, jokey, puns? Are they too long or too short? Do they stand out and grab your attention because they are in capital letters, a larger size of print, a different colour or perhaps a different typeface?

Content/language: Does it try to tell you too much or too little? Is it easy to understand or does it use technical language? Does it play on your emotions and can you pick out specific words or phrases to back up what you think about this? Does it use long or short sentences, do they seem punchy or sloppy? Who is giving you the information? Are they biased or neutral? Do they give you facts or opinions?

Presentational devices: Do they use questions and answers, listed points, speech bubbles with pictures of celebrities or the 'person in the street' giving their approval to the product or cause? Or does it seem to be written by an 'invisible' expert? Does the leaflet have boxes, tables, sections, gaps to give the eye a break? What effect do these things have?

You will not be expected to go into this much detail, but if you can comment on just a few of these things you will boost your marks. Concentrating on the language and devices used to deliver the information are the most important things.

Task time

Imagine that you work for the Meat Marketing Board, and would prefer things to remain as they are. Make a list of points you would use in a letter to headteachers to counter the Vegetarian Society's campaign.

You have made an appointment to see the head cook in your school to ask if you can have more vegetarian choices for school lunch. Make a short list of the points you wish to make in order of priority to prompt you during the interview. How will you introduce the subject? How will you influence this person and remain in command of the situation?

Write a letter to your headteacher requesting a vegetarian alternative at school meal times. You will need to justify your argument.

The information sheet *Choice!* mentions a free *Action Sheet for Parents* which gives information on what they can do to help. Imagine you have the job of preparing it. Draw a spider diagram to show the sort of information that could be contained in the action sheet. Include information about the style and language and techniques you could use, and add brief suggestions for titles, pictures and layout.

Non-fiction

The Cull of the Wild

Carefully read through this section of a leaflet from the Vegetarian Society – *The Cull of the Wild*.

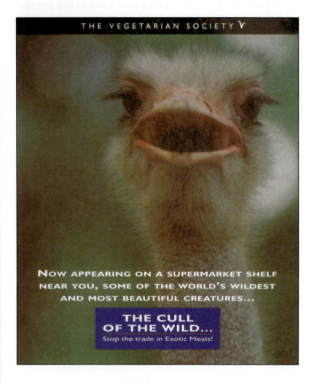

Over to you

Write a short paragraph summarising the issues.

Why does the Vegetarian Society think the importing of exotic meats into Britain should be stopped? Explain your position on the subject.

Write a letter to a supermarket objecting to their stocking exotic meats.

Now look at the *Ostrich Farming Information Sheet* from Foodstuffs supermarket chain. Comment on the question-and-answer device used, and the tone of the sheet.

Write a reply from the supermarket to accompany the information sheet and justify your company's position.

Hint: You might include some of the following points:

- The meat comes from selected suppliers.
- Your suppliers meet strict standards for import/rearing/culling of exotic meats.
- The shop is there to provide customers with what they want, not to make moral judgements.
- The company must keep up with competitors.
- It is for a trial period.
- It is because of consumer confidence following the British beef crisis.
- Demand is on the increase.

WELCOME TO THE MEAT INDUSTRY'S LATEST SICK JOKE: EXOTIC MEAT.

Ostrich, llama, crocodile, bison, kangaroo — taken from the zoo or the wildlife park to the butcher's slab in the blink of an eye.

Will the slaughter stop here? It's doubtful. Some marketing managers have already started exploring an even wider range of 'exotic' meats, including zebra and giraffe.

BIZARRE AND BARBARIC.

A nasty new fashion has hit the high street. A butcher selling kangaroo sausage was a finalist in the 1995 Sausage of the Year Competition. A delicatessen in Newcastle has developed a llama sausage and also stocks bison, ostrich and crocodile meats.

All over Britain people are importing, breeding and slaughtering rare and exotic animals — for meat!

HEADS IN THE SAND.

Ostriches are now farmed here in Britain. In a frenzy of breeding, incubating and mating, British ostrich farmers are beginning to market the meat and hides of their slaughtered birds.

But the abuses have already started. One farmer has been prosecuted for cruelty; his ostriches were found standing in 12 inches of their own dung. Twenty one ostriches recently suffocated during live transport to Manchester airport.

Naturally inquisitive and playful, ostriches can become bored and stressed on a farm. This can lead to disaster. Last year, two ostriches were found dead, one had swallowed 71 nails, another had ingested 2.5 metres of barbed wire in what an insurer of ostriches described as 'a strange kind of suicide'.

How do we slaughter these massive birds who would naturally live for up to 75 years? Hooded overnight prior to killing, they have their feet hobbled apart and then are doused with water before being stunned with a pair of electric tongs and bled to death.

Non-fiction

- An answer to any specific points you brought up in your letter of objection, for example, what measures the company takes to give nutritional/welfare information to customers.

Write an essay explaining the two sides of the exotic-meats debate without betraying where you stand on the issue.

Comment on the layout, language and style of *The Cull of the Wild* leaflet. How does it try to influence your thoughts and feelings about exotic meats?

Hint: Remember to look at the title, the picture, the language used. What effect do headings in capital letters have? Which has more impact – few words and a good picture with lots of boxes, or a straightforward presentation of information? Another common technique is to use speech bubbles asserting particular points of view – especially of celebrities. For example:

OSTRICH FARMING
Information sheet

FOODSTUFFS

Q: *How are the birds looked after?*
A: Far from being factory farmed, our ostriches are cared for as if they are in the wild. They graze on open land in groups, are given organic feed with vitamin supplements and have plenty of water.

Q: *Where are the ostriches farmed?*
A: At present our ostriches come from the United States because there are very few experienced ostrich farmers in Britain able to conform to our high standards of animal welfare. The birds are transported in strictly controlled conditions to minimise trauma.

Q: *Are the ostriches killed humanely?*
A: Yes, using internationally agreed guidelines for slaughter.

Q: *Is ostrich meat good for you?*
A: Yes – it is high in protein, low in cholesterol and contains far less fat than red meats and even less fat than chicken. It tastes delicious!

Q: *How far will Foodstuffs expand their stocks of exotic meats?*
A: We will continue to provide what our customers request, provided that suppliers, quality, price and welfare standards meet our high standards.

FOR MORE INFORMATION PLEASE WRITE TO:
FOODSTUFFS SUPERMARKETS, KANGAROO WAY, CROCTOWN, CC3 2TN

Non-fiction

D-Day

Compare these extracts from two leaflets: *Drugs & Solvents – You and your child* from the Department of Health (below), and *D mag* from the Health Education Authority (bottom).

Reflect on the language, tone and presentation of each piece. Then ask yourself how well fitted each piece is to its audience before you continue.

What do you think?

Do you think it is good to provide advice in two lists as below, or would two paragraphs of text be better? Give reasons for your answer.

What do you think of the way the designers of *D mag* have used different colours, sizes of print and typefaces? How does this differ from *Drugs & Solvents* and why?

Comment on the language in the 'How to help a friend ...' column below, paying particular attention to phrases such as, 'slagging them off', and 'what are mates for?'

Read *Drugs & Solvents* again. Why is it important for parents not to jump to conclusions if they notice possible signs of drug taking?

From the information given would you say that the leaflet is trying to be helpful to concerned parents, or just to stamp out drug taking? What gives you this impression?

Comment on the style of the *Drugs & Solvents* leaflet for parents. How effective is the faint, vertical title? What is the overall tone of the leaflet? What techniques does it use?

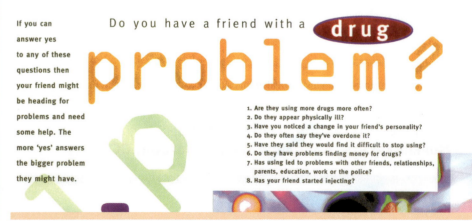

Non-fiction

Write the next page of the leaflet giving suggestions to a parent about how to talk to a child who may be taking drugs.

Hint: You could include some of these points – perhaps as do's and don'ts:

- Be firm, consistent and caring.
- Point out that most drugs are illegal.
- Try to understand the reasons why.
- Point out that your child's future health could be affected.
- Lecture and preach to your child on the problems of addiction.
- Put yourself in your child's shoes.
- Shout and display anger.
- Demand instant results.
- Spend some time with your child encouraging other interests.
- Scare your child with horror stories.
- Set a good example with, for example, smoking and drinking.
- Try to bully your child out of it.
- Tell your child you don't understand why, as he or she has had a good upbringing.
- Threaten to tell the police.

Try presenting your page in a word-processing/page design package on a computer. Think about how you can use fonts, formatting, tables, colour, etc. to enhance meaning and give importance to key parts of your text.

For your own notes

....

....

....

....

....

....

....

....

Review

Well done! You have completed the chapter. Now identify your strengths and weaknesses.

Checklist

Do you feel confident that you can:

		Yes	Not yet
1	Write a letter for a particular purpose? (pp. 44–46)	❑	❑
2	Comment on other people's diary entries and write your own? (pp. 47–52)	❑	❑
3	Write about your own life in an interesting way? (pp. 47–54)	❑	❑
4	Understand differences in style and tone by comparing texts by different writers on the same theme (pp. 55–56)	❑	❑
5	Write your own descriptions of places for different purposes and audiences? (pp. 60–67)	❑	❑
6	Tell the difference between fact and opinion? (pp. 68–71)	❑	❑
7	Follow an argument and say how effective it is? (pp. 72–73)	❑	❑
8	Make a chart to show both sides of an issue?	❑	❑
9	See how information is presented and say how effective it is?	❑	❑
10	Appreciate other writers' use of language and structure for different effects?	❑	❑
11	Write your own non-fiction for a wide variety of purposes and audiences?	❑	❑

If you've answered 'Not yet' to any question, skim-read some of the hints and tips in the chapter. If you are still not sure, ask your teacher.

Chapter 5: The media

Overview

To play an informed part in modern society, it's important to have some understanding of the media. That's why the media are included in every GCSE English Language syllabus. Here's what you'll understand by the end of this chapter:

- What is meant by 'media'.
- Why the media are important.
- The difference between fact and opinion.
- How reporting varies between different media.
- How 'emotive language' and reasoned argument are used to persuade.
- How presentation influences our interpretation of news stories.
- How advertisements persuade.
- How to write persuasively.

What is meant by 'media'?

About this section

This section tells you what is meant by 'media', why you need to understand the media, and the difference between fact and opinion.

The word *media* is the plural of *medium*. We normally use the phrase 'the media' to mean all the different forms in which information is conveyed, especially newspapers and magazines, television and radio, the Internet and the people involved in them.

Dr Wordsmith comments …

In sizes a medium comes *between* a small and a large; a spiritual 'medium' is said to communicate *between* spirits and living people; a 'mediator' tries to create understanding *between* individuals or groups; in society the 'media' are like a pipeline running *between* events and the people who want to know about them.

Why are the media important?

At one time news was carried slowly by travelling traders. Important news was carried by messengers on horseback, and proclaimed by the town-crier. Then came printing presses and news broadsheets – forerunners of modern newspapers. The first newspaper published in Britain was *The Times* in 1785. It was read by a relatively few wealthy people. Now new media technologies such as the Internet and digital TV are continually speeding up the transfer of information and giving more choice to audiences. These technologies affect content, style and presentation.

In additon, we can now all be involved in choosing our local and national government. Ours is a complex society. We need to be aware of changing laws, developments in education, science and the environment, and major events. We find out about these things largely through the media. However, the media don't simply present us with 'objective facts', as if we were seeing events ourselves. What they give us is a combination of **fact**, **opinion**, **persuasive argument** and **bias**. You will find out about all these in this chapter. Start a spider diagram about the media. Include sections on advertising, style, information, presentation and meaning. Add to it as you work through the chapter.

Fact and opinion

Facts are statements which can be proven beyond reasonable doubt to be true, and which are generally agreed to be true. Here are some examples:

- The sun gives out light and heat.
- Edinburgh is in Scotland.
- Football is a sport.

Opinions express a point of view, or a judgement:

- It's too hot today.
- Scotland should have its own government.
- Football is a great game.

Sometimes facts can be disputed, for example, in a court case. Sometimes they can appear to change: for example, it was once considered to be a fact that the sun went round the Earth. However, this doesn't make them opinions.

The media

Try this

Look at the statements which follow. Decide which are facts and which are opinions.

> School-leaving age is 16.
>
> Chelsea stand a good chance of winning the Cup.
>
> World population is increasing.
>
> Anyone who steals cars is an idiot.
>
> Polls show that 60 per cent of people are in favour of hanging.
>
> The Government is to blame for unemployment.

Try speaking for two minutes on a subject without expressing an opinion. Have a friend listen and note down any opinions. Choose from: Crime, Parents, Sport, Cruelty to animals, Religion.

Section round-up

By now you should know what is meant by 'media', why the media are important, and the difference between fact and opinion.

For your own notes

The media

Factual reporting and bias

About this section

This section compares two reports, from different media, relating to one news story. You will learn about:

● Objectivity and bias.

● Emotive language.

● The use of quotations.

'Swampy' captured the nation's imagination when he and other protesters tunnelled beneath the site of a proposed new road in Devon.

✪ Below are some of the terms the media used to describe him at the time. What opinion does each convey?

eco-warrior activist eco-terrorist mole hippy hero environmentalist trouble-maker

A media report shows **bias** when its presentation of facts is influenced – deliberately or not – by opinion or prejudice. An **objective** report is an unbiased one. **Emotive language** is language which aims to produce a particular emotional response in the reader. **Quotations** may seem objective, because they only reproduce someone else's words, but there may be bias in the selection of quotations, and in the context in which they are used.

Now read the news story below. Look particularly for:

• the basic facts

• how quotations are used

• any opinions expressed (you could mark them)

• emotive language.

RISK GROWS AS SWAMPY DIGS DEEPER

Part of the labyrinth of tunnels housing three protesters against the A30 road development collapsed yesterday, raising fears for their safety.

One, Swampy, 23, was at least 30 feet down and thought to be digging himself in deeper still. The partial collapse of roof supports and timbers in the tunnel where the 16-year-old girl known as Animal and a colleague, John Woodhams, were camped 24 hours earlier happened during the night near an area where professional tunnellers had been shoring up the network. No one was injured, but Under-Sheriff Trevor Coleman said yesterday: 'This is obviously a matter of great concern. It just emphasises the very dangerous nature of all the tunnels.

'The fact that there are three people and my tunnellers down there is helping to dry up the earth, so the risks (of collapse) are getting greater and greater.' Repeated requests from the bailiff's men for Swampy and his colleagues, Dave and Ian, to come out had been ignored, Mr Coleman said.

But the under-sheriff was considering a proposal from the A30 Action Group to allow one of their members to go in to speak to the men. The protesters' own lines of communications with the three were cut four days ago.

The Devon campaigners have called for a new inquiry into the A30 scheme, claiming it will eventually cost taxpayers £200m. It is being built under the Government's Design Build Finance and Operate scheme, whereby the road is privately funded and constructed and the cost repaid by the Government over 30 years.

In a move guaranteed further to infuriate environmentalists, the Government yesterday announced approval for a stretch of dual carriageway through countryside next to Fairmile, where the A30 protesters are making their last stand.

The 14 miles of road between Honiton in Devon and Ilminster in Somerset will run through the Blackdown Hills, an Area of Outstanding Natural Beauty.

It will connect to the A30 between Honiton and Exeter which is now being converted to dual carriageway, and where protesters have been evicted from three camps.

Paul Hamblin, of the Council for the Protection of Rural England, said: 'We can't think of a more provocative decision; this scheme would rank alongside Twyford Down in terms of its sheer damage to the landscape.' Simon Festing, of Friends of the Earth, said: 'It is appalling arrogance to give the go-ahead for yet more destructive road schemes while protesters are braving their lives in nearby tunnels to defend the countryside.'

Although both the Environment Secretary, John Gummer, and Transport Secretary, Sir George Young, gave the go-ahead for the £63m scheme yesterday following a public inquiry in 1995, no dates for its construction have been fixed and a start may be several years off.

Nick Schoon and Louise Jury

The media

News at 10

Below is a transcript of a *News at 10* report of Swampy's eventual emergence from the tunnels. Read it, looking especially at the things you looked for in the newspaper report, and at how the television presentation is different. Think, too, about what impression might have been made had the cameras shown other scenes – such as the tunnels themselves or local road congestion – or had other people been interviewed.

NEWS AT 10
Thursday 30 January

Trevor MacDonald: The last anti-roads protester who'd taken to the tunnels under the A30 extension came up blinking into the camera lights tonight, so the protest is over. The man known by the nickname Swampy may now be charged with obstruction under his real name, Danny Needs.
Robert Hall reports. [*Cut to scene; milling reporters*]

Hall: After seven days in a space barely large enough to turn round in, the man they nicknamed Swampy will spend tonight in police cells.

Interviewer at scene:
Why did you stop digging?

Swampy: Why did I stop digging? Because I felt that we'd made our point and I believed by coming out it was safer for all involved.

Hall: The first hint of an end to the stand-off came as negotiators emerged after a day which left Swampy isolated in his tiny tunnel. The sheriff's men had reached the first fugitive by tunnelling around him. Unable to lock himself in place, Muppet Dave was bussed off to face charges and an eventual reunion. A second man gave himself up on the promise of coffee and a cigarette. When the moment came to meet Swampy and his captors, curiosity caused something of a stampede. [*Shot of jostling reporters*]

Sheriff: I'm very pleased that they saw sense, that they saved anyone else putting themselves into danger, that the whole operation was carried out on an amicable and relatively friendly basis …

Hall: The campaigners move on. The next phase of this road improvement project has just been given the go-ahead. Robert Hall, News at 10, Devon.

Over to you

The newspaper report opposite includes very little emotive language, bias or opinion, outside of the quotations. One slight example is 'In a move guaranteed further to infuriate environmentalists …' This may be intended only to make what follows seem more exciting, but it does also give a particular view of environmentalists. However, news reports can be biased in what they don't say, as well as what they do say. They can present some facts and not others, or some opinions (either reported or in quotations) and not others. What evidence can you find of this in either of the reports given so far?

Hint: In the reports, quotations are given in red. What is the balance of pro-road and anti-road quotations given? What kind of facts might each side add to the facts given in the reports to back up their case?

Make notes on the effect made on the viewer of each of the following phrases used in the television report:

- 'blinking into the camera lights'
- 'a space barely large enough to turn round in'
- 'The sheriff's men had reached the first fugitive'
- 'something of a stampede'
- 'road improvement project'

Hint: One way to tackle this is to consider what differences alternative phrasing would make. For example, we could replace 'fugitive' with 'campaigner' without altering the basic facts, but what shift of attitude would this suggest?

Section round-up

If you've worked carefully through this section, you should now understand a lot more about objectivity and bias, selective use of quotations, and emotive language.

The media

Opinion and argument

About this section

This section looks at how the media present opinions and arguments. You will learn:

- The difference between opinion and bias.
- How writers structure their arguments.
- Some of the language and techniques used in arguing a case.

By now, you should know what **bias** is. (If not, turn back to p. 76.) An **opinion**, in the media, is a view held and openly expressed by the author, often backed up by **arguments** that aim to convince you, step by step, that the opinion is justified.

Word-play

Read the short news item below expressing an opinion about Swampy (see pp. 76–77), and the annotations beside it.

The language used in the piece is quite casual, even jokey – from the title onwards. Note, or circle, examples of this. What effect does this sort of language have?

Hint: This piece doesn't pretend to be objective, but the opinion is not presented in an entirely straightforward, open way. The language suggests that the protest is not to be taken seriously. Note especially, the clichés 'rough and ready', etc. (there's a similar one near the end).

Despite the casual tone of the piece, there is an argument. It begins with the statements annotated as 'statements of opinion presented as indisputable fact'. The next step in the argument is 'And yet it is hard to stifle admiration …' What is the writer implying about the protesters? How useful does the writer consider the protest to be?

Hint: 'And yet …' could read 'Despite this obvious truth that no sensible person could disagree with …'

(Answers on p. 88.)

Right or wrong?

In your exam you may be asked to comment on a longer piece of media prose, such as the one opposite from an article by Bel Mooney, who is also a novelist. Read it now. As you do, consider:

- the overall tone
- how the writer feels about protest, and about young people
- what conflicts she has between ideals and personal issues
- the real message of the piece.

Hint: Note that the piece is in the first person ('I've followed Animal's story …') and is unashamed about giving a personal view: it doesn't pretend to be objective. Note phrases such as 'you have to applaud such dogged determination and sheer guts in ones so young' (paragraph 5). Think about what sort of mother the writer is. What might her daughter say about her?

Word-play in the title suggests a fairly lightweight piece

Opening statement tells us the main theme – the nation's response to Swampy

Statements of opinion presented as indisputable fact

Comment on why Swampy's story appeals to people

The writer's own feelings

The nation digs you, Swampy

The British love an underdog and if the underdog is underground, like Swampy underneath the route of the A30, he is even more prized. Most people drive or rely on road transport. Most people accept that there have to be planning procedures, albeit rough and ready, which attempt to balance the various rural and urban, present and future interests. And yet it is hard to stifle admiration for the protesters' persistence and cunning. The spectacle of an under-sheriff being led a merry dance appeals to the Robin Hood in all of us. This saga will have to end, and ought to end long before there is any danger to life and limb. But for a couple of days at least, Swampy is a hero.

The media

Right or wrong, the young at least show some guts
Bel Mooney

Somebody once said that the bravest word you could see chalked on a wall is 'No!' The suffragettes marched shoulder to shoulder; civil rights demonstrators in the US followed Martin Luther King's dream; all over Eastern Europe at the end of the last decade people stood up and shouted 'enough is enough', in the face of the harshest totalitarian regimes.

Sixteen-year-old Ellenor Punch said 'No' too – when she left her school books, loving family and comfortable home, and buried herself for four days in squalid and terrifying tunnels. Known (mystifyingly) as 'Animal', she was one of five human moles trying to stop work on a 13-mile dual carriageway between Exeter and Honiton in Devon.

On Thursday night, 'Swampy', aged 23, also emerged from the underground labyrinth after 160 hours. He had been lying 18 ft below ground, 20 ft along a passage just small enough for him to squeeze into.

Explaining his protest to journalists he said: 'I feel it is the only way to get a voice these days. If I had written a letter to my MP would I have achieved all this? Would you lot be here? I think not.'

The important point to be made about Animal and Swampy is that, whether or not you agree with their ideas, you have to applaud such dogged determination and sheer guts in ones so young. Thank God for the idealism of youth. They are not stupid, or irresponsible. They are part of a growing number of young people who feel left out of normal political processes, and who are saying 'No!' to what they see as the wholesale destruction of the environment in the name of progress, business and the Great God Car. They care, and they will act, while the rest sit at home and do nothing.

I've followed Animal's story with fascination because it might have happened in my own family. She is the same age as my own daughter. In 1994 Kitty (then 14) became involved in the protests against the Batheaston bypass near our home.

I forbade her to take 'direct action', on grounds of safety – but I might as well have told the birds to stop singing. So I joined her, sharing her outrage at the destruction and loving our camaraderie. Shoulder to shoulder indeed – although we received some bruises for our pains. It was hard and I never thought we would stop the road, but I felt remade by the youthful idealism.

We have never regretted our actions and can't watch details of a protester's eviction on the news without knowing whose side we are on. Last year I felt a need to write about the experience, and decided to do it for the people who count – for teenagers. My novel* may lead some people to accuse me of encouraging the young to join road protests. Let them accuse. It so happens that the chief 'baddie' in the story is a protester, because I believe it is the duty of the novelist to be as even-handed as possible.

... We are told that the younger generation is apathetic, only interested in selfish pursuits, football culture, or in getting 'out of it' at raves. Not so. Talk to many teenagers and you will discover an anxiety about the world we live in, a real desire for leadership and inspiration, and a serious questing for answers to that old conundrum of the meaning of life. It is not good enough to dismiss this as 'single-issue politics', because in my experience there is a whole package of concerns. Moral values? Yes, these children care. They worry about our responsibility for the animal world, for the planet on which we (briefly) live, and for each other.

In primary schools you will hear eight-year-olds say they worry about things like 'poor people not having enough to eat'. 'Why do these things happen, Mummy?' Kitty used to ask me, watching the horrors of Bosnia on the news.

She once told me that the first stage of growing up is realising that your parents do not, after all, have the answers. They sit in their armchairs shrugging 'I dunno', while the kids in the wisdom of youth, cast a cold eye on the world and repeat, 'But why?'

There comes a point when parents cannot stop their children getting involved with real-life issues.

I have to be honest here, and say that had Kitty wanted to quit school and go to the A30 or Newbury protests I would have fought her, and not just because of the very real dangers. I would have said get your exams, get qualified, marshal the facts and argue with 'them' on their own terms, because there is more to these issues than shouting slogans.

But maybe Animal's parents were bolder than I am. Maybe they realised that what their daughter had chosen to do was in itself an education. No one can deny that her arguments were an impressive blend of idealism and hard facts.

At the core of it all is a passionate faith which, for many young people, seems to have replaced organised religion – and which at its worst becomes fanaticism. Protest is not just a negative; people do not take to the streets or trees or underground tunnels unless they are positive about what they do believe in.

Joining The Rainbow, (Methuen 1997)

Spaces have been added to the piece wherever it shifts to a new idea. Think of a sub-heading to sum up the content of each section. Write it in, or note it on paper. Think of a keyword for each section. Draw a spider diagram of the piece, giving each section keyword a separate branch. (Suggested headings and keywords on p. 88.)

Section round-up

This section has taught you about the relationship between opinion, bias and argument. You've also learned about some techniques of persuasion.

The media

Making an appeal

About this section

This section is about the ways in which a media writer can attempt to sway our opinion. You will learn about:

- Techniques used to gain our attention at the start of an article.

- The use of emotive language.

- Ways in which writers present an argument.

Read the extract on the right, which is the beginning of a magazine article about destruction of the natural environment by road building. As you read, ask yourself some questions. ✪ How does the writer try to make us care about Twyford Down and similar places? ✪ What criticism of the existing planning laws is he making? ✪ How does he anticipate opposing arguments? ✪ How does he feel about road building? ✪ What important point is he making about Sites of Special Scientific Interest?

Exam practice

An exam paper might ask you to 'Summarise the arguments presented in the piece, commenting on how the writer attempts to appeal to readers.' So how would you deal with this?

In the given extract, the first part of the question is relatively easy to answer. The writer argues that unique, beautiful natural habitats and species that depend on them are being destroyed by road developments, and that SSSI status gives insufficient legal protection to prevent this from happening: the Department of Transport usually gets its way, regardless of public opinion or inquiries. However, to get even a 'C' grade, you would need to make some comment on the writer's technique. To get an 'A' or a 'B' you would need to:

- comment in some detail on the writer's technique and style

- show understanding of how the piece is structured, and how the argument develops

- comment critically on technique, style and argument.

Against nature

It's a misty summer dawn. A pale sun rises slowly above a steep escarpment, sending long shadows across the dewy hillsides. A kestrel whirrs its wings; rooks caw in the brightening sky.

As the day warms, a butterfly floats past – it's a chalkhill blue, drawn by the rare pyramidal orchid half hidden in the grassland. And with the heat of the sun, the singing skylarks whirr upwards. This tranquil scene passes by in one of the most beautiful, unspoilt stretches of countryside in England.

… Only it's no longer unspoilt. A great wedge has been ripped out of the chalk hillside, and concrete and tarmac scar the wound. Rumbling articulated lorries drown the skylark song, exhaust fumes spew up the embankments. This is – or was – Twyford Down: once a tranquil refuge rich in rare butterflies and orchids, now a motorway cutting to help speed the traffic around Winchester.

There are, of course, endless examples of roads which have been driven through beautiful countryside – they have to be built somewhere, you might argue. But there is another, crucial dimension to Twyford Down. The M3 extension not only destroyed the hillsides, it devastated two Sites of Special Scientific Interest (SSSIs).

Near breaking point?

The idea of SSSIs is to protect and preserve vital habitats for some of our rarest plants and wildlife. But, as the destruction at Twyford Down demonstrated only too vividly, the protection of the Government agencies which designate and monitor the areas – English Nature, the Countryside Council for Wales, and Scottish Natural Heritage – is strictly limited. Occasionally they will prosecute private landowners who flout the law, developing land without proper planning permission. But if the Department of Transport decides the best route for a new road is straight through the middle of an SSSI, the chances are it will be able to go ahead. Despite a public outcry, an official inquiry and any number of protesters who might lie down in front of the bulldozers, there is no legal way to stop it.

Nick Trend

The media

Try this

Plan your answer to the question 'Summarise the arguments presented in the piece, commenting on how the writer attempts to appeal to readers.' Number your notes in the order in which you would include them in your answer.

Hint: This writer uses a popular and effective technique to draw us into the piece: he 'sets the scene'. Try to picture it. What details capture your imagination? What is the effect of the writer's choice of tense? What species are mentioned, and what is the effect of naming them? What is the overall mood of the first two paragraphs? Look especially at the adjectives – 'misty', 'pale', 'dewy', 'rare', 'tranquil'. Look, too, at the verbs – 'rises', 'whirrs', 'floats', etc.

Now look at how the mood changes in the third paragraph. Look at the emotive language:

> **'A great wedge has been ripped out … scar the wound … fumes spew up …'**
> **How is this meant to affect us?**

How effective is the contrast? Note the use of metaphor: no scarring or spewing in the ordinary sense is going on. Is it a fair use of emotive language? In your opinion, does it work, or is it excessive?

Compare '*Against nature*' with '*Drugs: the other road to disaster*'.

Hint: These are both openings. In addition to the points raised above, compare how each captures our attention and arouses our concern. In the second piece look especially at:

- the problems identified in each case
- the use of logical argument
- the use of statistics and expert evidence.

Drugs: the other road to disaster

As the Government renews its Christmas warnings against drink-driving it is oddly silent about an even greater road risk, a risk which is worrying the police and other experts – the drugged driver.

This is a peak period for 'party' drugs as well as stress-reducing medication. Both types can make drivers far more likely to have an accident than being just over the alcohol limit. Yet few users have any idea of the hazards of drugged driving; policemen, courts and even doctors know little about the risks; drug-driving laws are a shambles and the Government seems to do nothing to publicise the dangers. Moreover, if a drugged driver kills you, or a member of your family, this Christmas, the role of drugs won't even be a statistic. The figures for deaths caused by drugged driving aren't even collected.

Ironically, some of the most worrying evidence of driving impairment is for drugs prescribed to give peace of mind. Professor Ian Hindmarch and Dr John Kerr of the Surrey University's Human Psychopharmacology Unit, key researchers in this field, say the greatest risk of accidents may occur when taking some benzodiazepines (BZ) and tricyclates (TCA). They include some of the best known and widely prescribed anti-depressants, sleeping pills and tranquillisers. Last year more than 22 million prescriptions, in England alone, were handed out for them, yet they can impair crucial driving skills. In Dr Kerr's experiments, some TCAs slowed reaction times to a point where the emergency stopping distance was 15–60 per cent longer than if the driver was just over the limit for alcohol.

Moyra Bremner

Section round-up

So, what have you learned? More about emotive language and how it can be combined with logical argument; the importance of structure; how statistics and expert opinions persuade; and how to look at style and technique.

The media

From fact to comment

About this section

This section looks at a news story relating to drugs, and then at a feature giving an opinion on this story. You will learn:

- **More about facts, opinions, emotive language and argument.**
- **How to follow and criticise a writer's argument.**
- **About how the media decide what is newsworthy.**

Read the news story below carefully. Note the key facts it presents. Also consider:

- What use is made of quotations?
- What opinions are given?
- Are any opinions given outside of the quotations?
- How far do you agree with any of the opinions?

Now try this

Discuss with a friend how far you consider this to be a worthwhile news story, and why the media leapt on it (as they did) with such enthusiasm.

Hint: Readers like to hear about the famous. Reporters like short, memorable quotations – especially if they're likely to excite strong opinions.

What the public wants

Newspaper and magazine editors want to sell copies, so they will often try to make news stories sound exciting or controversial. They will also tend to express opinions with which the majority of their readers will agree.

The *Daily Mail* clearly felt that few of its readers would agree with Noel Gallagher's views on drugs, and that they were therefore fairly safe in condemning them. The annotated 'Comment' feature opposite argues against any moves to legalise drugs. Read it, and the margin notes, carefully to see how the argument is developed.

Fury at Gallagher drug outburst

Daily Mail reporter

Pop star Noel Gallagher triggered new outrage last night by claiming that taking drugs was as normal as 'getting up and having a cup of tea in the morning'.

The Oasis writer and guitarist's outburst came as he leapt to the defence of sacked singer Brian Harvey.

Harvey was thrown out of the band East 17 after claiming in an interview that Ecstasy was a safe drug which 'makes you a better person'.

Gallagher, 29, whose younger brother Liam received a police caution for possession of cocaine earlier this month, said Government arms sales were the real scandal.

He insisted most people in Britain took drugs and claimed several people in Parliament were cocaine or heroin addicts.

He said it was therefore hypocritical of MPs to lecture pop stars on their comments.

Anti-drugs campaigners angrily condemned Gallagher's stance.

The parents of Ecstasy victim Leah Betts pointed out that Oasis had been her favourite group – their hit Wonderwall was played at her funeral.

Mrs Janet Betts said: 'It's disgraceful. Noel Gallagher was her idol. Because of that, it makes his comments even worse.

'The danger is kids look up to a man like Noel Gallagher, particularly the most vulnerable 14 to 16-year-olds.

'Pop stars like him are in a position of responsibility, and to say something like this is unbelievable. He should have more sense. It makes me so angry.

'If Leah were still alive and she heard what he said, it could quite easily have made her think "Noel thinks it's OK, so it must be".'

Harvey was sacked by his fellow band members nearly two weeks ago after his comments drew condemnation from John Major in the House of Commons and led to radio stations banning their records.

The singer, who later apologised, told a radio interviewer he had once taken 12 Ecstasy tablets in a night.

Gallagher told BBC Radio Five Live's Entertainment News: 'If Brian Harvey did do 12 Es in one night – if he did do, and he's saying that he did – if he's being honest, then fair enough.

'If you can't be honest in this country then we might as well go and live in China, know what I mean?'

Gallagher added: 'There's people in the House of Parliament, man, who are bigger heroin addicts and cocaine addicts than anyone in this room right now.

'And it's all about honesty at the end of the day. If he done that, then fair enough – everybody does it, you know what I mean.

'As soon as people realise that the majority of people in this country take drugs, then the better off we'll all be.

'It's not like a scandalous sensation, or anything like that. Not when you've got our Government selling arms to people who go out and kill.

'Drugs is like getting up and having a cup of tea in the morning.'

The media

Margin notes (left):

- Choice of words hints at writer's view of Gallagher
- Good use of a statistic to make a point
- Illogical progression: idea that contempt for the law leads people to say it is bad – rather than the other way round
- Irony: writer pretends to be pro-legalisation in order to ridicule it by reducing the meaning of 'freedom' to frivolous drug-taking ('pop pills')
- Seems to argue that it was a mistake to legalise divorce, abortion and homosexuality. Are they really relevant to the drugs debate? What 'whole new culture of "gay rights"' is meant?
- Good comparison between alcohol and potential drug-related problems
- Cliché ending: 'But one thing is sure.'

COMMENT

Society must decide in the drugs debate

The *Daily Mail* makes no apology for returning today to Oasis guitarist Noel Gallagher and the question of drugs.

Gallagher seems to have persuaded himself that he has 'helped instigate an open and honest debate about drug abuse'. Very well. When liberal opinion is becoming increasingly vocal in its demand for drugs to be legalised, perhaps the issue needs debating.

On one thing, both sides of the argument can agree. Though vast sums have been spent in the campaign against drug abuse, though teachers warn and politicians rail, the battle is being hopelessly lost. In 1958 there were only 333 registered addicts in Britain. Today there are more than 25,000. And that takes no account of the millions who have experimented, sometimes disastrously, with narcotics.

Manifestly all the warnings and exhortations are being ignored. For countless youngsters, drugs like Ecstasy, cannabis and LSD are simply part of the culture. And when the law is held in such obvious contempt, the argument that it is bad and should be changed can sound seductive.

The reformers paint a glowing picture of what could happen. Drugs would lose their 'forbidden fruit' appeal to the young. At a stroke, the drug cartels would be put out of business. Burglaries and car thefts would be cut too, since junkies would no longer need to steal to feed their habit. Teenage prostitution would be reduced. Police resources would be freed for more pressing matters.

Government finances would improve dramatically, with scope for a whole range of new taxes. So why not let people smoke joints, pop pills and inject themselves? Isn't that what freedom is all about?

But make no mistake. Such a *laissez-faire* 'solution' would be anything but cost free. All drugs have damaging consequences. Soft drugs all too often lead inexorably to hard drugs. Can anybody seriously doubt that legalising such substances would lead to a catastrophic increase in addiction?

The reformers, of course, claim that nothing of the kind would occur. They should look at what has happened in the past, when taboos and legal restraints have been removed. Britain's divorce-rate is now a national disaster because of successive relaxations in the law. The Abortion Act was intended to deal only with extreme cases, but has led to abortion on demand. Legalising homosexual acts was intended to stop persecution, but has spawned a whole new culture of 'gay rights'.

That dismal pattern would certainly be repeated if drugs were legalised. We would risk creating a whole new generation of addicts. The social costs would be enormous. Many would die. Others would swamp NHS hospitals, at the taxpayer's expense. There would be even more fecklessness and crime.

Those who think drugs should become as acceptable as whisky or gin should reflect. Though Britain has had centuries of experience in trying to control the problems caused by drink, alcoholism is still at the root of countless human tragedies. How many more would be created with unrestricted and legal access to drugs?

Society itself will in the end have to decide if the risk of legalising these substances can ever be worth taking. But one thing is sure. The issues at stake are far more difficult, complex and far-reaching than anything imagined by Noel Gallagher with his preposterous belief that drug-taking is as normal as having a cup of tea.

Margin notes (right):

- Reason for this feature
- Sentence sounds impressive, but meaning is vague and not backed up by evidence
- Arguments for legalisation effectively anticipated
- Sweeping statements of opinion presented as indisputable fact
- Another rhetorical question (no answer expected). Writer in effect is saying, 'Surely no one in their right mind could disagree with me.' Is this an argument?
- Value judgement: more divorce doesn't necessarily mean more unhappiness
- Logic? If dead or 'swamping' hospitals, wouldn't be committing crimes to pay for drugs
- Final swipe at Gallagher to round off

A testing task

Making use of the margin notes, plan and write a critical appraisal of the *Daily Mail* comment feature, looking at what arguments the writer is putting forward, how effectively they are presented, and how they are likely to be received by the readers.

Section round-up

In addition to brushing up and expanding on what you've learned earlier, you've been finding out about how to follow and criticise a writer's argument, and how editors decide what is newsworthy.

83

The media

Presentation

About this section

This section looks at how presentation influences our understanding of the news. You'll learn:

- The importance of selection, placing and weighting of news stories.
- How pictures influence us.
- How headlines and captions can be biased.
- How the need to sell copies and make money affects news presentation.

Look closely at the front page of the *Guardian* below, and the notes.

Comment

In a newspaper, magazine, website or leaflet, presentation is very important. Words, illustrations and layout must work together to convey the intended message.

- Compare the presentation of news coverage in a newspaper and in the paper's website (use a search engine to find it). How do you account for the differences?

Advertisement for the paper: encourages you to buy the paper by mentioning some of its separate sections. The 'Editor' (which has a 'new look') summarises the week's news; the 'Guide' shows radio, TV, cinema and exhibitions.

Tasters: major features in the main sections, with authors' names.

Main story: The large typesize indicates that the editor sees this as the day's main story, though it is about a statement, by the German chancellor, rather than an event of immediate significance in itself. Other papers that day chose other main stories.

Eye-catching picture: a 71-year-old former banker revealing his body piercings in the Modern Primitives show in Germany. The German link with the main story is probably coincidental. Weekend papers often have a 'fun' picture or feature like this. In addition, none of the other stories is very visual, and none relates to a really major event just having taken place. Hence this picture, with its topical headline: 'Ouch! Lord of the rings'.

Second-place story: 'secondary' because it is about a report on a crash which took place over two years earlier, not about the crash itself.

Third-place story: the slightly smaller headline print and the bottom-of-page position put this third. Note the pun. What effect might a pun have in the other two headlines?

Advert for sister paper

Contents: especially useful in a large broadsheet paper.

Advertising: newspapers get a lot of income from advertising. Adverts target readers, so they can tell you about the paper's readership.

The media

Match the headlines

Headlines often show bias, or highlight different aspects of a news story to appeal to the readership. Picture captions do the same. Sometimes two papers use the same picture, but with captions that give quite different interpretations. The headlines below are for three different news stories. See if you can divide them into groups – one for each story. (Answers on p. 88.)

✪ How do the headlines within each group differ?

The death-trap on our doorstep

Prisons 'stretched to bursting-point'

Six contaminated in radioactive leak

Poor made scapegoat of Government incompetence, says charity boss

Nuclear plant puts safety first

ALL-CLEAR AT SELLAFIELD

THEY'VE ONLY GOT THEMSELVES TO BLAME

GOVERNMENT CRACKS DOWN ON SCROUNGERS

PENSIONER'S PERIL

INNER-CITY CRIME EPIDEMIC

Police efficiency praised

Single mothers face new hurdles in benefits race

Testing time

Collect several different newspaper articles about the same news story. Read each one carefully, comparing facts, coverage, bias, style and presentation of the story (where in the paper it is placed, size of headline, accompanying pictures and captions, etc.) This could form the basis of a piece of coursework, if your teacher approves.

Find a news story that interests you and that seems to be biased. Write your own version using the same facts, plus any others that you happen to know or have from other sources, giving an alternative view.

Take a news story where two opposing opinions are given (such as the Gallagher story on p. 82), or where you are aware of a controversy. With a partner, role-play two people involved arguing their case.

Section round-up

You've done some vital work on how presentation influences our understanding of a news story. Remember the importance of headlines, pictures and captions, selection and placing of stories, and the newspapers' need to sell copies.

The media

Tugging at heartstrings

About this section

This section focuses on a particular form of advertising: the charity appeal. You will learn:

- How different types of language can be used to persuade.
- How pictures and captions contribute to the overall effect.
- How charity appeals differ from other advertising.

Advertising is a big souce of media income. And, as noted on page 84, it can reveal a lot about the readership. Charities have to pay to advertise, though they may be charged less than businesses. Their advertisements are similar to those of businesses in that both groups want our money. Some of their techniques are similar, too. Both use language and images to **persuade**.

Study the advertisements on this and the next page. Consider how each appeals to its reader, bearing in mind the kind of language used, and the visual effect.

Comment

These advertisements all appeal in different ways. Look at the Crisis advertisement. Ask yourself:

- What does the illustration suggest?
- What effect will the double meaning in the caption have on readers?
- What is the intended effect of the repeated use of 'you …' in the first paragraph?
- Compare the two paragraphs. How might each appeal to readers in different ways?
- What feelings does the line 'I hear you, I'll help' play on?

Now look at the IFAW advertisement. Ask yourself:

- What emotive language is used? What phrases are particularly vivid?
- How does the repetition of the phrase 'every day' bring a negative note?
- Does the picture make you want to help, or turn over the page?

The media

Finally, look at the Oxfam advertisement, with its plain, unemotive language, with no picture. Ask yourself:

- What appeal does it make?
- What 'job' does each paragraph do?
- What use is made of bold type?

Now try this

Design and write a charity advertisement for a charity of your choice, real or made-up, using some of the techniques used in these advertisements.

Summarise the effect of each advertisement. Then look at ordinary commercial advertisements in newspapers and magazines. What types of appeal do they make? Make a chart of the different types.

Hint: Commercial advertising uses emotive phrases: 'Be the envy of all your friends …', 'For the man who knows what he wants', 'You want the best for them', 'Say goodbye to worry'.

Discuss with a friend which of the three charities you would be most likely to give to, and why.

Hint: You might consider whether an animal's suffering matters as much as a human being's, and how much you believe in the idea that 'charity begins at home'.

Oxfam
A rapid reaction force for Bosnia.

Bosnia's refugees have been run out of town. But they haven't run out of friends.

Oxfam has been working in Tuzla for over two years. Now we're reacting quickly, with shelter, clothing, blankets, health care and water for the most vulnerable. We are helping. But we need to do more.

Please help too. Join Oxfam's rapid reaction force.

Give a donation today.

Yes, I want to help Oxfam's work in former Yugoslavia. Here is my donation of:

£15 ☐   £50 ☐   £100 ☐   £250 ☐   £ _____

Mr, Mrs, Miss, Ms _____

Address _____

Postcode _____

Please send to: Oxfam, Room BC77, FREEPOST, Oxford OX2 7BR.

To donate by credit card
✆ **01865 312231**   OXFAM

Registered Charity No.202918

Section round-up

You've learnt about different types of charitable appeal, how they compare with ordinary advertising, and how images interact with words. Well done!

Dr Wordsmith's cure

Some people can't get the hang of sentences, they go on and on, never putting in a full stop, just using commas, this makes their writing difficult to read, are you one of them? A sentence is a set of words forming a statement that **makes sense in itself**. Unless it is a question or a command, it must convey information about an object: e.g. 'The boy (**subject**) walked quickly.' Begin a sentence with a capital. End it with a full stop.

The media

Review

This page pulls together what you've learnt in this chapter. Look at the diagram you started on page 74. If something doesn't make sense, go back to the appropriate section and skim-read it.

Checklist

Could you now:

		Yes	Not yet
1	Define 'media'? (p. 74)	❑	❑
2	Say why the media are important? (p. 74)	❑	❑
3	Tell the difference between a fact and an opinion? (p. 74)	❑	❑
4	Compare different media? (pp. 76–77)	❑	❑
5	Identify examples of emotive language and reasoned argument? (pp. 78–81)	❑	❑
6	Analyse the effect of presentation in a news story? (pp. 84–85)	❑	❑
7	Comment on techniques of persuasion in media advertising? (pp. 86–87)	❑	❑
8	Write persuasively yourself? (see especially p. 81)	❑	❑

If your answer to any of these questions is 'Not yet', look back at the pages indicated. If you're still unsure, ask your teacher for help.

Answers (p. 78)

Casual language: 'led a merry dance'; 'saga'; 'life and limb'; 'But for a couple of days'.

The writer implies that sensible people accept the planners' view that the A30 extension is necessary, and that the protesters are misguided – even if it's hard not to admire their efforts.

Answers (p. 79)

Possible sub-headings and keywords are:

- Saying 'No!' – NO!
- The protesters – PROTESTERS
- Young protesters bravely act on ideals – BRAVE
- Kitty's protest – KITTY
- The novel – NOVEL
- Young people concerned about the world – YOUTH

Answers (p. 85)

The three groups of headlines are:

Six contaminated in radioactive leak

All clear at Sellafield

Nuclear plant puts safety first

The death-trap on our doorstep

Inner-city crime epidemic

Police efficiency praised

Pensioner's peril

Prisons 'stretched to bursting-point'

Single mothers face new hurdles in benefits race

Government cracks down on scroungers

They've only got themselves to blame

Poor made scapegoat of Government incompetence, says charity boss

Literature from other cultures — Chapter 6

Overview

This heading covers poems, plays, stories and novels by writers who are not considered to be part of the English literary tradition. In this part of your course you will be asked to study works by American, Australian, African, Asian, Indian and European writers.

By the end of the chapter you will show that you can:

- Understand the content of texts from diverse cultures and traditions.
- Appreciate the distinctive qualities of texts from other cultures.
- Make relevant comparisons.

Short stories

About this section

When you have worked through this section you will feel confident about:

- Comparing two stories.
- Discussing aspects of life in different cultures.

An Astrologer's Day

This short story, 'An Astrologer's Day', is by the Indian writer R. K. Narayan. It is set in a fictitious town in Southern India.

An Astrologer's Day

Punctually at midday he opened his bag and spread out his professional equipment, which consisted of a dozen cowrie shells, a square piece of cloth with obscure mystic charts on it, a notebook and a bundle of palmyra writing. His forehead was resplendent with sacred ash and vermilion, and his eyes sparkled with a sharp abnormal gleam which was really an outcome of a continual searching look for customers, but which his simple clients took to be a prophetic light and felt comforted. The power of his eyes was considerably enhanced by their position – placed as they were between the painted forehead and the dark whiskers which streamed down his cheeks: even a half-wit's eyes would sparkle in such a setting. To crown the effect he wound a saffron-coloured turban around his head. This colour scheme never failed. People were attracted to him as bees are attracted to cosmos or dahlia stalks. He sat under the boughs of a spreading tamarind tree which flanked a path running through the Town Hall Park. It was a remarkable place in many ways: a surging crowd was always moving up and down this narrow road morning till night. A variety of trades and occupations was presented all along its way: medicine-sellers, sellers of stolen hardware and junk, magicians and, above all, an auctioneer of cheap cloth, who created enough din all day to attract the whole town. Next to him in vociferousness came a vendor of fried groundnuts, who gave his ware a fancy name each day, calling it Bombay Ice-Cream one day, and on the next Delhi Almond, and on the third Raja's Delicacy, and so on and so forth, and people flocked to him. A considerable portion of this crowd dallied before the astrologer too. The astrologer transacted his business by the light of a flare which crackled and smoked up above the groundnut heap nearby. Half the enchantment of the place was due to the fact that it did not have the benefit of municipal lighting. The place was lit up by shop lights. One or two had hissing gaslights, some had naked flares stuck on poles, some were lit up by old cycle lamps and one or two, like the astrologer's, managed without lights of their own. It was a bewildering criss-cross of light rays and moving shadows. This suited the astrologer very well, for the simple reason that he had not in the least intended to be an astrologer when he began life; and he knew no more of what was going to happen to others than he knew what was going to happen to himself next minute. He was as much a stranger to the stars as were his innocent customers. Yet he said things which pleased and astonished everyone: that was more a matter of study, practice and shrewd guesswork. All the same, it was as much an honest man's labour as any other, and he deserved the wages he carried home at the end of a day.

Literature from other cultures

He had left his village without any previous thought or plan. If he had continued there he would have carried on the work of his forefathers – namely, tilling the land, living, marrying and ripening in his cornfield and ancestral home. But that was not to be. He had to leave home without telling anyone, and he could not rest till he left it behind a couple of hundred miles. To a villager it is a great deal, as if an ocean flowed between.

He had a working analysis of mankind's troubles: marriage, money and the tangles of human ties. Long practice had sharpened his perception. Within five minutes he understood what was wrong. He charged three pies per question and never opened his mouth till the other had spoken for at least ten minutes, which provided him enough stuff for a dozen answers and advices. When he told the person before him, gazing at his palm, 'In many ways you are not getting the fullest results for your efforts,' nine out of ten were disposed to agree with him. Or he questioned: 'Is there any woman in your family, maybe, even a distant relative, who is not well disposed towards you?' Or he gave an analysis of character: 'Most of your troubles are due to your nature. How can you be otherwise with Saturn where he is? You have an impetuous nature and a rough exterior.' This endeared him to their hearts immediately, for even the mildest of us loves to think that he has a forbidding exterior.

Ask yourself some questions. ✪ **W**hat is being described? Who is the central character? What is he doing? Where is he doing it? ✪ **H**ow is he described? How are his clients described? How does he please his customers? ✪ What is the **E**ffect? What do you think about the astrologer?

Hint: When you write about texts from other cultures you will probably be commenting on local customs and traditions, or on rituals and beliefs. Note any details that may help you in this kind of answer.

Jot down your responses.

The nuts-vendor blew out his flare and rose to go home. This was a signal for the astrologer to bundle up too, since it left him in the darkness except for a little shaft of green light which strayed in from somewhere and touched the ground before him. He picked up his cowrie shells and paraphernalia and was putting them back into his bag when the green shaft of light was blotted out; he looked up and saw a man standing before him. He sensed a possible client and said: 'You look so careworn. It will do you good to sit down for a while and chat with me.' The other grumbled some vague reply. The astrologer pressed his invitation; whereupon the other thrust his palm under his nose, saying: 'You call yourself an astrologer?' The astrologer felt challenged and said, tilting the other's palm towards the green shaft of light: 'Yours is a nature …' 'Oh, stop that,' the other said. 'Tell me something worthwhile … .'

Our friend felt piqued. 'I charge only three pies per question, and what you get ought to be good enough for your money … .' At this the other withdrew his arm, took out an anna and flung it out to him, saying, 'I have some questions to ask. If I prove you are bluffing, you must return that anna to me with interest.'

'If you find my answers satisfactory, will you give me five rupees?'

'No.'

'Or will you give me eight annas?'

Literature from other cultures

'All right, provided you give me twice as much if you are wrong,' said the stranger. This pact was accepted after a little further argument. The astrologer sent up a prayer to heaven as the other lit a cheroot. The astrologer caught a glimpse of his face by the match-light. There was a pause as cars hooted on the road, *jutka*-drivers swore at their horses and the babble of the crowd agitated the semi-darkness of the park. The other sat down, sucking his cheroot, puffing out, sat there ruthlessly. The astrologer felt very uncomfortable. 'Here, take your anna back. I am not used to such challenges. It is late for me today … .' He made preparations to bundle up. The other held his wrist and said, 'You can't get out of it now. You dragged me in while I was passing.' The astrologer shivered in his grip; and his voice shook and became faint. 'Leave me today. I will speak to you tomorrow.' The other thrust his palm in his face and said, 'Challenge is challenge. Go on.' The astrologer proceeded with his throat drying up. 'There is a woman … .'

'Stop,' said the other. 'I don't want all that. Shall I succeed in my present search or not? Answer this and go. Otherwise I will not let you go till you disgorge all your coins.' The astrologer muttered a few incantations and replied, 'All right. I will speak. But will you give me a rupee if what I say is convincing? Otherwise I will not open my mouth, and you may do what you like.'

Ask yourself some questions. ✪ **W**hat happens? Who is the new character? ✪ **H**ow does he speak to the astrologer? How is the astrologer's reaction described? ✪ What is the **E**ffect? What atmosphere is created? How do you respond to what is happening?

Hint: Pick out some key words. Look for descriptions of **feelings** or **actions**.

Add to your notes.

After a good deal of haggling the other agreed. The astrologer said, 'You were left for dead. Am I right?'

'Ah, tell me more.'

'A knife has passed through you once?' said the astrologer.

'Good fellow!' He bared his chest to show the scar. 'What else?'

'And then you were pushed into a well nearby in the field. You were left for dead.'

'I should have been dead if some passer-by had not chanced to peep into the well,' exclaimed the other, overwhelmed by enthusiasm. 'When shall I get at him?' he asked, clenching his fist.

'In the next world,' answered the astrologer. 'He died four months ago in a far-off town. You will never see any more of him.' The other groaned on hearing it. The astrologer proceeded.

'Guru Nayak –'

'You know my name!' the other said, taken aback.

'As I know all other things. Guru Nayak, listen carefully to what I have to say. Your village is two days' journey due north of this town. Take the next train and be gone. I see once again great danger to your life if you go from home.' He took out a pinch of sacred ash and held it out. 'Rub it on your forehead and go home. Never travel southward again, and you will live to be a hundred.'

'Why should I leave home again?' the other said reflectively. 'I was only going away now and then to look for him and to choke out his life if I met him.' He shook his head regretfully. 'He has escaped my hands. I hope at last he dies as he deserved.' 'Yes,' said the astrologer. 'He was crushed under a lorry.' The other looked gratified to hear it.

Literature from other cultures

The place was deserted by the time the astrologer picked up his articles and put them into his bag. The green shaft was also gone, leaving the place in darkness and silence. The stranger had gone off into the night, after giving the astrologer a handful of coins.

It was nearly midnight when the astrologer reached home. His wife was waiting for him at the door and demanded an explanation. He flung the coins at her and said, 'Count them. One man gave all that.'

'Twelve and a half annas,' she said, counting. She was overjoyed. 'I can buy some jaggery and coconut tomorrow. The child has been asking for sweets for so many days now. I will prepare some nice stuff for her.'

'The swine has cheated me! He promised me a rupee,' said the astrologer. She looked up at him. 'You look worried, what is wrong?'

'Nothing.'

After dinner, sitting on the pyol, he told her, 'Do you know a great load is gone from me today? I thought I had the blood of a man on my hands all these years. That was the reason why I ran away from home, settled here and married you. He is alive.'

She gasped. 'You tried to kill!'

'Yes, in our village, when I was a silly youngster. We drank, gambled and quarrelled badly one day – why think of it now? Time to sleep,' he said, yawning, and stretching himself on the pyol.

Ask yourself some questions. ✪ **W**hat is the twist in the story? ✪ **H**ow does the astrologer know his customer's name and history? How are the astrologer's reactions described? ✪ What is the **E**ffect on you? What do you think about the way the astrologer deals with the danger he faces?

Finish your notes on this extract.

Test yourself

Here are some examples of the kind of question you might get in your exam. You could practise writing answers, or you could make full plans. Remember that planning is the key to a good answer.

What do you learn from the story about the customs and beliefs described?

Hint: Look at your notes on the astrologer's appearance, the way he plies his trade and what his clients are like. Your answer could include some of the following points:

- the description of the astrologer – personal appearance, dress, use of shells, etc.
- the description of the place where he works – the other trades and occupations

- his customers' belief in astrology
- his customers' willingness to believe him
- the acceptance of bargaining/negotiation.

What do you think about the astrologer and the way he works?

Hint: Look at the important things we are told about what he says and does. Think about the writer's attitude to the character. Decide what you think or feel about his behaviour. Your answer could include the following:

- his lack of knowledge of astrology
- he feels he gives people what they want and so earns his money
- he works from a knowledge of human nature
- he had to leave his village after quarrelling and leaving a man for dead
- he gives a quick-witted reply to keep himself out of danger
- he is relieved to know the man is alive after all
- the writer uses phrases like 'Our friend'; his wife's response shows he is not naturally violent.

92

Literature from other cultures

Dead Men's Path

This short story, 'Dead Men's Path', is by the African writer Chinua Achebe. The story is set in Nigeria, and focuses on the conflict between the old way of life and the modern attitudes to the world.

When you have read the first extract ask yourself some questions. ✪ **W**hat is the situation described? ✪ **H**ow is Michael Obi described? How is Nancy described? ✪ What is the **E**ffect on you? What do you think of them?

Hint: Look for key words to sum up the attitudes of Michael and Nancy. Notice any **words** or **ideas** that are **repeated**.

Make notes on your responses, as a diagram if you wish.

Dead Men's Path

Chinua Achebe

Michael Obi's hopes were fulfilled much earlier than he had expected. He was appointed headmaster of Ndume Central School in January 1949. It had always been an unprogressive school, so the mission authorities decided to send a young and energetic man to run it. Obi accepted this responsibility with enthusiasm. He had many wonderful ideas and this was an opportunity to put them into practice. He had had sound secondary school education which designated him a 'pivotal teacher' in the official records and set him apart from the other headmasters in the mission field. He was outspoken in his condemnation of the narrow views of these older and often less educated ones.

'We shall make a good job of it, shan't we?' he asked his young wife when they first heard the joyful news of his promotion.

'We shall do our best,' she replied. 'We shall have such beautiful gardens and everything will be just modern and delightful …' In their two years of married life she had become completely infected by his passion for 'modern methods' and his denigration of 'these old and superannuated people in the teaching field who would be better employed as traders in the Onitsha market'. She began to see herself already as the admired wife of the young headmaster, the queen of the school.

The wives of the other teachers would envy her position. She would set the fashion in everything … Then, suddenly it occurred to her that there might not be other wives. Wavering between hope and fear, she asked her husband, looking anxiously at him.

'All our colleagues are young and unmarried,' he said with enthusiasm which for once she did not share. 'Which is a good thing,' he continued.

'Why?'

'Why? They will give all their time and energy to the school.'

Nancy was downcast. For a few minutes she became sceptical about the new school; but it was only for a few minutes. Her little personal misfortune could not blind her to her husband's happy prospects. She looked at him as he sat folded up in a chair. He was stoop-shouldered and looked frail. But he sometimes surprised people with sudden bursts of physical energy. In his present posture, however, all his bodily strength seemed to have retired behind his deep-set eyes, giving them an extraordinary power of penetration. He was only twenty-six, but looked thirty or more. On the whole, he was not unhandsome.

'A penny for your thoughts, Mike,' said Nancy after a while, imitating the woman's magazine she read.

'I was thinking what a grand opportunity we've got at last to show these people how a school should be run.'

Ndume School was backward in every sense of the word. Mr Obi put his whole life into the work, and his wife hers too. He had two aims. A high standard of teaching was insisted upon, and the school compound was to be turned into a place of beauty. Nancy's dream-gardens came to life with the coming of the rains, and blossomed. Beautiful hibiscus and allamanda hedges in brilliant red and

Literature from other cultures

yellow marked out the carefully tended school compound from the rank neighbourhood bushes.

One evening as Obi was admiring his work he was scandalised to see an old woman from the village hobble right across the compound, through a marigold flower-bed and the hedges. On going up there he found faint signs of an almost disused path from the village across the school compound to the bush on the other side.

'It amazes me,' said Obi to one of his teachers who had been three years in the school, 'that you people allowed the villagers to make use of this footpath. It is simply incredible.' He shook his head.

'The path,' said the teacher apologetically, 'appears to be very important to them. Although it is hardly used, it connects the village shrine with their place of burial.'

'And what has that got to do with the school?' asked the headmaster.

'Well, I don't know,' replied the other with a shrug of the shoulders. 'But I remember there was a big row some time ago when we attempted to close it.'

'That was some time ago. But it will not be used now,' said Obi as he walked away. 'What will the Government Education Officer think of this when he comes to inspect the school next week? The villagers might, for all I know, decide to use the schoolroom for a pagan ritual during the inspection.'

Heavy sticks were planted closely across the path at the two places where it entered and left the school premises. These were further strengthened with barbed wire.

Three days later the village priest of Ani called on the headmaster. He was an old man and walked with a slight stoop. He carried a stout walking-stick which he usually tapped on the floor, by way of emphasis, each time he made a new point in his argument.

'I have heard,' he said after the usual exchange of cordialities, 'that our ancestral footpath has recently been closed …'

'Yes,' replied Mr Obi. 'We cannot allow people to make a highway of our school compound.'

'Look here, my son,' said the priest, bringing down his walking-stick, 'this path was here before you were born and before your father was born. The whole life of this village depends on it. Our dead relatives depart by it and our ancestors visit us by it. But most important, it is the path of children coming in to be born …'

Mr Obi listened with a satisfied smile on his face.

'The whole purpose of our school,' he said finally, 'is to eradicate just such beliefs as that. Dead men do not require footpaths. The whole idea is just fantastic. Our duty is to teach your children to laugh at such ideas.'

'What you say may be true,' replied the priest, 'but we follow the practices of our fathers. If you re-open the path we shall have nothing to quarrel about. What I always say is: let the hawk perch and let the eagle perch.' He rose to go.

'I am sorry,' said the young headmaster. 'But the school compound cannot be a thoroughfare. It is against our regulations. I would suggest your constructing another path, skirting our premises. We can even get our boys to help in building it. I don't suppose the ancestors will find the little detour too burdensome.'

'I have no more words to say,' said the old priest, already outside.

Two days later a young woman in the village died in childbed. A diviner was immediately consulted and he prescribed heavy sacrifices to propitiate ancestors insulted by the fence.

Obi woke up next morning among the ruins of his work. The beautiful hedges were torn up not just near the path but right round the school, the flowers trampled to death and one of the school buildings pulled down. That day the white supervisor came to inspect the school and wrote a nasty report on the state of the premises but more seriously about the 'tribal-war situation developing between the school and the village, arising in part from the misguided zeal of the new headmaster.'

Literature from other cultures

Ask yourself some questions. ✪ **W**hat is Michael's objection to the path? What is his attitude to the priest's explanation? ✪ **H**ow is the conflict between them described? ✪ What is the **E**ffect on you – do you sympathise with Michael, or with the villagers? Do you think Michael deserves the report he gets?

Finish your notes.

Practice time

Plan or write answers to these questions on the story.

What impression do you gain of Michael Obi's character and beliefs?

Hint: Use your notes to help you to identify the important ideas about the character. Key points you might refer to include:

- he is ambitious
- he is progressive
- he openly criticises other people's narrow views.

Which of these characters do you feel most sympathy for: Michael Obi; Nancy Obi; the priest?

Hint: Take each character in turn and decide for each the points in their favour and the points against. Write a paragraph on each one, then give your opinion and conclusion. Points you could refer to include:

- Michael's enthusiasm for his progressive ideas
- his lack of tolerance for the villagers' beliefs

- Nancy's support of her husband
- Nancy's lack of confidence
- the priest's duty to support the villagers
- his duty to mediate between the villagers and Michael Obi.

Compare the two short stories. You should include:

- the part played in each story by distinctive customs and beliefs
- the thoughts and feelings of the characters
- your response to each story.

Imagine that you are either Guru Nayak from 'An Astrologer's Day' or Nancy Obi from 'Dead Men's Path'. Write a letter to a friend in which you describe your feelings about the events described in the story.

What about customs and superstitions from your own culture? Prepare a short talk about any that you find interesting. You could focus on particular days, such as St Valentine's Day and Shrove Tuesday.

Section round-up

You have come to the end of this section – well done. You have:

- **Compared two texts from other cultures.**
- **Shown understanding of their particular qualities.**
- **Demonstrated personal response and insight.**

For your own notes

....

....

....

....

Literature from other cultures

Poems

About this section

This section gives you two poems that you can use to help you to practise your exam technique or as part of a coursework unit.

By the end of this section you will be able to:

- Discuss poems from diverse cultures.
- Appreciate their distinctive features.
- Respond to the writers' thoughts and feelings.

Poem at Thirty-Nine

This poem is by Alice Walker, a modern American writer.

Over to you

Write a commentary on 'Poem at Thirty-Nine'. You should comment on:

- the impression you receive of the father
- the impression you receive of the daughter
- how the writer uses form and language to express her thoughts and emotions.

Hint: Look at the notes and comments opposite, and add any ideas of your own. Remember to check the question and make sure that you can say something about every part of it.

Poem at Thirty-Nine

How I miss my father.
I wish he had not been
so tired
when I was
born.

Writing deposit slips and checks
I think of him.
He taught me how.
This is the form,
he must have said:
the way it is done.
I learned to see
bits of paper
as a way
to escape
the life he knew
and even in high school
had a savings
account.

He taught me
that telling the truth
did not always mean
a beating;
though many of my truths
must have grieved him
before the end.

How I miss my father!
He cooked like a person
dancing
in a yoga meditation
and craved the voluptuous
sharing
of good food.

Now I look and cook just like him:
my brain light;
tossing this and that
into the pot;
seasoning none of my life
the same way twice; happy to feed
whoever strays my way.

He would have grown
to admire
the woman I've become:
cooking, writing, chopping wood,
staring into the fire.

Poem at Thirty-Nine

Literature from other cultures

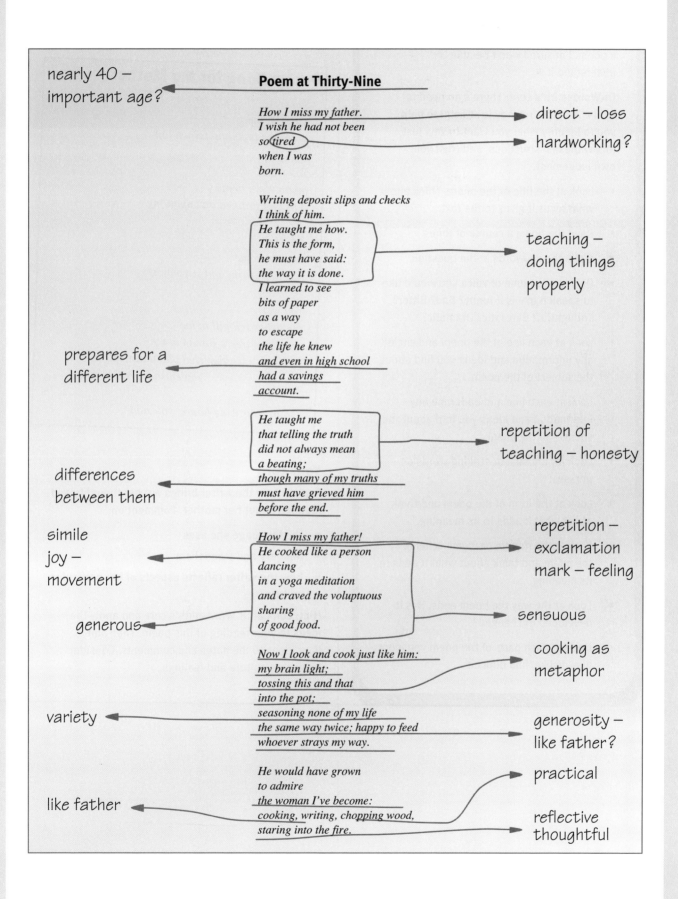

Literature from other cultures

Medicine Box

Ailment: I just go blank when I have to read a poem. I'm sure I won't be able to understand it.

Dr Wordsmith's cure: There's no need to worry. A simple remedy is at hand to help you to identify what you want to say. Just follow these instructions, and trust your own judgement.

- Look at the title of the poem. Think about what focus it gives to the text.
- Read the poem a couple of times.
- Circle the keywords in the question.
- Decide what tone of voice you would like to speak it in – is it funny? Sad? Bitter? Thoughtful? Sarcastic? Dramatic?
- Look at each line of the poem and circle any information and ideas you find about the subject of the poem.
- Look at each line and underline any information and ideas you find about the speaker of the poem.
- Look for unusual or striking words or phrases.
- Look at the form of the poem and think about what it adds to its meaning.
- Look at the rhythm or rhyme scheme of the poem and think about what it adds to its meaning.
- Look at the way the poem ends. Has it developed or changed?
- Decide which parts of the poem you most like/dislike/find difficult.

Praise Song for My Mother

Here is another poem showing a child's view of a parent, this time a mother. 'Praise Song for My Mother' is by the Caribbean poet Grace Nicholls.

Praise Song for My Mother

You were
water to me
deep and bold and fathoming

You were
moon's eye to me
pull and grained and mantling

You were
sunrise to me
rise and warm and streaming

You were
the fishes red gill to me
the flame tree's spread to me
the crab's leg/the fried plantain smell
        replenishing replenishing

Go to your wide future, you said

Your turn

Explain how the writer brings out her thoughts and feelings about her mother. Comment on:

- the language she uses
- imagery and symbolism
- how the writer reflects aspects of her particular culture.

Hint: Look at Dr Wordsmith's cure and apply the ideas to your reading of this poem. Then add your ideas to the notes and comments. Consider language, culture and feelings.

Literature from other cultures

Dr Wordsmith says ...

You will get credit for the effective use of terminology such as **simile** and **metaphor** (see p. 108). Remind yourself what these expressions refer to. A word of warning – remember to **comment** on the particular feature of language you are describing. Don't just pin labels on words.

Instead of saying 'The poet says her mother was like sunrise. This is a metaphor,' say something like, 'I find the metaphor of sunrise very effective because it suggests that her mother was ...'

Section round-up

Well done. You have shown that you can:

- Appreciate poems from different cultures.
- Identify distinctive features of language.
- Express personal response.

Review

Checklist

Check that you now feel confident about the following:

		Yes	Not yet
1	Discussing texts from different cultures.	☐	☐
2	Identifying specific aspects of texts from other cultures.	☐	☐
3	Expressing personal opinion based on the texts.	☐	☐

If your answer to any of these questions is 'Not yet', look back at the chapter or ask your teacher for help.

Now try this

Which of the two poems do you prefer? Refer to the texts to illustrate your comments.

Chapter 7 Drama

Overview

This chapter separately explores examples of drama from the period before 1914 and from the period after 1914. By the end of the chapter you will:

- Understand the importance of the social, cultural and historical context of drama.
- Appreciate the way that dramatists use language.
- Be able to comment on characterisation.
- Be able to respond critically to dramatic texts.

The individual and society

About this section

This section looks at extracts from two plays which deal with ideas about the values and ideas which influence human behaviour.

A View from the Bridge

A View from the Bridge by the American writer Arthur Miller, published in Great Britain in 1955, is set in New York, in the Italian-American community. At the time millions of Italians had travelled to America, the land of opportunity, looking for work and a better standard of living. However, there was a clampdown on this practice and laws restricting immigration were enforced. As a result, there was a brisk trade in illegal entry into the country.

In this extract, Eddie Carbone, his wife Beatrice and his niece Catherine are awaiting the arrival of Beatrice's cousins, who are being smuggled into the country from Italy. They will be working on the docks illegally and staying secretly with the Carbones.

CATHERINE:	He's bringin' them ten o'clock, Tony?
EDDIE:	Around, yeah. [*He eats.*]
CATHERINE:	Eddie, suppose somebody asks if they're livin' here. [*He looks at her as though already she had divulged something publicly. Defensively*] I mean if they ask.
EDDIE:	Now look, Baby, I can see we're gettin' mixed up again here.
CATHERINE:	No, I just mean … people'll see them goin' in and out.
EDDIE:	I don't care who sees them goin' in and out as long as you don't see them goin' in and out. And this goes for you too, B. You don't see nothin' and you don't know nothin'.
BEATRICE:	What do you mean? I understand.
EDDIE:	You don't understand; you still think you can talk about this to somebody just a little bit. Now lemme say it once and for all, because you're makin' me nervous again, both of you. I don't care if somebody comes in the house and sees them sleepin' on the floor, it never comes out of your mouth who they are or what they're doin' here.
BEATRICE:	Yeah, but my mother'll know –
EDDIE:	Sure she'll know, but just don't you be the one who told her, that's all. This is the United States government you're playin' with now, this is the Immigration Bureau. If you said it you knew it, if you didn't say it you didn't know it.
CATHERINE:	Yeah, but Eddie, suppose somebody –
EDDIE:	I don't care what question it is. You – don't – know – nothin'. They got stool pigeons all over this neighbourhood, they're payin' them every week for information, and you don't know who they are. It could be your best friend. You hear? [*To BEATRICE*] Like Vinny Bolzano, remember Vinny?

100

Drama

BEATRICE:	Oh, yeah. God forbid.
EDDIE:	Tell her about Vinny. [*To* CATHERINE] You think I'm blowin' steam here? [*To* BEATRICE] Go ahead, tell her. [*To* CATHERINE] You was a baby then. There was a family lived next door to her mother, he was about sixteen –
BEATRICE:	No, he was no more than fourteen, 'cause I went to his confirmation in Saint Agnes. But the family had an uncle that they were hidin' in the house, and he snitched to the Immigration.
CATHERINE:	The kid snitched?
EDDIE:	On his own uncle!
CATHERINE:	What, was he crazy?
EDDIE:	He was crazy after, I tell you that, boy.
BEATRICE:	Oh, it was terrible. He had five brothers and the old father. And they grabbed him in the kitchen and pulled him down the stairs – three flights his head was bouncin' like a coconut. And they spit on him in the street, his own father and his brothers. The whole neighbourhood was cryin'.
CATHERINE:	Ts! So what happened to him?
BEATRICE:	I think he went away. [*To* EDDIE] I never seen him again, did you?
EDDIE:	[*rises during this, taking out his watch*] Him? You'll never see him no more, a guy do a thing like that? How's he gonna show his face? [*To* CATHERINE, *as he gets up uneasily*] Just remember, kid, you can quicker get back a million dollars that was stole than a word that you gave away. [*He is standing now, stretching his back.*]
CATHERINE:	Okay, I won't say a word to nobody, I swear.

For you to do

Answer the following questions. If you have time you can practise writing full answers, or alternatively you could make full plans, or discuss your responses with a friend.

What do you gather from the passage about Eddie, Beatrice and Catherine and the relationship between them?

Hint: In drama, you rely on what the characters do and say rather than on what the writer tells you about them. Read through the extract and **listen in your head** to what the characters say and the way they speak the lines. Make a chart to show your impressions.

What do you learn from the extract about values and customs in the Italian-American community?

Hint: When you think about the nature of a cultural group, look for what its members **believe** in and what they think is **important**. Your answer could include:

- the importance of trust
- the code of honour – not giving information away
- the importance of the family
- the disgrace of betrayal.

Imagine that you are directing this scene. Explain to each of the actors how he or she should speak and move. Make clear what dramatic effect you want to create.

The seeds of the drama are sown at the beginning of the play. Try to predict the kind of development that might take place. Which of these ideas contained in the extract are most likely to be significant:

- the necessity for secrecy and the fear of the Immigration Bureau
- where Vinny Bolzano went
- Catherine's anxiety that she will give something away
- Eddie's insistence on trust and honour?

Drama

An Inspector Calls

An Inspector Calls by J.B. Priestley was written in 1945, but the drama is set in 1912, before the beginning of World War I. The play concerns a wealthy industrial family, the Birlings, who live in a Midlands industrial town. Under the interrogation of the mysterious Inspector Goole, it emerges that each member of the family has been involved with a young woman who has committed suicide.

a) A man has to make his own way - has to look after himself – and his family too, of course, when he has one – and so long as he does that he won't come to much harm. But the way some of these cranks talk and write now, you'd think everybody has to look after everybody else, as if we were all mixed up together like bees in a hive – community and all that nonsense.

b) I can't accept any responsibility. If we were all responsible for everything that happened to everybody we'd had anything to do with, it would be very awkward, wouldn't it?

c) Go and look for the father of the child. It's his responsibility.

d) I don't see that it's any concern of yours how I choose to run my business.

e) A man has to look after himself.

f) We don't live alone. We are members of one body. We are responsible for each other.

Try this

Read the statements above made by characters in the play. Underline key words. Write a sentence explaining what themes you think that the play will explore. What do you think will be the areas of conflict in the drama?

Remind yourself of the year in which the play is set. What is the dramatic effect of the following statements?

a) 'There's a lot of wild talk about possible labour trouble in the near future.'

b) 'In 1940 ... you'll be living in a world that'll have forgotten all these Capital versus Labour agitations and all these silly war scares.'

c) 'You'll hear some people say that war is inevitable. And to that I say – fiddlesticks!'

d) 'This new liner ... the Titanic ... unsinkable, absolutely unsinkable.'

Section round-up

You are now familiar with some of the themes and ideas characteristic of post-1914 drama. Take a break before travelling back in time.

Drama

Macaroons and cucumber sandwiches

About this section

In this section you will experience two very different types of drama, both written before 1914. The first passage is from a powerful and controversial play about marriage, society and relationships. The second extract also presents ideas about marriage and society, but in a light and amusing style.

A Doll's House

This extract is from *A Doll's House*, a play by the Norwegian writer Henrik Ibsen, published in 1879. The play aroused furious controversy at the time because of its presentation of a woman fighting against male-dominated society. Here, Nora has been Christmas shopping.

NORA: Hide the Christmas tree away carefully, Helene. The children mustn't see it till this evening when it's decorated. [*to the porter, taking out her purse*] How much?

PORTER: Fifty öre.

NORA: There's a crown. Keep the change.
[*The porter thanks her and goes. Nora shuts the door. She continues to laugh quietly and happily to herself as she takes off her things. She takes a bag of macaroons out of her pocket and eats one or two; then she walks stealthily across and listens at her husband's door.*]

NORA: Yes, he's in. [*She begins humming again as she walks over to the table, right.*]

HELMER: [*in his study*] Is that my little sky-lark chirruping out there?

NORA: [*busy opening some of the parcels*] Yes, it is.

HELMER: Is that my little squirrel frisking about?

NORA: Yes!

HELMER: When did my little squirrel get home?

NORA: Just this minute. [*She stuffs the bag of macaroons in her pocket and wipes her mouth.*] Come on out, Torvald, and see what I've bought.

HELMER: I don't want to be disturbed! [*A moment later, he opens the door and looks out, his pen in his hand.*] 'Bought', did you say? All that? Has my little spendthrift been out squandering money again?

NORA: But, Torvald, surely this year we can spread ourselves just a little. This is the first Christmas we haven't had to go carefully.

HELMER: Ah, but that doesn't mean we can afford to be extravagant, you know.

NORA: Oh yes, Torvald, surely we can afford to be just a little bit extravagant now, can't we? Just a teeny-weeny bit. You are getting quite a good salary now, and you are going to earn lots and lots of money.

HELMER: Yes, after the New Year. But it's going to be three whole months before the first pay cheque comes in.

NORA: Pooh! We can always borrow in the meantime.

HELMER: Nora! [*crosses to her and takes her playfully by the ear*] Here we go again, you and your frivolous ideas! Suppose I went and borrowed a thousand crowns today, and you went and spent it all over Christmas, then on New Year's Eve a slate fell and hit me on the head and there I was …

NORA: [*putting her hand over his mouth*] Sh! Don't say such horrid things.

HELMER: Yes, but supposing something like that did happen … what then?

NORA: If anything as awful as that did happen, I wouldn't care if I owed anybody anything or not.

HELMER: Yes, but what about the people I'd borrowed from?

NORA: Them? Who cares about them! They are only strangers!

HELMER: Nora, Nora! Just like a woman! Seriously though, Nora, you know what I think about these things. No debts! Never borrow! There's always something inhibited, something unpleasant, about a home built on credit and borrowed money. We two have managed to stick it out so far, and that's the way we'll go on for the little time that remains.

NORA: [*walks over to the stove*] Very well, just as you say, Torvald.

HELMER: [*following her*] There, there! My little singing bird mustn't go drooping her wings, eh? Has it got the sulks, that little squirrel of mine? [*Takes out his wallet.*] Nora, what do you think I've got here?

NORA: [*quickly turning round*] Money!

HELMER: There! [*He hands her some notes.*] Good heavens, I know only too well how Christmas runs away with the housekeeping.

NORA: [*counts*] Ten, twenty, thirty, forty. Oh, thank you, thank you, Torvald! This will see me quite a long way.

HELMER: Yes, it'll have to.

NORA: Yes, yes, I'll see that it does. But come over here, I want to show you all the things I've bought. And so cheap! Look, some new clothes for Ivar … and a little sword. There's a horse and a trumpet for Bob. And a doll and a doll's cot for Emmy. They are not very grand but she'll have them all broken before long anyway. And I've got some dress material and some handkerchiefs for the maids. Though, really, dear old Anne Marie should have had something better.

HELMER: And what's in this parcel here?

NORA: [*shrieking*] No, Torvald! You mustn't see that till tonight!

HELMER: All right. But tell me now, what did my little spendthrift fancy for herself?

NORA: For me? Puh, I don't really want anything.

103

Drama

Task time

Plan or write answers to these questions, or discuss them with a friend.

What impression of Nora and Helmer and the relationship between them do you gain from the passage?

Hint: Look at what each character does and says. Decide what this tells you about each person. Here are some of the things you might notice first about Nora:

- Nora laughs and hums.
- She 'stealthily' listens at her husband's door.
- She doesn't want Helmer to see that she has been eating macaroons.

What do these points suggest about Nora, and about her relationship with Helmer?

Look at the way Helmer talks to Nora. Consider:

- the names he calls her
- his attitude to her spending money
- his attitude to her eating macaroons.

What do these points suggest about the way Helmer sees Nora?

What do you discover from the extract about values and customs in the society Ibsen portrays?

Hint: Look for attitudes and beliefs. Think about:

- the position of men and women – who seems to have the power?
- the accepted behaviour of husbands and wives
- the importance of money.

Which of these ideas from the opening of the play are likely to be significant:

- Nora's liking for macaroons
- Nora and money
- Helmer's feeling that he doesn't know where Nora's money goes
- Helmer's dislike of debt
- Helmer's power over Nora?

The Importance of Being Earnest

This is the beginning of *The Importance of Being Earnest* by Oscar Wilde, published in 1899.

Morning-room in Algernon's flat in Half Moon Street. The room is luxuriously and artistically furnished. The sound of a piano is heard in the adjoining room.

LANE *is arranging afternoon tea on the table, and after the music has ceased,* ALGERNON *enters.*

ALGERNON: Did you hear what I was playing, Lane?

LANE: I didn't think it polite to listen, sir.

ALGERNON: I'm sorry for that, for your sake. I don't play accurately - anyone can play accurately - but I play with wonderful expression. As far as the piano is concerned, sentiment is my forte. I keep science for Life.

LANE: Yes, sir.

ALGERNON: And, speaking of the science of Life, have you got the cucumber sandwiches cut for Lady Bracknell?

LANE: Yes, sir. *(hands them on a salver)*

ALGERNON: *(inspects them, takes two, and sits down on the sofa)* Oh!...by the way, Lane, I see from your book that on Thursday night, when Lord Shoreman and Mr Worthing were dining with me, eight bottles of champagne are entered as having been consumed.

LANE: Yes, sir; eight bottles and a pint.

ALGERNON: Why is it that at a bachelor's establishment the servants invariably drink the champagne? I ask merely for information.

LANE: I attribute it to the superior quality of the wine, sir. I have often observed that in married households the champagne is rarely of a first-rate brand.

ALGERNON: Good heavens! Is marriage so demoralising as that?

LANE: I believe it is a very pleasant state, sir. I have had very little experience of it myself up to the present. I have only been married once. That was in consequence of a misunderstanding between myself and a young person.

ALGERNON: *(languidly)* I don't know that I am much interested in your family life, Lane.

LANE: No, sir, it is not a very interesting subject. I never think of it myself.

ALGERNON: Very natural, I am sure. That will do, Lane, thank you.

LANE: Thank you, sir.

(LANE goes out.)

ALGERNON: Lane's views on marriage seem somewhat lax. Really, if the lower orders don't set us a good example, what on earth is the use of them? They seem, as a class, to have absolutely no sense of moral responsibility.

Drama

Task time

Which of the following words can be applied to the kind of humour in the passage?

> *slapstick   wit   farce   wordplay   irony*

Find examples where the dialogue gains its effect from the unexpected or inverted use of a word or phrase.

How do you think that the actors playing Algernon and Lane should speak? Make notes on accent, pace, pitch and intonation. Mark up the script extract with any particular instructions.

Section round-up

Now you have worked through this section you can:

- Appreciate the social and cultural setting of a drama text.
- Respond to characterisation and dramatic effect.

Review

Congratulations on reaching the end of the chapter.

Checklist

Are you confident about:

		Yes	Not yet
1	The importance of context in drama?	❑	❑
2	Using textual evidence?	❑	❑
3	Discussing themes?	❑	❑
4	Appreciating the use of language?	❑	❑

If your answer to any of these questions is 'Not yet', look back at the chapter or ask your teacher for help.

For your own notes

Chapter 8 — Shakespeare

Overview

What do you already know about Shakespeare? Perhaps more than you think. Here's what you'll know by the end of this chapter:

- **Why he's worth the effort.**
- **All you need to know about his life and times.**
- **How he used prose and poetry.**
- **How to write about his poetic style.**
- **How to explore his characters.**
- **How to look at scenes in context.**
- **Some of his themes and how to write about them.**
- **How to review a performance.**

Why bother with the Bard?

Why make the effort to read 400-year-old plays? For a start, you may need 'a written response' to a Shakespeare play in your coursework folder. It could be, for example, an essay on a character or theme, or on Shakespeare's use of words; an analysis of a scene in the context of the whole play; an account of the play from one character's viewpoint; or a review of a performance. You could also focus on Shakespeare in an oral coursework assignment.

All these options are covered in this chapter. Your teacher will set coursework, but you may have more choice if you ask to do some of the options here. At any rate, working through this chapter will greatly increase your enjoyment of Shakespeare, and help you with whatever coursework you do.

The more interesting reason for bothering with Shakespeare is that he was the greatest literary genius ever to write in English! He has a finely tuned sense of drama, a deep understanding of character, and an astonishing way with words (see pp. 108–109).

Shakespeare's characters, dramatic technique and poetic use of language have influenced most, if not all, writers in English who come after him – for example, the novelists Hardy and Dickens, and the poet T. S. Eliot. Shakespeare is the central figure in the English literary heritage.

Task time

Start a spider diagram with the sections: types, style, theatre, performance, why, who and coursework. Add to it as you work through the chapter.

Shakespeare wrote about the same issues and emotions that capture our imagination and fill our conversation – and our television screens – nowadays. Jot down what you think these might be. Think about power, friendship, greed. . . . Look out for these themes in the extracts used in this chapter and in any Shakespeare play you study in your coursework.

For your own notes

Shakespeare

Background

About this section

This section explains the historical and cultural influences on Shakespeare's plays – their 'context'. It tells you:
- The basic facts about Shakespeare's life.
- What the Elizabethan theatre was like.
- The types of plays Shakespeare wrote.

Shakespeare's father was a glove-maker, and the young Shakespeare probably met a wide variety of people, from illiterate labourers to nobles. He later portrayed – and wrote for – the whole social range (see 'Style and language' p. 108). He went to school, but probably learnt more from listening to people, and from observation – especially of the local countryside. Descriptions of nature appear in some of his most beautiful speeches.

The Elizabethan theatre

Shakespeare's plays are meant to be seen, not just read. Try to see at least one performance of the play you're studying, and buy or hire a video or DVD. Bear in mind the following points about Elizabethan theatre:

- There was little scenery, and no lighting effects, though music was used to help create a mood. The scene had to be created largely by the words.

A contemporary Elizabethan sketch of the Swan Theatre on Bankside, London

- Female roles were played by boys – one reason why they have relatively few lines, though there are some very important female characters, such as Lady Macbeth. Another reason is that Elizabethan women led less dramatic lives than men. They weren't involved in war, politics or business; few had much power – Elizabeth I was an exception.
- Audiences were probably rowdier than modern ones. People drank beer and ate oranges, and many were standing. Therefore few Shakespeare plays present major characters or vital information until the audience has had a chance to settle down. Comedy (in tragedies, comic relief) was an important way of holding interest.

Types of play

Shakespeare wrote four types of play:

- **Comedy**: emphasising humour, often with confusions and people in disguise, and with happy endings (usually marriages), and no deaths (e.g. *Twelfth Night*).
- **Tragedy**: focusing on a tragic hero (or couple) whose nobility or achievement we admire, and whose downfall and death through a weakness or error, coupled with fate, arouses our sympathy (e.g. *Macbeth*, *Romeo and Juliet*).
- **History**: based on historical characters and conflicts, sometimes with tragic elements (e.g. *Henry V*).
- **Romances** or **'problem'** plays: the later plays, featuring magic, mystery, moral lessons and unlikely happy endings (e.g. *The Tempest*).

Comedy and tragedy, the types you are most likely to study, have their roots in classical (ancient) Greek drama.

Question time

Decide which type of play you're studying. How do its characteristics emerge in the play? Does it have characteristics of other types as well?

Write a first-person account of an Elizabethan performance of the play you're studying, as if you're actually there. Include as many details as you can remember.

Section round-up

By now you should know:
- What makes Shakespeare so special.
- What the Elizabethan theatre was like.
- What types of play Shakespeare wrote.
- Where comedy and tragedy originated.

Shakespeare

Style and language

About this section

This section and the next will show you Shakespeare's influence on the English language, and give you a toolkit to help you understand and write about his style. You'll learn:

- What Shakespeare gave to the English language.
- How he uses poetry and prose.
- The secret of his wide appeal.
- All about imagery, rhythm and word-play.

New words and well-worn phrases

Have you ever heard any of these phrases? 'Being cruel to be kind.' 'There's method in his madness.' 'It's vanished into thin air.' 'He won't budge an inch.' 'Fair play/foul play.' 'Don't stand on ceremony.' 'Fool's paradise.' 'My own flesh and blood.' 'Good riddance!'

You've guessed it – they're Shakespeare's. He was also an inventor and populariser of new words. The words *accommodation*, *assassination*, *dire*, *dislocate*, *horrid*, *obscene*, *submerged* and *vast* are just a few he helped to fix in our language.

Poetry and prose

Shakespeare's plays are a mixture of **poetry** (verse) and **prose** (ordinary writing without rhymes or fixed line-lengths). Lowly characters, like Launcelot Gobbo in *The Merchant of Venice*, speak in prose. Nobles speak in prose only if speaking informally – or if they've gone mad (like Lady Macbeth and King Lear).

Shakespeare's normal verse style is **blank verse** ('blank' means 'non-rhyming'). It usually has five pairs of syllables to a line, with the stress on each second syllable. Blank verse is also called unrhymed **iambic pentameter**. Why? Each pair of syllables is called an 'iambus'; and there are five pairs to a line (Greek *pente* (five), as in 'pentagon' and 'pentathlon'). **Note:** Sometimes a speech is rounded off with a **rhyming couplet**.

Rich and poor

Shakespeare had to appeal both to the nobility and to ordinary, uneducated people. We'll look at an example from *Macbeth*. The guilt-racked murderer Macbeth fears that not even the entire ocean will wash the blood from his hands.

Read these lines aloud:

> 'this my hand will rather
> The multitudinous seas incarnadine,
> Making the green one red.'

Multitudinous and *incarnadine* suggest the seriousness of the crime, and the vast, rolling depths of the sea – and would appeal to the more sophisticated nobles. They would know that *incarnadine* (make crimson, like a red *carn*-ation) comes from the Latin for 'flesh': *carnis*.

✪ Why is this so appropriate? The last line is down-to-earth Anglo-Saxon English. It contrasts with the earlier line, and spells out its meaning for the uneducated.

Imagery

Images are word pictures that bring ideas to life, often by highlighting similarities, describing a character's behaviour, or something abstract, like love, as if it were something we could see and touch. Shakespeare uses four types:

1. **Similes** compare two things similar in one important way; e.g. 'he doth bestride the narrow world/Like a Colossus' (*Julius Caesar*). Similes often include *like*, but not always: 'It seems she hangs upon the cheek of night/As a rich jewel in an Ethiop's ear' (*Romeo and Juliet*, Act 1, Scene 5).

2. **Metaphors** describe a thing as if it actually is something else: 'Life's but a walking shadow, a poor player/That struts and frets his hour upon the stage' (*Macbeth*, Act 5, Scene 5).

3. **Comparisons** measure one thing against another: 'As violently as hasty powder fir'd/Doth hurry from the fatal cannon's womb' (*Romeo and Juliet*, Act 5, Scene 1).

4. **Personification**: describing something as if it were a person, e.g. 'The gray-ey'd morn smiles on the frowning night' (*Romeo and Juliet*, Act 2, Scene 3).

Shakespeare matches imagery to themes (central ideas). In *Macbeth* the animal imagery reflects Macbeth's inhuman crime. In (3) above, the war image fits the theme of conflict. Look out, too, for images from seafaring, tailoring and falconry.

Word music

Shakespeare fits rhythm to sense. A downcast Macbeth sees a bleak, monotonous future: 'Tomorrow, and tomorrow, and tomorrow'. When Macduff announces that he was 'from his mother's womb/Untimely ripped', the line itself is cut short. The sound of the words is important, too, especially **alliteration**: repetition of a sound, usually at the beginnings of words; e.g. 'big-bellied with the wanton wind' (*A Midsummer Night's Dream*, Act 2, Scene 1).

Shakespeare

Word-play

Shakespeare excels at the favourite kind of Elizabethan word-play – the **pun**: the use of a word with two meanings, or of two similar-sounding words, where both meanings are appropriate in different ways. Often the punning is competitive:

> MERCUTIO: ... dreamers often lie.
> ROMEO: In bed asleep, while they do dream
>   things true.
>   (*Romeo and Juliet*, Act 1, Scene 4)

Look out, too, for **oxymorons** (opposites): 'O heavy lightness, serious vanity ... Feather of lead, bright smoke, cold fire, sick health' (*Romeo and Juliet*, Act 1, Scene 1).

Review time

Make a note of who speaks prose in the play you're studying, and when.

Read some blank verse aloud, tapping out the syllables and noting any variations.

Find examples of each type of image. Consider why each is appropriate.

Find some puns in the play you're studying. Work out exactly what they mean. Make up your own.

Dr Wordsmith says ...

Blanking out on blank verse? Try this:

- **Iam-buses** always come in pairs;

 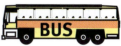

- **Pentameter**: write it on your fingers and thumbs. Use them to count syllables per line.

Section round-up

By now you should understand Shakespeare's greatest strength – his mastery of language, especially his poetry and prose, vocabulary and imagery.

For your own notes

Shakespeare

Antony and Cleopatra

About this section

This section focuses on the difference between descriptive prose and Shakespeare's verse. It gives you a chance to apply what you've learnt from pages 108–109.

First, read the prose description of Cleopatra, an Elizabethan translation from the Roman writer Plutarch.

Shakespeare turned this into poetry. Read his version below – first skim-read it to get a rough idea of its content and mood; then read it to see how the scene and the ideas develop and how the lines relate to each other. Then read it more slowly. Finally, read it out loud.

✪ What details are the same in both versions? (You could draw linking lines.) How do the styles differ? Note examples of technique as shown on pages 108–109. What do they achieve?

Note its content and language. (**Note**: *poop*: rear part of the barge; *amorous*: loving; *divers*: many; *yarely*: nimbly.)

… she disdained to set forward otherwise, but to take her barge in the river of Cydnus, the poop whereof was of gold, the sails of purple, and the oars of silver, which kept strike in rowing after the sound of the music of flutes, hautboys, citherns, viols, and such other instruments as they played upon in the barge. And now for the person of herself: she was laid under a pavilion of cloth of gold of tissue, apparelled and attired like the goddess Venus, commonly drawn in picture: and hard by her, on either hand of her, pretty fair boys apparelled as painters do set forth god Cupid, with little fans in their hands, with the which they fanned wind upon her. Her ladies and gentlewomen also, the fairest of them were apparelled like the nymphs Nereids (which are the mermaids of the waters) and like the Graces, some steering the helm, others tending the tackle and ropes of the barge, out of the which there came a wonderful passing sweet savour of perfumes, that perfumed the wharf's side, pestered with innumerable multitudes of people. Some of them followed the barge all alongst the river's side: others also ran out of the city to see her coming in.
So that in the end, there ran such multitudes of people one after another to see her, that Antonius was left post alone in the market place, in his imperial seat to give audience …

The barge she sat in, like a burnish'd throne,
Burn'd on the water. The poop was beaten gold;
Purple the sails, and so perfumed that
The winds were lovesick with them. The oars
  were silver,
Which to the tune of flutes kept stroke, and
  made
The water which they beat to follow faster,
As amorous of their strokes. For her own
  person,
It beggar'd all description. She did lie
In her pavilion, cloth of gold of tissue,
O'er-picturing that Venus where we see
The fancy outwork Nature. On each side her
Stood pretty dimpled boys, like smiling Cupids,
With divers-coloured fans, whose wind did
  seem
To glow the delicate cheeks which they did
  cool,
And what they undid, did …
Her gentlewomen – like the Nereids,
So many mermaids – tended her i' the eyes
And made their bends adornings. At the helm
A seeming mermaid steers. The silken tackle
Swell with the touches of those flower-soft
  hands,
That yarely frame the office. From the barge
A strange invisible perfume hits the sense
Of the adjacent wharfs. The city cast
Her people out upon her: and Antony,
Enthron'd i' the market place, did sit alone, …
Whistling to the air; which, but for vacancy,
Had gone to gaze on Cleopatra too,
And made a gap in nature.

110

Shakespeare

What follows is a personal response to this Shakespeare passage by a student at the start of the GCSE course. Read it first with the notes below covered. ✪ What do you think is good about it? What improvements could be made? Now look at the notes.

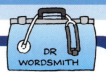

Dr Wordsmith's diagnosis

This is an articulate and sensitive response. Its two weaknesses are:

1. It doesn't look at the language closely enough. For example the alliteration in 'The water which they beat to follow faster' suggests the sound of the oars, while the line's extra syllable means we have to speed up at the end, like the water. And note the pun on *strokes*.

2. It mentions the visual splendour, but overlooks the other senses (flutes, perfume, flower-soft hands ...). And note the wondrous way in which the fans seem to cool Cleopatra's cheeks and make them glow at the same time.

> I like this passage because of all the vivid descriptions. I think the part where Enobarbus describes Cleopatra and the barge which she lies in is extremely effective.[1] The image of a splendid, dramatic boat, shining bright gold on the water, is created. The alliteration of 'The <u>b</u>arge she sat in, like a <u>b</u>urnished throne,/ <u>B</u>urn'd on the water' adds to the effect.[2] I imagine the boat with billowing sails, purple because it is the colour of love and dreams.[3] The ship is magic, romantic, almost unreal. The display of it is like a monument to love, which mesmerises all the people around, and the water and air.
>
> Cleopatra herself is too beautiful to put into words,[4] so there is not much description of her, apart from her being Venus-like in appearance, wrapped up in gold cloth which makes her seem like a goddess, with the mythical, beauteous mermaids and perfect little Cupid-like boys with their coloured fans attending her.
>
> I like the way there is a 'gap in nature'. Because of this dreamy love-filled boat, all of nature stops as it is marvelled upon by everyone and everything.[5]

[1] Better to say 'is extremely effective in creating an image of ...'.

[2] Alliteration: well-spotted.

[3] Also royal colour.

[4] Good point: her beauty is hinted at; her features are not described.

[5] Interesting interpretation, but a closer look at the sense is needed: the air itself would have gone to see Cleopatra, had this not created a vacuum – an impossible 'gap in nature'.

Your turn

What impression is made by the picture of Antony, left alone, 'Whistling to the air'?

Write your own response to a passage in the Shakespeare play you're studying – or write notes directly onto a photocopy of the passage. Give close attention to style and language.

Section round-up

You've had a hands-on experience of Shakespeare's poetry and compared it to prose, and you've seen one student's essay.

Shakespeare

Character

> **About this section**
>
> This page and the next look at how to approach characters in Shakespeare. You will learn:
> - The importance of dramatic purpose and types of character.
> - How characterisation differs in different types of play.
> - What questions to ask.
> - How to tackle different types of character study.

Many students make the mistake of treating Shakespeare's characters as if they were real people. They do portray real human problems and emotions, but remember – they also have a *dramatic* purpose. Without Lady Macbeth, Macbeth would not murder a king. If Lord Capulet, Juliet's father, were more easy-going, *Romeo and Juliet* would not be a tragedy.

Many characters, too, are recognisable as types: villains, like Iago in *Othello* and Don John in *Much Ado About Nothing*; paternal authority figures, like Egeus in *A Midsummer Night's Dream* – they are not meant to be completely realistic. The most lifelike ('fully rounded') characters are in the tragedies and histories (see p. 107). Comedies are concerned with social relationships; tragedies are associated more with individuals' inner conflict and development.

Here is a checklist of questions. For 'X' read whatever character you want to explore:

- How realistic is X, and how realistic is X meant to be?
- What is X's dramatic role?
- What are X's motives and problems?
- How does X develop?
- How do you feel towards X?
- What can be said for and against X?

Another way to explore a character is with a spider diagram. Start with connections, motives and development.

Romeo and Juliet

One possible type of coursework involves telling the story of a play from the viewpoint of one character. The extract below does this.

It is from Humphrey Carpenter's excellent *Shakespeare without the Boring Bits*, which also covers other Shakespeare plays.

Told by Juliet's Nurse

Some people have said it was all our fault, me and Friar Lawrence. They say grown-ups shouldn't meddle in the affairs of youngsters like my poor little Juliet and her Romeo. But me, I say it was just bad luck.

They'd both be alive today, poor dears, if their families hadn't been fighting, fighting all the time. There must have been some reason why the Capulets – that's Juliet's family, where I worked – and the Montagues began quarrelling in the first place. But nobody can remember what it was. They'd been squabbling for years and years. So when the Capulets gave a party at their big house in Verona, none of them would have dreamt of inviting a Montague. Oh dear, no!

But one of the Montagues invited himself. I'm talking about young Romeo. A fine good-looking lad he was, and in those days he fancied a girl called Rosaline. He knew she'd be at the party, and it was a fancy dress affair, so he put on a mask and slipped in uninvited. The saucy boy!

He was spotted, though, by Lady Capulet's nephew, a fiery young fellow called Tybalt, who was always picking fights with the Montagues in the market-place. He recognized Romeo beneath the mask. And off he trotted to tell his uncle Lord Capulet that one of the enemy had gate-crashed! But my lord – I call him that because he was my employer, you see, dear – my lord had had a few drinks, and was feeling merry, and told Tybalt it didn't matter. And then what should happen but Romeo went and caught sight of my little Juliet, and fell in love with her on the spot.

Shakespeare

I say 'little', but she was quite grown up really. Just a few days short of her fourteenth birthday. And there's many a girl in Verona was married by the time she was fourteen. But my lord, her father, didn't want her to rush into marriage. There was a decent young nobleman called Paris, who'd taken a proper fancy to little Juliet. But my lord Capulet told him he'd have to wait a couple of years before marrying her. No one asked Juliet what *she* thought about it. It was always the father that decided who put the wedding ring on their daughter's finger. Which is why Friar Lawrence was really being very naughty when he … but I'm jumping ahead, dear.

Tasks

Underline the phrases that reveal the Nurse's character. What picture do you get of her?

Practise giving a short talk on a character using a diagram in place of notes.

With a partner, role-play a character being interviewed, either at the end of the play's action, or at a crucial stage during the play.

With a partner, role-play two characters discussing the play's events, and how they feel about each other, and about other characters.

Section round-up

By now you should have an insight into Shakespeare's characters and how to explore them, and be able to apply it to the play you're studying.

For your own notes

....

....

....

....

....

....

....

Shakespeare

Comparisons

> ### About this section
>
> In GCSE English you will often be asked to make comparisons. This is because doing so highlights the qualities of each thing being compared.

Read the passages that follow. The first is from *Macbeth* (Act 2, Scene 4): Macbeth has murdered the King.

> *Enter* ROSS *and an* OLD MAN.
>
> OLD MAN Threescore and ten I can remember well:
> Within the volume of which time I have seen
> Hours dreadful and things strange; but this sore night
> Hath trifled former knowings.
>
> ROSS Ah, good father,
> Thou seest, the heavens, as troubled with man's act,
> Threaten his bloody stage: by the clock, 'tis day,
> And yet dark night strangles the travelling lamp;
> Is't night's predominance, or the day's shame,
> That darkness does the face of earth entomb,
> When living light should kiss it?
>
> OLD MAN 'Tis unnatural,
> Even like the deed that's done. On Tuesday last,
> A falcon, towering in her pride of place.
> Was by a mousing owl hawk'd at and kill'd.
>
> ROSS And Duncan's horses, – a thing most strange and certain, –
> Beauteous and swift, the minions of their race,
> Turn'd wild in nature, broke their stalls, flung out,
> Contending 'gainst obedience, as they would make war with mankind.
>
> OLD MAN 'Tis said they ate each other.
>
> ROSS They did so; to the amazement of mine eyes,
> That look'd upon't.

This extract is from *Julius Caesar* (Act 1, Scene 3): nothing terrible has happened yet. ✪ What makes us think that it will?

> *Rome. A Street.*
> *Thunder and Lightning. Enter, from opposite sides,* CASCA, *with his sword drawn, and* CICERO.
>
> CIC Good-even, Casca: brought you Caesar home?
> Why are you breathless? and why stare you so?
>
> CASCA Are not you mov'd, when all the sway of earth
> Shakes like a thing unfirm? O Cicero,
> I have seen tempests, when the scolding winds
> Have riv'd the knotty oaks; and I have seen
> The ambitious ocean swell, and rage, and foam,
> To be exalted with the threat'ning clouds:
> But never till to-night, never till now,
> Did I go through a tempest dropping fire.
> Either there is a civil strife in heaven;
> Or else the world, too saucy with the gods,
> Incenses them to send destruction.
>
> CIC Why, saw you anything more wonderful?
>
> CASCA A common slave, – you know him well by sight, –
> Held up his left hand, which did flame and burn
> Like twenty torches join'd; and yet his hand,
> Not sensible of fire, remain'd unscorch'd.
> Besides, – I ha' not since put up my sword, –
> Against the Capitol I met a lion,
> Who glar'd upon me, and went surly by,
> Without annoying me: and there were drawn
> Upon a heap a hundred ghastly women,
> Transformed with their fear; who swore they saw
> Men, all in fire, walk up and down the streets,
> And yesterday the bird of night did sit,
> Even at noon-day, upon the market-place,
> Hooting and shrieking.

Try this

How do the Old Man and Casca give weight, in their opening lines, to what they report?

Underline or list the strange things in each report. Look for images of light and dark, weather, and animals. (What bird appears in both accounts?)

Act out the passages with a partner. Try different interpretations of mood and character.

Write a comparison of the passages.

Hint: Exam boards expect you to be aware of social and historical context. Most of Shakespeare's audience

114

Shakespeare

would find it easy to believe that killing a king – Macbeth's crime against God and nature – would be echoed by unnnatural events. *Julius Caesar* contains similar ideas, but with more emphasis on the events as signs of things to come.

Relationships

Read and compare the following passages. The first comes from *Much Ado About Nothing* (Act 4, Scene 1), the second from *Macbeth* (Act 1, Scene 7). In both a woman tries to persuade a man to kill someone.

BEATRICE I am gone, though I am here; there is no love in you; nay I pray you let me go.

BENEDICT Beatrice –

BEA In faith, I will go.

BEN We'll be friends first.

BEA You dare easier be friends with me than fight with mine enemy.

BEN Is Claudio thine enemy?

BEA Is he not approved in the height a villain, that hath slandered, scorned, dishonoured my kinswoman? O that I were a man! What, bear her in hand until they come to take hands, and then with public accusation, uncovered slander, unmitigated rancour – O God that I were a man! I would eat his heart in the market-place.

BEN Hear me, Beatrice

BEA Talk with a man out at a window! A proper saying!

BEN Nay, but Beatrice –

BEA Sweet Hero! She is wronged, she is slandered, she is undone.

BEN Beat –

BEA Princes and counties! Surely a princely testimony, a goodly count, Count Comfect, a sweet gallant surely! O that I were a man for his sake, or that I had any friend would be a man for my sake! But manhood is melted into curtsies, valour into compliment, and men are only turned into tongue, and trim ones too: he is now as valiant as Hercules that only tells a lie and swears it. I cannot be a man with wishing, therefore I will die a woman with grieving.

BEN Tarry, good Beatrice. By this hand I love thee.

BEA Use it for my love some other way than swearing by it.

BEN Think you in your soul the Count Claudio hath wronged Hero?

BEA Yea, as sure as I have a thought, or a soul.

BEN Enough! I am engaged, I will challenge him.

LADY M Was the hope drunk
  Wherein you dress'd yourself? Hath it slept since?
  And wakes it now, to look so green and pale
  At what it did so freely? From this time
  Such I account thy love. Art thou afeard
  To be the same in thine own act and valour
  As thou art in desire? Wouldst thou have that
  Which thou esteem'st the ornament of life,
  And live a coward in thine own esteem;
  Letting I *dare not* wait upon I *would*,
  Like the poor cat i' the adage?

MACBETH Pr'ythee, peace:
  I dare do all that may become a man;
  Who dares do more is none.

LADY M What beast was't, then,
  That made you break this enterprise to me?
  When you durst do it, then you were a man;
  And, to be more than what you were, you would
  Be so much more the man. Nor time nor place
  Did then adhere, and yet you would make both:
  They have made themselves, and that their fitness now
  Does unmake you. I have given suck, and know
  How tender 'tis to love the babe that milks me:
  I would, while it was smiling in my face,
  Have pluck'd my nipple from his boneless gums,
  And dash'd the brains out, had I so sworn as you
  Have done to this.

MACBETH If we should fail –

Review time

How do these passages, and the two relationships, compare? Make a chart of your ideas.

Section round-up

You've seen how comparisons can help you to focus.

Shakespeare

Themes

About this section

This section suggests ways to approach themes (central ideas) in Shakespeare, focusing on *Romeo and Juliet* and *The Merchant of Venice*.

If you're asked to focus on a play's themes, first draw a diagram of all the themes, and think about how they connect. Look back to the themes you thought of on page 106. ✪ Which of them appear in the play you're studying? You may be asked to deal with a pair of related themes. Sometimes themes are so closely related as to be like two sides of one coin, like those explored in the essay reproduced in part below. Read it now, together with the notes on what's good about it and what could be improved.

'Here's much to do with hate, but more with love.' How are the themes of love and hate presented in 'Romeo and Juliet'? Is it a play about love or hate?

'Romeo and Juliet' is a play that tells a tragic love story that all at once can be an unrealistic, fictional tale of something long ago and far away and a stark, cold example of real life that is easy to relate to. It shows how love and hate can be closely linked and in this story, need one to fuel the other.[1] As Romeo says to Benvolio:

'Here's much to do with hate, but more with love.' Act I, Sc 1

Romeo, after only 172 lines of the play, sums up more or less the whole story. By saying it, Romeo is describing both his unhappy, lovesick mood and the scene of a recent street brawl before him, recognising how similar they are. His love for Rosaline was making him just as unhappy as the hatred around him. He sees how both love and hate are powerful emotions and how either of them can just as easily bring about wreck and ruin, as they can happiness.[2] I want to explore love and hate relationships in the play and see how they are linked to each other and what similarities they have.

The central relationship in the play is of the 'star-crossed lovers', alias Romeo and Juliet. Their love is frenzied and passionate and of course rushed, endangered and cursed from the very start.[3] In fact, the whole relationship, from the meeting and the first kiss to their dramatic and desperate twin suicides, takes place within four days.[4] When they first meet in the house of Capulet, it is love at first sight. I feel that they fall for each other in such a big way for a variety of reasons: the hatred between their two feuding families being one of them. Romeo had just been rejected by Rosaline, which left him vulnerable and susceptible to falling in love; he was on the rebound. Juliet was also vulnerable on account of her being emotionally starved through a lack of love and care from her parents. Another relevant factor was their ages, which would have been reason enough for their impetuous actions and behaviour.[5]

Right from the beginning their love was overshadowed by the hatred going on around them. The love would not have been rushed or secretive if they were not always in constant fear of being found out. It would have developed in the way that was typical to society then, such as a dowry, wooing and the meeting and blessing of parents.[6] Their controversial love was certainly doomed from the start.

'My only love sprung from my only hate.' Act I, Sc 5, Line 135

Juliet says this when she finds that the man that she has met, kissed and subsequently fallen in love with is from an opposing family and that their prodigious love is surely not to be. What she is saying is that the only man she has ever loved happens to be the son of the family she has been bred and taught to hate from birth, in fact her 'only hate'.

Shakespeare

1 Important insight, developed later.

2 Good example of love leading to unhappiness.

3 Should say why 'cursed from the start'. Mention Romeo's misgiving before meeting Juliet (Act 1, end of Scene 4).

4 Timing – good point.

5 Insight into characters' backgrounds.

6 Shows awareness of historical and cultural context.

The essay goes on to comment on: Shakespeare's language; hate and kinship (focusing on Tybalt); and how Juliet gets more love from her nurse than from her parents.

✪ If you're studying *Romeo and Juliet*, how far do you agree with the essay? If not, how do love and hate feature in the play you're studying?

Now read the extract below, from *The Merchant of Venice*, Act 3, Scene 1. It focuses on the theme of Jewishness. ✪ What broader theme does this relate to? What other theme is closely related?

> SHYLOCK: He [Antonio] hath disgraced me and hindered me of half a million; laughed at my losses, mocked at my gains, scorned my nation, thwarted my bargains, cooled my friends, heated mine enemies! and what's his reason? I am a Jew! Hath not a Jew eyes? Hath not a Jew hands, organs, dimensions, senses, affections, passions? Fed with the same food, hurt with the same weapons, subject to the same diseases, healed by the same means, warmed and cooled by the same winter and summer as a Christian is? If you prick us, do we not bleed? If you tickle us, do we not laugh? If you poison us, do we not die? And if you wrong us, shall we not revenge? If we are like you in the rest, we will resemble you in that.

Test yourself

What, according to Shylock, is Antonio's attitude to Jews? What is Shylock's attitude to Christians, and to his own Jewishness? What do you think is Shakespeare's attitude to Jews?

Hint: In Shakespeare's time, Christians believed that money-lending for profit was immoral, and yet they often needed loans for trade. Prejudice against Jews meant that they became money-lenders because other occupations were closed to them. Elizabeth I had a Jewish doctor, Roderigo Lopez, but in 1593 he was accused of trying to poison her, and hanged. In about 1590, Christopher Marlowe wrote a play, *The Jew of Malta*, featuring a villainous Jew.

Section round-up

You've assessed one student's work on themes, and seen how themes can be connected. You've also seen a good example of how a theme can be put in historical context. Well done!

117

Shakespeare

Performance

> **About this section**
>
> This page and the next guide you through what to look for and comment on in a Shakespeare production. Before continuing, think about:
> - In what ways can one production of a play differ from another?
> - What makes a good production?

It is highly desirable for you to see a stage production of the Shakespeare play you're studying. Two productions – or perhaps one stage and one film version – would be even better.

Points to consider

- **Characters**. How does the interpretation of characters compare with how you see them? For example, Macbeth could be seen as a monster or as a victim of evil. Ask yourself how the characters could have been played differently.
- **Acting**. Do the actors seem to fit their parts? Is the acting convincing? Do the actors put energy and meaning into their lines?
- **Set design**. 'Setting' – where the action occurs at any one time – is very important in Shakespeare. Often, a particular type of action and mood is associated with each setting: e.g. *A Midsummer Night's Dream* (a court – law, a wood – magic and nature), *The Merchant of Venice* (Rialto – business, Belmont – love). Does the set design (perhaps enhanced by lighting) reflect the mood?
- **Costumes**. Are they Elizabethan, historically realistic (e.g. togas for *Julius Caesar*), modern? Do they reflect the characters and overall interpretation? Do they enhance the set?
- **Music and sound**. What use is made of music and sound effects to create mood?
- **Updating**. Has the director tried to update the play or give it a new twist? For example, one production of *Macbeth* had Macbeth and his followers as Buddhists, with Macbeth willingly submitting to execution at the end. A production of *Romeo and Juliet* might be set in Northern Ireland, with Protestant and Catholic families.

If considering a film, is it just a screen version of a stage production, or does it make use of realistic settings?

Costume design for Phebe in *As You Like It*

Set design for *As You Like It*

Shakespeare

Task time

Read the extract from a student essay on *Romeo and Juliet*. What impression do you get of the production described? Do you agree with the author's comments? What ideas do you have for a production of this play?

The staging of 'Romeo and Juliet' is exceedingly significant to the way that love and hate are indicated in the storyline. There would have to be contrasting colours for scenes of love and kindness and for malevolence and conflict. (When we saw the play, the company used red and white Spanish costumes and lighting to symbolise the two rival families; they applied red and white for love scenes and red and black for scenes containing hate and violence; I feel that these were good colour choices that gave the right overall effect. I think that red was chosen because it can be both sensual and romantic, yet hateful and threatening at the same time.) Casting is also extremely important for the success of such a play as 'Romeo and Juliet'. For example, the actors playing the two lovers are essentially required to be youthful and good-looking to promote the image of adolescent purity and innocence, which makes it easier to relate to. This leads me to speculate on how they coped in Shakespearian times when only males were permitted on stage.

Consider how the play you're studying should be produced. Make a spider diagram, using the headings given in the case study for the main branches.

Choose a soliloquy to act out on your own, or a dialogue to act out with a partner. Practise different interpretations.

Case study

Review notes for production of *As You Like It*

- **Characters:** Mostly as expected. Orlando and Rosalind as enthusiastic innocents. Perhaps overdone. Not enough difference between two dukes – played by same actor. (Why?) Jaques played as a likeable poser.

- **Acting:** Some scenes too slow, especially Orlando. Oliver excellent – his conversion convincing. Rosalind's breakdown and scream when exiled very moving.

- **Set design:** Should have been a clear distinction between Court and Forest of Arden – wasn't! Dangling model sheep and birdsong didn't quite do it. Scaffolding with lots of wheels – why? Perhaps wheel of fortune?

- **Costumes:** Dark, angular, rigid costumes for court. Exiles in forest done like travellers or New York winos (hats and coats) round cooking-pot. Dazzling contrast of Rosalind's wedding dress at end. Phebe like Little Miss Muffet in Doc Martens boots!

- **Music and sound:** Songs done like a boy band video. Sheep baas by off-stage actors quite amusing. Music and lighting used effectively to capture magic of falling in love.

- **Updating:** New elements introduced – Touchstone the Fool doing impressions of TV comedians (slightly too often). Martext's removal of altar, candles, cloth and six-foot madonna from his suitcase (via a trapdoor!) very funny.

Section round-up

You've now got all the information you need to make an informed judgement on a Shakespeare production, and to write about it for coursework.

Shakespeare

Review

This page pulls together what you've learnt in this chapter. If you've been adding to a spider diagram of the chapter as you've been working through it, use it to remind yourself of what you've learnt. If something doesn't make sense, go back to the appropriate section and skim-read it.

Checklist

Could you now:

		Yes	Not yet
1	Say when Shakespeare uses prose instead of verse? (p. 108)	❑	❑
2	Think of three examples of Shakespeare's plays being influenced by the times in which he lived? (pp. 114–117)	❑	❑
3	Draw a diagram for one major character in a Shakespeare play?	❑	❑
4	Define blank verse, imagery, metaphor, simile, personification, comparison, alliteration, pun? (pp. 108–109)	❑	❑
5	Name the main themes in the play you're studying?	❑	❑
6	List features to focus on in a Shakespeare production? (pp. 118–119)	❑	❑

If your answer to any of these questions is 'Not yet', look back at the pages indicated. If you're still unsure, ask your teacher for help.

Poetry — Chapter 9

Overview

Do you feel faint when poetry is mentioned? Don't worry! There's a lot of it about. Just read this chapter, and you'll soon feel much better. You'll be able to:

- Read poems and get an idea of what they mean.
- Work out the main purpose of a poem.
- Recognise some common types of poem.
- Recognise some of the techniques poets use.
- Explain how poetic techniques add to the meaning of a poem.
- Make helpful notes on the text of poems you are studying.
- Read, talk and write about poems written before this century.
- Read, talk and write about modern poems.
- Identify – and write about – similarities and differences between two poems with a similar subject.
- Prepare yourself for writing about poems from different cultures.
- Write a good piece of coursework about poems you have studied.
- Produce good essays about poems under exam conditions.
- Read poems for fun and pleasure.

When studying poetry, you need to consider format, purpose, language and themes.

Before 1914

About this section

You will read through and analyse two poems on a similar theme, comparing them and looking at a GCSE student's piece of coursework on them.

121

Poetry

Gone but not forgotten

Relax and read through the two poems on the next two pages – 'Remember' by Christina Rossetti and 'Remembrance' by Emily Brontë.

Ignore the comments on *Remembrance* for a few minutes. Then skim-read through the rest of the section to get a feel for what you'll be doing.

> ### Remember
>
> Remember me when I am gone away,
> Gone far away into the silent land;
> When you can no more hold me by the hand,
> Nor I half turn to go yet turning stay.
> Remember me when no more day by day
> You tell me of our future that you planned:
> Only remember me; you understand
> It will be late to counsel then or pray.
> Yet if you should forget me for a while
> And afterwards remember, do not grieve:
> For if the darkness and corruption leave
> A vestige of the thoughts that once I had,
> Better by far you should forget and smile
> Than that you should remember and be sad.

Make a chart to compare the poems, starting with time, characters, setting, form and use of the words 'remember'/'remembrance'.

For your own notes

....

....

....

....

〰️ cold/dead/grief
෴ light/life/happiness

Remembrance

Cold in the earth, and the deep snow piled above thee!
Far, far removed, cold in the dreary grave!
Have I forgot, my Only Love, to love thee,
Severed at last by Time's all-severing wave?

Time making her forget him. Does it?

Now, when alone, do my thoughts no longer hover
Over the mountains, on that northern shore
Testing their wings where heath and fern-leaves cover
Thy noble heart for ever, ever more?

Metaphor she compares her thoughts to flying birds

Cold in the earth, and fifteen wild Decembers
From those brown hills have melted into spring:
Faithful indeed is the spirit that remembers
After such years of change and suffering!

She can't forget. Or, only for a little time

Sweet Love of youth, forgive if I forget thee
While the World's tide is bearing me along:
Sterner desires and darker hopes beset me,
Hopes which obscure, but cannot do thee wrong!

Metaphor she is carried into the future by time, which moves her along just as the sea keeps moving

No later light has lightened up my heaven,
No second morn has ever shone for me;
All my life's bliss from thy dear life was given,
All my life's bliss is in the grave with thee.

But when the days of golden dreams had perished
And even Despair was powerless to destroy
Then did I learn how existence could be cherished,
Strengthened and fed without the aid of joy.

Then did I check the tears of useless passion,
Weaned my young soul from yearning after thine;
Sternly denied its burning wish to hasten
Down to that tomb already more than mine.

She stopped herself from wanting to die + be with him

And even yet, I dare not let it languish,
Dare not indulge in memory's rapturous pain;
Once drinking deep of that divinest anguish,
How could I seek the empty world again?

Poetry

Learn to make notes

Read 'Remembrance' on page 123 again, this time taking notice of the comments added to it to prepare you for the next task.

Now read 'Remember' on page 122 again carefully. You may find it useful to read the words aloud. As you read, make notes on the poem using the notes already made on 'Remembrance' as a guide. You might find it helpful to enlarge the page on a photocopier – it's easier to mark and you can write whatever you like on it in full, glowing colour.

Hints:

- Underline (or highlight) important words and short phrases.
- Jot down words next to your underlinings to explain your thoughts and interpretations.
- A straight line in the margin shows that a whole line of the poem (or more) seems very important.
- Wavy lines to underline words, or in the margin to mark whole lines of the poem, show you find those parts difficult to understand.
- Question marks in the margin mean you find some of the ideas in that part of the poem rather odd, or you disagree with what the poet seems to be saying.
- Exclamation marks in the margin mean you strongly agree, or are especially impressed, with an idea in that part of the poem.
- Different colours could be used to highlight words expressing different emotions, for example yellow for happiness and blue for grief.

Your turn

See what ideas you can add to your chart from page 122 now. Colour code the entries in a way that reflects the colours you used for notes on the text.

In more depth

A television programme about the poetry of Victorian women poets is planned. You have been asked to suggest four visual images for each poem (which could be still pictures, or moving film or video) to be shown on the screen while 'Remember' and 'Remembrance' are read aloud.

Working with others

Discuss ideas with a friend and decide on a total of about ten images which you think would help viewers understand the poems in more depth. Images could include:

- the poets
- suitable settings – specify
- things that suggest the passing of time – clocks, calendars
- abstract images – like coloured patterns which suggest emotions
- symbols such as hearts and roses to suggest love.

For your own notes

Poetry

A student's work

Now you have studied the two poems 'Remember' and 'Remembrance', look at how GCSE student Sophie Woodrow tackles a piece of coursework on the two poems (see pages 122–123). Don't worry if you don't think you could write an essay as good as this one yet – your work will improve with practice. The comments show what your teacher is looking for.

Task

Explain in your own words what the two poems tell us about the poets' thoughts and feelings about death.

A comparison between 'Remembrance' by Emily Brontë and 'Remember' by Christina Rossetti

These two poems are based on the ambivalent [1] theme of death, and convey the feelings of a bereaved lover. Although both poets are speaking directly to their lovers, the obvious difference is that Emily Brontë describes her experiences after the death of her lover, while Christina Rossetti is imagining her own death, and what effect it might have on her lover. Neither poem describes death in a graphic or direct way, rather they use images of love, time and place, to convey the grief and recovery process which happens when a loved one dies. [2]

In both poems images of time act as metaphors for the divide created [3] between someone who has died, and the living. This is evocatively described by Brontë as "Time's all severing wave". This sentiment appears in Rossetti's poem, as the worry that time will cause her lover to forget her after her death, this is apparent in the reiteration of the words "Remember me", throughout the poem. [4]

The theme of place links strongly to images of time within each poem, as physical distance is something which can also separate two people. Rossetti describes herself as "gone far away", while Brontë talks in a similar way of her lover as "Far, far removed". While

describing this physical distance, both poets also convey to the reader that spiritual planes of thought can transcend physical ones. Rossetti writes in the hope that she can remain in her lover's imagination after her death; Brontë shows the power of her spiritual love by describing her thoughts as hovering, "over the mountains, on that northern shore". [5]

Brontë creates a strong atmospheric setting in "Remembrance" through reference to landscapes and the seasons. The poem is given a mournful tone through the use of images describing her lover's grave, it is "cold in the earth" covered over in "deep snow", and set in a "nothern shore", giving a strong impression of the sorrow she feels when she thinks of her lover. [6]

As Rossetti imagins her lover after her death, and the things he will loose with her, she builds a lucid picture of the relationship they share in the present. Yet she sees a time ... "When you can no longer hold me by the hand", nor "Tell me of the things you planned", she describes the things that occur "day by day", realising that a time will come when "It will be late to counsel then or pray". She creates for the reader the image of a bonding relationship, and what happens when death and time sever those bonds. [7]

---

1   This is an odd word to use – don't try too hard to be clever! Otherwise a good introduction which says what you are going to write about.

2   The two poems are being compared and points about similarities and differences made.

3   Awareness of imagery.

4   Awareness of language, apt quotation, recognition of the use of the technique of repetition.

5   Recognition of how the poets feel and what they are trying to express.

6   Awareness of atmosphere.

7   More sound analysis of the effect of language and the passage of time.

125

Poetry

Although "Remembrance" is a poem about a death, it can be described as essentially a love poem, written with elegiac qualities. This is shown in the startling contrast between images associated with love and death, throughout the poem. Brontë describes her life in the past with her lover as "golden dreams", then carries on to say that with his death, the dreams have "perished". Her life with him has been "bliss", but has now lost all meaning. She uses the metaphor ... "All my lives bliss is in the grave with thee", to convey this. She also expresses her devotion by saying ... "No later light has lighted up my ~~life~~ heaven". The repetition of the word "No" in the first two lines of the fifth verse, followed by the repetition of the contrasting word "All", is a technique which emphasises the absoluteness of her love. These contrasts in imagery create a very strong, yet tender feeling of her love. [8]

"Remember" as the title of Rossetti's poem appears almost as a command, then again, the repetition of the words "Remember me", serves to enforce this feeling. In the first eight lines the poet is forcefully concerned that her lover should "Remember", in the last six lines, however, she offers us a strange contradiction to this. She states that it would be "Better by far" that her lover should "forget" her, and "smile", than "remember and be sad".

The structure of this poem, is traditional sonnet form, which Rossetti has used purposely to ~~its~~ emphasise the progression of thought in the poem; the first eight

lines are about remembering, while the last six, with a different rhythm, are about forgetting. This shows the journey from grief to recovery, in the bereavement of her lover. [9]

The concise structure of "Remembrance" charts the poet's grieving process, from the time when her lover died fifteen years ago, then how time has made memory uncertain, as the "world's tide" bears her along. Acknowledging this natural tendency, she asks ... "Have I forgot my only love to love thee?"

She relates her gradual gaining of strength, as she learns that "existence could be cherished, strengthened and fed without the aid of joy". In the last verse she resists the temptation to "indulge in memories rapturous pain". Knowing that she must look forward to the future even though she can only see the world as empty.

In her poem "Remember", Rossetti also makes this realisation. In the first part of the poem she demonstrates the theory that in life you look forward .... "day by day you tell me of the future that you planned", while it is death that makes you look through the "darkness and corruption", into the "silent land" of those who can only exist in the past.

Of the two poems Brontë's relates most clearly the emotions of grief and recovery. "Remember", seems to touch more lightly on these themes, not exploring them in such depth, or using such lucid imagery to communicate its message. [10]

---

8 Perceptive analysis of the effect of poetic techniques.

9 Recognition of poetic form and its appropriateness to what is being expressed.

10 Conclusion sums up but could go further.

A well-structured essay. The ideas in the main body of the essay are organised in paragraphs – and each point made is supported by evidence from the poem.

The student's personal response to the poems is backed up by her insight into their meaning. She has explained the choices the poets have made about what kind of verse form to use and why this suits each poem's message. She remembers to talk about the language of the poems and the use of some poetic techniques, with explanations of how these communicate the poet's ideas and feelings. The conclusion could go further.

✪ Did you have a preference for one poem or the other?

Section round-up

Look back at the list of points in the overview section on page 121 and see if you feel more confident that you can tackle some of those points.

Poetry

Modern poetry

About this section

You will be studying just one longer poem. It is called 'Not My Best Side' by U. A. Fanthorpe, and is about the three characters you can see in the painting of *Saint George and the Dragon* by Paolo Uccello (1397–1475).

Different voices

Take a good, long look at the painting, then read the poem on page 128, and skim-read the rest of the section. Start a diagram with the sections: dragon, virgin, St George and horse. Add notes to each of these headings.

Uccello: *Saint George and the Dragon*, The National Gallery

Poetry

Not My Best Side

I

Not my best side, I'm afraid.
The artist didn't give me a chance to
Pose properly, and as you can see,
Poor chap, he had this obsession with
Triangles, so he left off two of my
Feet. I didn't comment at the time
(What, after all, are two feet
To a monster?) but afterwards
I was sorry for the bad publicity.
Why, I said to myself, should my conqueror
Be so ostentatiously beardless, and ride
A horse with a deformed neck and square
  hoofs?
Why should my victim be so
Unattractive as to be inedible,
And why should she have me literally
On a string? I don't mind dying
Ritually, since I always rise again,
But I should have liked a little more blood
To show they were taking me seriously.

II

It's hard for a girl to be sure if
She wants to be rescued. I mean; I quite
Took to the dragon. It's nice to be
Liked, if you know what I mean. He was
So nicely physical, with his claws
And lovely green skin, and that sexy tail,
And the way he looked at me,
He made me feel he was all ready to
Eat me. And any girl enjoys that.
So when this boy turned up, wearing
  machinery,
On a really *dangerous* horse, to be honest,
I didn't much fancy him. I mean,
What was he like underneath the hardware?
He might have acne, blackheads or even
Bad breath for all I could tell, but the dragon –
Well, you could see all his equipment
At a glance. Still, what could I do?
The dragon got himself beaten by the boy,
And a girl's got to think of her future.

III

I have diplomas in Dragon
Management and Virgin Reclamation.
My horse is the latest model, with
Automatic transmission and built-in
Obsolescence. My spear is custom-built,
And my prototype armour
Still on the secret list. You can't
Do better than me at the moment.
I'm qualified and equipped to the
Eyebrow. So why be difficult?
Don't you want to be killed and/or rescued
In the most contemporary way? Don't
You want to carry out the roles
That sociology and myth have designed for
  you?
Don't your realise that, by being choosy,
You are endangering job-prospects
In the spear- and horse-building industries?
What, in any case, does it matter what
You want? You're in my way.

Focus your thoughts

Does the poem make you see the painting differently? In what way?

Hint: Does the poem make the characters come to life? Can you imagine yourself there? Does it help you to form an opinion about any of the figures?

Re-read the poem, making notes on the text (to remind yourself how to do this, look again at page 124).

Read section I of the poem – then look at the dragon in the painting. It might help to enlarge the picture on a photocopier.

Read section II – then look at the virgin.

Read section III – then look at the knight.

How does the title of the poem relate to all three characters? Does it have more than one meaning? Note down your thoughts in the margin next to the title.

Add to your diagram, summing up your main impressions of the appearance, thoughts and personalities of dragon – virgin – knight.

Poetry

Focus on form

The poet makes use of a form called **dramatic monologue** – that is, the poet writes in the voice of a particular character, not herself. One poetry critic, Simon Rae, said that 'capturing another person's voice convincingly is not easy, and Fanthorpe gets mixed results from the form.'

Underline all the words the dragon uses which give you the impression that he is quite an educated and intellectual character.

Underline all the words the virgin uses which show she is silly, self-centred and judges others on their outward appearance only.

Underline all the words the knight uses which show he is obsessed with his qualifications and equipment. Where do jargon words similar to the ones he speaks occur in real life?

Now look carefully at the way the lines of the poem are broken up. Fanthorpe makes use of a technique called *enjambement* – where the sense of what she is saying is split between two or more lines of the poem. Sometimes this means that a line of the poem will begin with one or two words which are the end of a sentence. It helps to emphasise those words and draws your attention to them. Underline three examples of this from each section of the poem (there are nine examples altogether).

Imitate the form

Write the dramatic monologue the horse might have added to the other three voices of the poem.

- **Make sure he has a distinctive character reflected in his choice of words.**
- **Make sure he comments on his feelings about each of the other three characters in the picture.**
- **Try to imitate Fanthorpe's distinctive use of enjambement.**

Working with others

Working with a friend, interview one, or more, of the characters from the painting as if they are guests on a television chat show. The interviewer's questions should:

- **get them talking about their experience of events before and at the time of the scene shown in the painting**
- **ask them to give their opinions of each other.**

The characters' answers should reflect the personality, opinions and manner they are shown to have in the poem.

Make comparisons

How effective do you find U. A. Fanthorpe's dramatic monologues in this poem? Compare the three characters she has created, commenting on the differences between the way each talks about him or herself.

Hint: In your writing, you may wish to comment on:

- What a dramatic monologue is, and where the original idea for the poem is to be found.
- How the language used in the three sections of the poem helps to communicate the personalities, opinions and feelings of the three characters.
- How Fanthorpe's use of enjambement draws the reader's attention to specific words and ideas in the poem.
- Your personal response to the poem – did you enjoy it? Does the use of dramatic monologue work? Are the three characters Fanthorpe has created convincingly different?

For your own notes

....

....

....

....

....

....

....

Section round-up

You have examined a witty, modern poem, tried out different poetic techniques yourself, and perhaps had some fun.

Poetry

Valentines

> **About this section**
>
> You will look at two poems which express similar ideas within a different form. They are 'I Wouldn't Thank You for a Valentine' by Liz Lochhead and 'Valentine' by Carol Ann Duffy. Read both poems several times before you try to answer the questions.

I Wouldn't Thank You for a Valentine

(Rap)
I wouldn't thank you for a Valentine
I won't wake up early wondering if the postman's been.
Should 10 red-padded satin hearts arrive with a sticky sickly saccharine
Sentiments in very vulgar verses I wouldn't wonder if you meant them.
Two dozen anonymous Interflora roses?
I'd not bother to swither over who sent them!
I wouldn't thank you for a Valentine.

Scrawl SWALK across the envelope
I'd just say 'Same Auld Story
I canny be bothered deciphering it –
I'm up to here with Amore!
The whole Valentine's Day Thing is trivial and commercial,
A cue for unleashing clichés and candyheart motifs to which I personally am not partial.'
Take more than singing Telegrams, or pints of Chanel Five, or sweets,
To get me ordering oysters or ironing my black satin sheets.
I wouldn't thank you for a Valentine.

If you sent me a solitaire and promises solemn,
Took out an ad in the Guardian Personal Column
Saying something very soppy such as 'Who loves ya, Poo?
I'll tell you, I do, Fozzy Bear, that's who!'
You'd entirely fail to charm me, in fact I'd detest it
I wouldn't be eighteen again for anything, I'm glad I'm past it.
I wouldn't thank you for a Valentine.

If you sent me a single orchid, or a pair of Janet Reger's in a heart-shaped box and declared your Love Eternal
I'd say I'd not be caught dead in them they were politically suspect and I'd rather something thermal.
If you hired a plane and blazed our love in a banner across the skies;
If you bought me something flimsy in a flatteringly wrong size;
If you sent me a postcard with three Xs and told me how you felt
I wouldn't thank you, I'd melt.

Thanks, but no thanks

List the images used in Liz Lochhead's poem.

What is the effect of alliteration (repetition of the first sound or sounds in a word) in this poem?

Notice that this poem is written in Rap. How does the rap rhythm affect the poem?

Hint: Read through the poem aloud and check line endings. Which rhyme, and is this consistent through each **verse**/**stanza**? How well do you think this kind of verse form suits the poem's message?

Poetry

Valentine

Not a red rose or a satin heart.

I give you an onion.
It is a moon wrapped in brown paper.
It promises light
like the careful undressing of love.

Here.
It will blind you with tears
like a lover.
It will make your reflection
a wobbling photo of grief.

I am trying to be truthful.

Not a cute card or a kissogram.

I give you an onion.
Its fierce kiss will stay on your lips,
possessive and faithful
as we are,
for as long as we are.

Take it.
Its platinum loops shrink to a wedding-ring,
if you like.
Lethal.
Its scent will cling to your fingers,
cling to your knife.

Veggie Valentine

What qualities in the onion does Carol Ann Duffy bring out to suggest that it is a fitting token of love?

Comment on these images:

- 'a moon wrapped in brown paper'
- 'a wobbling photo of grief'
- 'platinum loops.'

Comment on the structure of 'Valentine'.

Hint: How many parts does the poem divide into? What effect do the single lines have on the tone of sincerity the poet is trying to express? What do you notice about each stanza? How is the theme of the poem developed by its structure?

Comparisons

What similarities and differences do you notice between the two poems?

What images do the poets prefer? Which do they object to and why?

A television programme about modern women poets is planned. Suggest four visual images for each poem (which could be still pictures, or moving film or video) to be shown on the screen while these two poems are being read.

Across time

Look back to the two poems, 'Remember' and 'Remembrance' on pages 122 and 123. Pick out five things which are similar and five things which are different in the two pairs of poems from two different centuries.

Could these two Valentine's poems have been by the Victorian poets? Could the two earlier poems, 'Remember' and 'Remembrance', have been written now? What makes each pair of poems characteristic of the age in which they were written?

Which of the four poems do you prefer and why? Discuss with a friend.

Section round-up

You have looked at similarities and differences in several poems and considered their imagery in some depth.

Poetry

Using your senses

About this section

You will be reading two poems by Seamus Heaney: 'Digging' and 'The Early Purges'. Skim-read both pages, take a look at the tasks and then read the poems.

Digging

Between my finger and my thumb
The squat pen rests; snug as a gun.

Under my window, a clean rasping sound
When the spade sinks into gravelly ground:
My father, digging. I look down

Till his straining rump among the flowerbeds
Bends low, comes up twenty years away
Stooping in rhythm through potato drills
Where he was digging.

The coarse boot nestled on the lug, the shaft
Against the inside knee was levered firmly.
He rooted out tall tops, buried the bright edge deep
To scatter new potatoes that we picked
Loving their cool hardness in our hands.

By God, the old man could handle a spade.
Just like his old man.

My grandfather cut more turf in a day
Than any other man on Toner's bog.
Once I carried him milk in a bottle
Corked sloppily with paper. He straightened up
To drink it, then fell to right away

Nicking and slicing neatly, heaving sods
Over his shoulder, going down and down
For the good turf. Digging.

The cold smell of potato mould, the squelch and slap
Of soggy peat, the curt cuts of an edge
Through living roots awaken in my head.
But I've no spade to follow men like them.

Between my finger and my thumb
The squat pen rests.
I'll dig with it.

The Early Purges

I was six when I first saw kittens drown.
Dan Taggart pitched them, 'the scraggy wee shits',
Into a bucket; a frail metal sound,

Soft paws scraping like mad. But their tiny din
Was soon soused. They were slung on the snout
Of the pump and the water pumped in.

'Sure isn't it better for them now?' Dan said.
Like wet gloves they bobbed and shone till he sluiced
Them out on the dunghill, glossy and dead.

Suddenly frightened, for days I sadly hung
Round the yard, watching the three sogged remains
Turn mealy and crisp as old summer dung

Until I forgot them. But the fear came back
When Dan trapped big rats, snared rabbits, shot crows
Or, with a sickening tug, pulled old hens' necks.

Still, living displaces false sentiments
And now, when shrill pups are prodded to drown
I just shrug, 'Bloody pups'. It makes sense:

'Prevention of cruelty' talk cuts ice in town
Where they consider death unnatural,
But on well-run farms pests have to be kept down.

Poetry

Focus on the five senses

Re-read the poems, underlining or highlighting with five different colours the details which appeal to the five senses of sight, hearing, touch, smell and taste.

In the margins, note down where Heaney uses alliteration (repetition of the first sound or sounds in a word) or onomatopoeia (words which imitate a sound). Decide why he does this. Is it to draw attention to, or emphasise, important words? Or is it to make you imagine what he heard himself at the time?

Now look for places in the poems where Heaney uses similes (comparisons where you say something is like or the same as something else: look for the key words, *like* and *as*).

When Heaney uses similes, are the comparisons aimed to appeal to one of the five senses, to help the reader imagine more vividly how something looked or what it felt like to touch? Note down your thoughts in the margin.

Read through the poems – and your own notes – one more time. Draw a diagram, collecting together words and drawings of ideas from the poems for each of the five senses.

Review and talk

Which details appealing to one of your five senses help to make Heaney's description of his memories more vivid?

The final five or six lines of both these poems move on from Heaney's memories. He explains how the experiences he tells of affect his thoughts and beliefs now. What does he say at the end of 'The Early Purges'? How does his attitude differ from his reaction as a child? How does the title of the poem relate to this experience?

Now re-read the ending of 'Digging'. Can you make any sense of the metaphor in the last line (when he says he will 'dig' with his pen – comparing it with his father's spade)?

What is he explaining about how his life is different from, but also similar to, the way his father and grandfather lived?

Review and write

Spend a maximum of 40 minutes writing an essay to answer the question below and aim to write about two sides of A4. If you're really short of time, make an essay plan of what you would include in your answer. It may be worthwhile to write one or two paragraphs using this plan.

In both these poems Heaney uses words to describe what he experiences with his senses – things he sees, hears, smells and touches. Explain how these details help you to imagine the events and how the poet feels about them.

Hint: You may wish to write about:

- how the poems recapture memories and link them with the present
- details which appeal to the different senses – and how these are sometimes added to by other techniques such as similes and onomatopoeia
- how the experiences described change the way Heaney thinks and feels
- how you respond to the events and ideas described in each poem.

Section round-up

You have compared two poems by the same poet concentrating on the poetic devices he uses to achieve his effects.

For your own notes

....

....

....

....

....

....

....

Poetry

Encounters with animals

About this section

You will prepare yourself for writing about poems from different cultures in the exam and for coursework.

Skim-read both poems, take a look at the tasks, then read the poems more closely. They are: 'The Field-Mouse' by Gillian Clarke and 'Night of the Scorpion' by Nissim Ezekiel.

The Field-Mouse

Summer, and the long grass is a snare drum.
The air hums with jets.
Down at the end of the meadow,
far from the radio's terrible news,
we cut the hay. All afternoon
its wave breaks before the tractor blade.
Over the hedge our neighbour travels his field
in a cloud of lime, drifting our land
with a chance gift of sweetness.

The child comes running through the killed
    flowers,
his hands a nest of quivering mouse,
its black eyes two sparks burning.
We know it will die and ought to finish it off.
It curls in agony big as itself
and the star goes out in its eye.
Summer in Europe, the field's hurt,
and the children kneel in long grass,
staring at what we have crushed.

Before day's done the field lies bleeding,
the dusk garden inhabited by the saved voles,
frogs, a nest of mice. The wrong that woke
from a rumour of pain won't heal,
and we can't face the newspapers.
All night I dream the children dance in grass,
their bones brittle as mouse-ribs, the air
stammering with gunfire, my neighbour turned
stranger, wounding my land with stones.

Night of the Scorpion

I remember the night my mother
was stung by a scorpion. Ten hours
of steady rain had driven him
to crawl beneath a sack of rice.
Parting with his poison – flash
of diabolic tail in the dark room –
he risked the rain again.
The peasants came like swarms of flies
and buzzed the name of God a hundred times
to paralyse the Evil One.
With candles and with lanterns
throwing giant scorpion shadows
on the mud-baked walls
they searched for him: he was not found.
They clicked their tongues.
With every movement that the scorpion made
his poison moved in Mother's blood, they said.
May he sit still, they said. May the sins of your
    previous birth
be burned away tonight, they said.
May your suffering decrease
the misfortunes of your next birth, they said.
May the sum of evil
balanced in this unreal world
against the sum of good
become diminished by your pain.
May the poison purify your flesh
of desire, and your spirit of ambition,
they said, and they sat around
on the floor with my mother in the centre,
the peace of understanding on each face.
More candles, more lanterns, more neighbours,
more insects, and the endless rain.
My mother, twisted through and through,
groaning on a mat.
My father, sceptic, rationalist,
trying every curse and blessing,
powder, mixture, herb and hybrid.
He even poured a little paraffin
upon the bitten toe and put a match to it.
I watched the flame feeding on my mother.
I watched the holy man perform his rites
to tame the poison with an incantation.
After twenty hours
it lost its sting.

My mother only said
Thank God the scorpion picked on me
and spared my children.

Poetry

The Field-Mouse

Highlight the events that the poet experiences during 'The Field-Mouse' at different times of the day.

Underline details from each stanza which remind us of events taking place away from the immediate setting of this poem.

What connections does the poet make between these two sets of events – especially in the final four lines of the poem?

Night of the Scorpion

Highlight the events the poet tells you about at the beginning of 'Night of the Scorpion' which explain how his mother was stung.

The middle of the poem tells of various ideas people tried, to stop the poison affecting the mother. Underline:

- three things the neighbours did
- two things the father did
- two things the priest did.

What do you think cured her in the end?

Circle two words or phrases the poet uses to describe the neighbours, his father and the priest which communicate his different opinions of these people and their behaviour. Who does he seem to be criticising the most?

Focus your thoughts

Highlight important words and phrases in both poems. Make brief notes on the text of your associations with these words.

Make a chart of similarities and differences you notice in these two poems.

Add details to your chart about the customs and beliefs of each poet's culture.

Finally, look again at the way each poem ends and make sure your chart records the similarity between the women's reactions.

Task time

Write the dialogue that these two women might have if they meet. Their conversation will bring out the similarities and differences in the poems and could include:

- how the season of the year led to their memorable encounter with an animal
- what happened at that moment, and how each felt
- what happened afterwards – the way other people react to what happened
- how the experiences brought out feelings of mother-love – and how these feelings bridge their different cultures.

Write a paragraph explaining which poem made the biggest impression on you and why.

For your own notes

....
....
....
....
....

Section round-up

In this section you have had an opportunity to bring together most of the techniques for looking at poetry that you have covered in the previous pages. Well done!

135

Poetry

Drafting

About this section

You will be preparing to write about the development of William Blake's poetry for coursework, or to compare ideas expressed in two contrasting poems as part of the exam.

This final section on poetry is a little different from the others. Here you will be able to see the process of drafting that Blake went through in the writing of his famous poem, 'The Tyger', as well as reading the final versions of both 'The Tyger' and its partner poem, 'The Lamb'.

Skim-read this section, read the various versions of the poem, and take a look at the tasks you will be completing.

1   First Draft

The Tyger

Tyger Tyger burning bright
In the forests of the night
What immortal hand or eye
~~Dare Could~~ frame thy fearful symmetry

~~Burnt in~~
~~In what~~ distant deeps or skies
~~The cruel~~ ~~Burnt the~~ fire of thine eyes
On what wings dare he aspire
What the hand dare seize the fire

And what shoulder & what art
Could twist the sinews of thy heart
And when thy heart began to beat
What dread hand & what dread feet

~~Could fetch it from the furnace deep~~
~~And in thy horrid ribs dare steep~~
~~In the well of sanguine woe~~
~~In what clay & in what mould~~
~~Were thy eyes of fury roll'd~~

Where   where
~~What~~ the hammer ~~what~~ the chain
In what furnace was thy brain

                    dread grasp
What the anvil what ~~arm~~
~~arm grasp clasp~~
Dare ~~Could~~ its deadly terrors
~~clasp~~

        ~~grasp~~ clasp

Tyger tyger burning bright
In the forests of the night
What immortal hand & eye
                    frame
Dare ~~form~~ thy fearful symmetry

2   Additions to the First Draft

On the opposite page of Blake's notebook there is another draft of the second stanza, all of it crossed out, and a draft of a stanza he had added to his first draft.

Burnt in distant deeps or skies
The cruel fire of thine eyes
Could heart descend or wings aspire
What the hand dare seize the fire

    dare he ~~smile laugh~~
And ~~did he laugh~~ his work to see

        ankle
~~What the shoulder what the knee~~
Dare
~~Did~~ he who made the lamb make thee
When the stars threw down their spears
And water'd heaven with their tears

136

Poetry

3 Second Draft

Tyger Tyger burning bright
In the forests of the night
What immortal hand & eye
Dare frame thy fearful symmetry

And what shoulder & what art
Could twist the sinews of thy heart
And when thy heart began to beat
What dread hand & what dread feet

When the stars threw down their spears
And water'd heaven with their tears
Did he smile his work to see
Did he who made the lamb make thee

Tyger Tyger burning bright
In the forests of the night
What immortal hand & eye
Dare frame thy fearful symmetry

4 Final Version
The Tyger

Tyger! Tyger! burning bright
In the forests of the night,
What immortal hand or eye
Could frame thy fearful symmetry?

In what distant deeps or skies
Burnt the fire of thine eyes?
On what wings dare he aspire?
What the hand dare seize the fire?

And what shoulder, & what art,
Could twist the sinews of thy heart?
And when thy heart began to beat,
What dread hand? & what dread feet?

What the hammer? what the chain?
In what furnace was thy brain?
What the anvil? what dread grasp
Dare its deadly terrors clasp?

When the stars threw down their spears,
And water'd heaven with their tears,
Did he smile his work to see?
Did he who made the Lamb make thee?

Tyger! Tyger! burning bright
In the forests of the night,
What immortal hand or eye
Dare frame thy fearful symmetry?

Focus on 'The Tyger'

Work through these questions with a friend and make notes about your ideas on the text of each draft of the poem.

Re-read the final version of 'The Tyger' a couple of times – preferably aloud.

Now read the first draft – especially the original fourth stanza, which is completely crossed out. Notice that the first line of this crossed-out stanza actually completes the question: 'What dread hand and what dread feet/ Could fetch it from the furnace deep?'

Why do you think Blake got rid of this stanza? Does it leave the end of the third stanza not making sense? Does it sound unfinished? Or does it have a new meaning?

Look at the places where Blake is undecided whether to use *could* or *dare* in the first draft. In the final draft he uses 'could' at the beginning of the poem and 'dare' at the end. Why do you think he decided to do this? What change of feeling about 'The Tyger' does it show?

Read through the additions to the first draft. Compare this version of the second stanza with the first and final drafts. Why do you think Blake thought it was not as good as his first draft? How is its meaning slightly altered by the changes in the words?

Read the new stanza added to the first draft. How does this create a gentler tone in the poem – especially if you compare it with the stanza removed from the first draft?

Compare the second draft with the final draft. In particular, read the final draft stanzas two and four. How does missing these out alter the tone of the poem?

137

Poetry

Read the final draft, aloud, once more. Sum up in three keywords how Blake feels when he imagines the 'tyger'.

Create an illustrative diagram which explores ideas in 'The Tyger', including sketches of some of the memorable visual images of fire, forests, heaven, Earth and parts of the body.

Review and write

Studying the different drafts of 'The Tyger' not only helps us to understand Blake's feelings about the animal and its Creator more fully, it also gives us an idea of how his feelings altered as he moved towards the final draft.

Using your notes and your diagram, explain how your study of the draft versions has helped you to see more clearly what Blake is saying in this poem. You may wish to write about:

- how stanzas which were added or deleted alter the meaning of the poem
- how alteration of a single word may sometimes change the meaning of a line, or a stanza
- different feelings about the 'tyger', comparing the first to the final draft
- different feelings about the Creator of the 'tyger', comparing the first to the final draft
- your personal response to the poem, and the thought Blake put into writing it.

For your own notes

....
....
....
....
....
....
....

The Lamb

(Innocence)

    Little Lamb, who made thee?
    Dost thou know who made thee?
Gave thee life, and bid thee feed,
By the stream and o'er the mead?
Gave thee clothing of delight,
Softest clothing, woolly, bright?
Gave thee such a tender voice,
Making all the vales rejoice?
    Little Lamb, who made thee?
    Dost thou know who made thee?

    Little Lamb, I'll tell thee,
    Little Lamb, I'll tell thee:
He is called by thy name,
For he calls Himself a Lamb.
He is meek, and He is mild;
He became a little child.
I a child, and thou a lamb,
We are called by His name.
    Little Lamb, God bless thee!
    Little Lamb, God bless thee!

Poetry

Innocence and Experience

'The Tyger' is just one of many paired poems which Blake included in a book called *Songs of Innocence and Experience*. Before you study its pair, 'The Lamb', it will probably help to think about the words *Innocence* and *Experience*.

For each word, make a list of the words and images you associate with it.

You may like to consider which list some of these words belong to:

fear wonder dark trust hate joy awe love
sorrow little curse gentle adult dread bless
death hope light massive

Which list does 'The Tyger' belong to? Why? How many of your own words and images are similar to those in the poem?

Focus on contrasts

Read 'The Lamb', aloud, a couple of times. Which words and images in your list are similar to those in the poem?

Notice that both poems include many questions. Is their subject matter different? Are any of them answered? Do they have a different effect on the tone of each poem? Add notes on both texts which make these differences of tone and meaning clear to you.

Review and talk

Working with a partner, debate which of the Creators of the two animals you might feel more inclined to worship.

Hint: You will find plenty of evidence in the two poems which makes it clear how you would benefit by being looked after or protected. You might also wish to consider which Creator more deserves respect, and which one's world you would find more interesting to live in.

Review and write

Use your lists and annotations as the basis for an essay. You should spend a maximum of 40 minutes on the essay below and aim to write about two sides of A4. Here is the title:

> *What important differences are shown between the makers of the tiger and the lamb – and the animals themselves?*

Hint: You may wish to comment on:

- how the animals are described and how this affects your feelings about each one
- what the poems tell us about the differences between the animals' Creators
- how ideas of innocence and experience are linked with the animals and their Creators
- any interesting words and phrases bringing out these ideas
- how your interpretation of the poems changed as you re-read, and compared them to each other
- which of the poems made more of an impression on you and why.

Section round-up

Now you have considered the anatomy of a poem from first draft to final version. You should have improved your skill at looking into similarities and differences in pairs of poems.

139

Poetry

Review

Well done! You have reached the end of the poetry chapter. If you have worked your way through it carefully, you should be able to say 'Yes' to some of the questions below.

Checklist

Can you:

		Yes	Not yet
1	Read and re-read poems until you understand at least some of them?	❏	❏
2	Say what dramatic monologue is? (p. 129)	❏	❏
3	Imitate the form of some poems? (p. 129)	❏	❏
4	Say what enjambement is? (p. 129)	❏	❏
5	Understand some of the processes that go on in drafting a poem? (pp. 136–139)	❏	❏
6	See how changing a few words or lines can alter the tone of a poem? (pp. 136–139)	❏	❏
7	Recognise some of the techniques poets use?	❏	❏
8	Explain how poetic techniques add to the meaning of a poem?	❏	❏
9	Make helpful notes on the text of poems you are studying?	❏	❏
10	Read, talk and write about poems written before 1914? (pp. 122–126)	❏	❏
11	Read, talk and write about modern poems? (pp. 127–129)	❏	❏
12	Identify – and write about – similarities and differences between two poems with a similar subject? (pp. 130–131)	❏	❏
13	Identify – and write about – similarities and differences between two poems written by the same poet? (pp. 132–133)	❏	❏
14	Feel confident writing about poems from different cultures?	❏	❏
15	Write a good piece of coursework about poems you have studied?	❏	❏
16	Enjoy poetry?	❏	❏

If your answer is 'Not yet' to any of these, look back at the appropriate sections to remind yourself. If you're still unsure, ask your teacher for help.

Drafting and proofing — Chapter 10

Overview

This chapter focuses on improving written work by drafting and proofreading. It looks at the 'mechanics' of English, especially spelling and punctuation. It covers:

- Drafting.
- Sequencing and paragraphing.
- Proofreading.
- Punctuation.
- Spelling.

Why do we need to do it?

Few good pieces of writing find their way into print exactly as they were first written. Writers change their minds. They write a 'first draft', and then put it aside for a while. When they look at it again, they can see much more clearly where they've made mistakes, and how the first draft can be improved. Look back to pages 136–137 for an example. In an exam you won't have time to draft and redraft a whole essay, although you may find it worth drafting the first and last paragraphs.

'Proofreading' is the checking stage when you know you've got your writing more or less right – paragraphs in order, arguments (or, in a story, events) linked together, quotations in place. You give it a final read for spelling, punctuation and grammar – in fact, the things you'll find in the grid below. To identify your weaknesses, check at least ten pages of your **marked** written work. Whenever you find a mistake of the kind listed in the grid, make a mark in pencil (so you can re-use it to check your progress). Then total your mistakes to see where you need to focus.

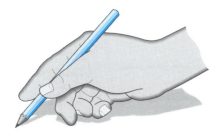

Mistakes made	How often	Total
Capitals omitted for 'I', names or new sentence		
Commas used where there should be a new sentence		
Apostrophes of ownership (e.g. *boy's/boys'*)		
Contractions (e.g. *don't, can't, didn't*)		
Word confusions (e.g. *their/there; accept/except*)		
Misuse of ible/able/uble (e.g. *possible/impassable*)		
Single/double letter spellings (e.g. *access*)		
Plurals misspelt (e.g. *tomatoes, daisies*)		
Other spellings		
Awkward word order		

Drafting and proofing

Write first time

Here's a drafting exercise. Read the passage below (out loud if it helps) and see what's been changed in the first paragraph, and why. Then redraft the remainder.
Sequencing and **paragraphing** are important.
Sequencing is putting ideas – and therefore sentences and paragraphs – in order.

Paragraphs divide writing into manageable sections. Begin a new one wherever there is a major step forward in your sequence of ideas or events. Use shorter paragraphs for web pages or leaflets.

Drafting exercise

In the unchecked text below, you will need to move one sentence, and insert one paragraph break. If you change a phrase in a sentence, make sure that the sentence still makes sense. (Suggested new version on page 149.)

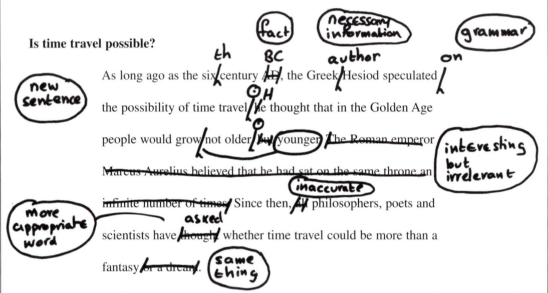

Time travel would be in theory possible if we could travel at speeds approaching the speed of light. Einstein also proved that gravity warps space itself, and that, since time can only be measured relative to space, in a sense it warps time. In fact it has been shown that if one of a pair of very accurate atomic clocks is flown at high speed round the world, it fell slightly behind the one left behind. Einstein proved that time, at the speed of light, stands still. Physicist Stephen Hawking reckons that time travel could take place inside 'black holes' in space. Gravity is so strong that nothing can escape its pull, and space is infinitely warped. This kind of time travel could only take us forward in time. Most people agree that backward time travel is unquestionable because of the 'grandmother paradox', this states that time travel cannot occur because if you went back you could, in theory, kill your granny and never get born.

Drafting and proofing

Proofreading

About this section

This section focuses on the final stage of checking your written work. It suggests ways to increase your accuracy and improve your presentation.

What is proofreading?

If you're writing coursework, proofreading comes after the second draft. At this point you should be looking mainly for mistakes in spelling, punctuation and grammar. However, you may still come across bigger problems, such as a paragraph that needs to be moved or deleted. If so, or if you spot a lot of minor errors,

you'll need to produce another draft – at least of any pages affected. If you've word-processed your work, this will be a relatively easy task. But do keep a copy of the original file as a back-up. If using *Word*, you may find the 'Track Changes' option helpful (on Tools menu). Ask your teacher if any of your coursework has to be handwritten.

In an exam, allow 5–10 minutes to proofread. If you find that a whole section needs to be moved, mark it clearly with an arrow.

Proofreading exercise

In the piece below, the first paragraph has been proofread. Correct the rest yourself. Look especially for the types of mistake listed on page 141. If you're uncertain of spellings, check them in a dictionary. If you can't remember how dialogue is punctuated, find some in a novel. (Check your corrected version carefully against the one on page 149.)

Ian had planned to take julie to a indian restaraunt near there office. By six oclock he was wandering what to wear, by seven he was allready geting nervous. Its going to be allright he told him self, trying desparately to feel nonshalant.

He turned up five minuets early at the adress shed given him - 7 minorca terrace. She's managed to find acommodation in a pleasant tree lined street just over the river. Taking a few deep breaths he wrang the bell, to his surprise it played god save the queen. In a moment, Julie was at the door. Ians' face felt hot. 'Hallo,' he said she said hallo back and thier was a moments unsertain hesitation.

'Do you want to come in.' 'Er, no ... lets just go straihgt to the restaraunt?'

At the restaurant, they ordered Curry. Ian was emmbarased that he couldnt pronounce the names of the dishes. He asked Julie what she wanted? She chose chicken korma and he decided on a vindaloo, with potato's and tomatoes.

Ive never eaten Indian before he admitted later. That curry was so hot it was almost indelible, but I couldent of faced the embarasment of sending it back.

Later she pictured his face, bright scarlet even in the lowlit restaurant. She smiled to herself. A bit of color suited him, she decided.

143

Drafting and proofing

Punctuation

> ### About this section
> This section helps you brush up on punctuation, focusing on:
> - Commas, dashes and full stops.
> - Capitals.
> - Question and exclamation marks.
> - Colons and semicolons.
> - Apostrophes.
> - Speech marks.

Why is punctuation important?

Nobody ever won a Nobel Prize for punctuation. On the other hand, if your punctuation is poor, your readers will find it hard to understand your writing, or will at least be distracted from its sense. For GCSE you will be expected to punctuate at least well enough to make your meaning clear.

Commas and full stops

The commonest punctuation mistake at GCSE is using a comma (or even no punctuation at all) in place of a full stop and capital. Look at these words:

'Sally ran towards the phone.'

This is a sentence because it's a complete statement. It has a subject (Sally) and an active verb (ran). Without these, it wouldn't be a proper sentence. 'Sally ran' is a sentence, but 'towards the phone' is not. Try another one:

'Sally ran towards the phone, it stopped ringing as she reached it.'

This is wrong. You could write: 'Sally ran towards the phone. It stopped ringing as she reached it.' Or for a smoother effect, you could write: 'Sally ran towards the phone, but it stopped ringing as she reached it.'

Commas, dashes and clauses

A **comma** is useful in dividing up parts of a sentence – clauses – to make the sense clear:

'I asked Dave, who works in a garage.'

Without the comma, this could mean 'Dave who works in a garage, not Dave the plumber'. A separate clause in the middle of a sentence can also be divided off by commas:

'The car, which had been poised on the edge of the cliff, toppled over at that moment.'

Reading aloud is a good guide. Try reading the sentence above, first with the commas, then without. What's the difference?

Dashes can be used in a similar way, where a slightly more dramatic effect is required. They can also be used to make a deliberate break in the flow of sense:

'The young man – he might have been 15 – turned to face me.'

Capitals

What's the capital of England? Answer – **E**. It's not much of a joke, but it might help you remember the important point that names – of places, people, makes of cars, football teams, etc. – begin with a capital letter.

A useful guide is that giving something a capital makes it more *specific*. The word 'dog' doesn't need a capital, any more than any other species of animal, but your pet poodle Fifi does! Likewise, it's 'My **mum** doesn't like housework,' but 'I think **Mum** prefers mountaineering.'

Question and exclamation marks

A **question mark** goes at the end of a question. Easy? Decide whether the following is right or wrong:

'He asked if I wanted it with chips or without.'

This is correct. There's no question mark, because the question is reported. On the other hand, you would write, 'Do you want it with chips or without?'

Normally an **exclamation mark** only goes after an exclamation – usually a few words spoken with feeling, often an order:

'Come here! You blithering idiot! Oi! Get out!'

However, some 'questions' that aren't really questions get an exclamation mark, too (see illustration).

144

Drafting and proofing

Colons and semicolons (: ;)

You can get away without using these, but they can be useful. A **colon** gives the sense that something is about to follow on as a direct consequence of what's gone before. It's like blowing a little trumpet to announce someone:

> 'Here's what we took with us: one fork, one spoon, and a teabag.'

> 'It turned out I'd wasted my time: she'd already left.'

A **semicolon** is stronger than a comma, but not as strong as a full stop. It's particularly useful to divide two balanced halves of a sentence, in place of 'but':

> 'Some people hate haggis; personally, I can't get enough of it.'

Apostrophes

Here are some correct uses of apostrophes:

> *she's, you'd, I'd, didn't, couldn't, wouldn't, can't* (to show something's been left out, but note spelling of *won't* – will not)

> 'The teacher's hair stood on end. The pupils' work had gone.' (one teacher, two or more pupils)

Never insert an apostrophe just because a word is plural: *tomatoes, potatoes, fishes, bananas, menus* – none of these needs an apostrophe. Also remember *1990s*, not *1990's*.

Dialogue

Dialogue can help to bring a piece of writing to life. Here's how to punctuate it:

> 'What colour's your lipstick?' asked Sonia.

> 'Plum, I think,' murmured Jane.

> 'Taste nice?'

> 'Not bad.'

For more complicated cases, see how it's done in any good novel. Remember, though, that American punctuation in dialogue is slightly different from standard English!

Quotations

Long quotations are best presented as a separate block of text without quote marks. Shorter quotations are best presented like this:

> Macbeth's line, 'Tomorrow, and tomorrow, and tomorrow,' shows his despair.

For quotations within a quotation, use double quote-marks, like this:

> I said, 'Macbeth's line, "Tomorrow, and tomorrow, and tomorrow," shows his despair.'

Test yourself

Copy out a few paragraphs from a good novel, a newspaper article, or your anthology, leaving out all punctuation and capitals. Or copy text from a reliable website, paste it into a *Word* document and remove the punctuation. Then (perhaps the next day) try to correct it. Compare it with the original and note your mistakes. Review this section to put them right.

For your own notes

....

....

....

....

....

....

....

145

Drafting and proofing

Spelling

About this section

This section looks at a variety of typical spelling mistakes, and suggests how to use mnemonics and your computer spellcheck to correct them.

Why spelling is important

In Shakespeare's time, spelling wasn't important. Shakespeare even spelt his own name in a variety of different ways. However, since the invention of the printing press, and modern typesetting, people have got used to seeing words spelt consistently. If your spelling is odd, your readers will be distracted from what you want them to concentrate on – your sense and style.

Spelling rules

Some spellings can be remembered by rhymes, or by conjuring up mental pictures to help you remember. These memory techniques are called **mnemonics**.

Pronunciation is also helpful, often providing the key to whether or not a word has a double letter in the middle:

tinny/tiny	*spinner/spiny*	*dinner/diner*
bitter/biter	*tiller/tiler*	*foggy/fogey*

It can also help you tell whether a word has an 'e' on the end or not:

dot/dote	*spat/spate*	*tot/tote*
writ/write	*mat/mate*	*shin/shine*

A lot of these words turn into 'ing' words in a consistent way. Those without the 'e' usually double their last letter, those with an 'e' don't:

dotting/doting	*totting/toting*
matting/mating	*winning/wining*
ragging/raging	*ratting/rating*

Mnemonics

Mnemonics (from Mnemosyne, the Greek goddess of memory) are very useful in spelling, particularly if you make up your own. Probably the best known is:

> 'I before E, except after C, but only when the sound is EE.'

Think of words like:

brief	*belief*	*chief*	*thief*	*mischief*	*siege*

and like:

receipt	*receive*	*deceive*
ceiling	*(after C)*	

and like:

weir	*freight*	*their*
weight	*height*	*(no 'ee' sound)*

Mental pictures (draw them if it helps) can also be useful, especially if they're striking, absurd or funny. You might combine them with a sentence. For example, you might remember 'assessment' by saying 'I musn't make an ass of myself in my assessment,' and picturing someone with an ass's head. Your own will work best for you.

able, ible, uble

No, it's not a witches' incantation, it's a group of commonly confused word endings. How confident are you about these?

comfortable	*suitable*	*forgivable*	*fashionable*
believable	*passable*		

inedible	*indelible*	*incredible*	*horrible*
indefensible	*forcible*	*possible*	

soluble	*voluble*

Groupings

Spelling grouping is also worth bearing in mind. When you look at spelling corrected in your written work, see if the words fit into categories, such as:

bought	*brought*	*drought*	*throughout*
caught	*fraught*	*haughty*	*naughty*
rough	*tough*	*enough*	*cough*

These can also be turned into mnemonics (see above).

Drafting and proofing

Perplexing plurals

Here are some hints on spelling plurals correctly.

If a noun stem ends in *ch*, *sh*, *s*, or *x*, add *es* to make the plural:

watches *lashes* *losses* *foxes*

If it ends in a *y* after a consonant (not a vowel), replace it with *ies*:

nappies *puppies* *babies* *flies*

If it ends in *o* after a vowel, just add *s*:

radios *studios* *videos* *rodeos*

If it ends in *o* after a consonant, add *es*:

tomatoes *potatoes* *desperadoes*

Never use apostrophes to make a plural: 'Buy some tomato's.' is **wrong**!

Spellchecks

A computer spellcheck will help you to get your spellings right. But don't let it make you lazy. You won't be able to use it in the exam, and there are lots of other occasions when you'll have to rely on memory. Get to know exactly what your spellcheck does, and make sure it is using English (UK) spelling, such as *colour*, rather than US *color*. (To change this in *Word*, click on Tools > Language > Set language and choose *English UK*.) It won't catch simple word confusions (such as *bought* and *brought*), and it will probably offer you silly alternatives to names – such as *Emu* for *Emma*.

✪ Which of the following errors will your spellcheck catch?

> 'Wether your a restuarant chef or a member of the publick, you cant beat are prices for all kinds of snakes and finger food.'

Try it out and see if you were right.

All down to you

You can read endless lists of commonly misspelt words, but in the end you'll learn from your own mistakes.

Whenever you have a spelling mistake marked by your teacher, write the correct version out, and make an effort to learn it, preferably using a mnemonic.

Start now by making a list, in the space below, of words you've got wrong more than once in marked work.

147

Drafting and proofing

Confusions

About this section

This section gives a checklist of commonly confused words and suggests ways to remember them.

Sounds like …

Most of these pairs of words sound similar to each other – though if you listen carefully there is often a slight difference. Study the list and examples below. Then cover the examples and test yourself by seeing if you can write sentences using the words correctly. Use a dictionary if any of the meanings are unclear to you.

accept/except	I **accept** your offer – **except** that I insist on paying.
access/excess	There's no **access** to anyone with **excess** baggage.
affect/effect	The rain won't **affect** us indoors. You'll spoil the **effect**.
complement/compliment	The flavours **complement** each other: my **compliments** to the chef!
continual/continuous	We were **continually** arguing. Old printers use **continuous** paper.
discreet/discrete	Diplomats are **discreet**. Wales isn't England – it has a **discrete** identity.
knew/new	I **knew** you'd found someone **new**.
lead/led	You now **lead** me where I once **led** you.
licence/license	A driving **licence** (noun) doesn't **license** (verb) you to kill.
lose/loose	I'd hate to **lose** my **loose** change.
passed/past	I **passed** (verb) a ghost from my **past** (noun) on the way here.
practise/practice	Try to **practise** (verb) every day – **practice** (noun) makes perfect.
principal/principle	The new school **principal** has no **principles**.
quiet/quite	Do be **quiet** – you're making me **quite** ill.
stationary/stationery	The train is **stationary**. A **stationery** shop sells paper.
there/their/they're	Look over **there** and you'll see **their** clothes: **they're** swimming.
thorough/through	The police were **thorough** in going **through** my drawers.
to/too/two	Thanks **to** you it's **too** late to find a room with **two** beds.
uninterested/disinterested	You seem **uninterested** in my beer mat collection. I have nothing to gain – I'm a **disinterested** observer.
who's/whose	**Who's** the culprit? **Whose** muddy boots are these?
your/you're	**Your** brother's a criminal, and **you're** almost as bad.

Making up mnemonics

Mnemonics – techniques to assist your memory – will help you remember spellings. Here are some to start you off – but making up your own will be most effective for you.

'It's tOO wet to wOO.' 'Not tHERE – HERE!'

'Mark my eXcess baggage with an X.'

'The ambassador's parrot was too discrEEt to scrEEch.'

'I was LED into the SHED.'

'I ACCidentally used my ACCess card.'

'THOR was ROUGH but THOROUGH.'

Drafting and proofing

Answers (p. 142)

As long ago as the sixth century BC, the Greek author Hesiod speculated on the possibility of time travel. He thought that in the Golden Age people would grow younger, not older. Since then, philosophers, poets and scientists have asked whether time travel could be more than a fantasy.

Einstein proved that at the speed of light, time stands still. Time travel would in theory be possible if we could travel at speeds approaching the speed of light. Einstein also proved that gravity warps space itself, and that, since time can only be measured relative to space, in a sense it warps time. In fact it has been shown that if one of a pair of very accurate atomic clocks is flown at high speed round the world, it falls slightly behind the one that has remained stationary.

Physicist Stephen Hawking has suggested that time travel could take place inside 'black holes' in space, where gravity is so strong that nothing can escape its pull, and space is infinitely warped. However, this kind of time travel could only take us forward in time. Most people agree that backward time travel is out of the question because of the 'grandmother paradox'. This states that time travel cannot occur because if you went back in time you could, in theory, kill your grandmother, so that you could never be born in the present time.

For your own notes

....
....
....
....
....
....
....

Answers (p. 143)

Ian had planned to take Julie to an Indian restaurant near their office. By six o'clock he was wondering what to wear, and by seven he was already getting nervous. It's going to be all right, he told himself, trying desperately to feel nonchalant.

He turned up five minutes early at the address she'd given him – 7 Minorca Terrace. She'd managed to find accommodation in a pleasant tree-lined street just over the river. Taking a few deep breaths, he rang the bell. To his surprise it played 'God Save the Queen'. In a moment, Julie was at the door.

Ian's face felt hot.

'Hallo,' he said.

She said 'Hallo' back, and there was a moment's uncertain hesitation.

'Do you want to come in?'

'Er, no … let's just go straight to the restaurant.'

At the restaurant, they ordered curry. Ian was embarrassed that he couldn't pronounce the names of the dishes. He asked Julie what she wanted. She chose chicken korma and he decided on a vindaloo, with potatoes and tomatoes.

'I've never eaten Indian before,' he admitted later. 'That curry was so hot it was almost inedible, but I couldn't have faced the embarrassment of sending it back.'

Later she pictured his face, bright scarlet even in the low-lit restaurant. She smiled to herself. A bit of colour suited him, she decided.

How did you do?

In the drafting exercise, there's room for individual preferences. In the proofreading exercise, it's more a matter of simple 'right or wrong' (although there is one 'optional spelling' here: *hallo/hello*). You probably won't have caught every mistake, but if you make a note of the ones you missed, try to see why they're wrong, and avoid them in your own work, you'll learn fast.

149

Drafting and proofing

Review

Checklist

Do you now know:

		Yes	Not yet
1	What you need to check at 'draft' level? (p. 142)	❑	❑
2	What you need to check at 'proofreading' level? (pp. 141, 143)	❑	❑
3	How to use paragraphing correctly? (p. 142)	❑	❑
4	When to use commas, full stops and capitals? (p. 144)	❑	❑
5	When to use semicolons, colons and dashes? (pp. 144–145)	❑	❑
6	When to use question and exclamation marks? (p. 144)	❑	❑
7	How to punctuate dialogue and quotations? (p. 145)	❑	❑
8	What spellings or groups of spellings you need to learn? (pp. 146–147)	❑	❑
9	What your computer spellcheck will and won't do? (p. 147)	❑	❑
10	The differences between commonly confused words? (p. 148)	❑	❑
11	How to use mnemonics to improve your spellings? (p. 148)	❑	❑

If your answer is 'Not yet' to any of these, look back at the appropriate sections to remind yourself. If you're still unsure, ask your teacher for help.

Useful websites

www.englishbiz.co.uk (good all-purpose site; 'quick' and full guides, and free downloads)

www.shunsley.eril.net/armoore (very good for literature and media)

www.s-cool.co.uk (clear revision help, with simple tests)

www.learn.co.uk (*Guardian* newspaper's education site)

www.bbc.co.uk/schools/gcsebitesize/english (sound tests and revision material)

www.sparknotes.com (summaries and commentaries on key texts)

www.schoolsnet.com (highly visual interactive revision material on key texts)

www.shakespeare-online.com/essays (essays, sources, timelines, FAQs)

http://the-tech.mit.edu/Shakespeare (full texts of Shakespeare plays)

For your own notes

....

....

....

....

....

....

....

Index

accent 3, 67

advertising 86–87

alliteration 61, 108, 111, 130, 133

Anglo-Saxon 1–2

apostrophes 145

argument 78

audience 60–61

autobiography 53–54

beginnings 8

bias 76–77, 85

biography 55–56

blank verse 108–109

capitals 144

characterisation 7, 10–13, 95, 112–113

charity appeals 86–87

Chaucer, Geoffrey 2

clichés 78

colons 145

commas 144

communication, purposes of 2–4

confused words 148

conjunctions 10

context, social and historical 7, 17, 20–23, 40, 117

coursework 1, 7, 112

dashes 144

dialogue 40, 145

diaries 47–52

drafting 136–138, 141–150

drama 100–120

drugs 72–73, 81–83

emotive language 80–81

endings 8

English

development of 1–2

non-standard 3, 67, 72

enjambement 129

environmental issues 76–80

exclamation marks 144

fact 74

fiction 6

full stops 144

headlines 85

humour 66–67

hyphens 49

imagery 22, 30, 33, 98, 108

information 68–74

instructions 42

irony 5, 19

Latin 2

letters 43–46

link words 8

media 74–88

memory 146

metaphor 99, 108

monologue, dramatic 129

narrative style 20, 40

National Curriculum 1

newspapers 74, 76–85

non-fiction 4, 42–73

Normans 2

objectivity 78

Old Norse 1

onomatopoeia 133

opinion 74, 78–79

oxymorons 109

paragraphs 142

paraphrasing 4

parts of speech 6

personification 108

plot and structure 7

poetry 96–99, 121–140

presentational devices 71, 73, 86–87

proofreading 141–143

punctuation 144–145

puns 109

question marks 144

questions, asking 4

quotations 33, 76, 145

rap 130

reading 4–7

semicolons 10, 145

sentences 60, 144

setting and atmosphere 7, 20–24

Shakespeare, William 106–120

background 107

and English language 2, 108

style 108–109, 110

theatre 107, 118–119

themes 116–117

types of play 107, 112

similes 22, 33, 99, 108, 133

speaking and listening 2–4

spelling 146–147

style and language 7, 60–61, 108–109, 110

technological language 2

travel writing 60–67

Valentines 130–131

vegetarianism 68–71

viewpoint 7

Vikings 1

writing 7–8, 60–61

151